PEIRCE'S PHILOSOPHICAL PERSPECTIVES

PEIRCE'S PHILOSOPHICAL PERSPECTIVES

by
VINCENT G. POTTER

Edited by VINCENT M. COLAPIETRO

Fordham University Press
New York
1996

Copyright © 1996 by FORDHAM UNIVERSITY PRESS
All rights reserved.
LC 96-1328
ISBN 0-8232-1615-2 (hardcover)
ISBN 0-8232-1616-0 (paperback)
ISSN 1073-2764
American Philosophy Series No. 3
Vincent M. Colapietro, Editor
Vincent G. Potter (1929-1994), Founding Editor

Library of Congress Cataloging-in-Publication Data

Potter, Vincent G.
  Peirce's philosophical perspectives / by Vincent G. Potter ; edited by Vincent M. Colapietro.
    p. cm. — (American philosophy series, ISSN 1073-2764 ; no. 3)
  Includes bibliographical references.
  ISBN 0-8232-1615-2 (hardcover); ISBN 0-8232-1616-0 (paperback)
  1. Peirce, Charles S. (Charles Sanders), 1839-1914.
I. Colapietro, Vincent Michael, 1950- . II. Title. III. Series.
B945.P44P63 1996
191—dc20   96-1328
                                                                      CIP

Printed in the United States of America

CONTENTS

Abbreviations	vii
Foreword	ix
To the Reader	xxvii

1. Charles Sanders Peirce: An Overview — 1
2. Peirce's British Connection — 17
3. Peirce on Normative Science — 37
4. Action Through Thought: The Ethics of Inquiry — 65
5. Normative Science and the Pragmatic Maxim — 78
6. Peirce's Pragmatic Maxim: Realist or Nominalist? — 91
7. Peirce on "Substance" and "Foundations" — 103
8. Peirce on Continuity — 117
9. Objective Chance: Lonergan and Peirce on Scientific Generalization — 124
10. C. S. Peirce and Religious Experience — 141
11. "Vaguely Like a Man": The Theism of Charles S. Peirce — 155
12. C. S. Peirce's Argument for God's Reality: A Pragmatist's View — 169

Appendix: Response to Hartshorne's "Peirce and Religion" — 195
Bibliography — 205
About the Author — 211

ABBREVIATIONS

In general, quotations from Peirce's works are taken from of the *Collected Papers of Charles Sanders Peirce*, vols. I–VI, ed. Charles Hartshorne and Paul Weiss (Cambridge: The Belknap Press of Harvard University Press, 1931–1935); vols. VII–VIII, ed. Arthur Burks (Cambridge: The Belknap Press of Harvard University Press, 1958). References are by volume and paragraph.

MS The Charles S. Peirce Papers, microfilm edition, Cambridge: Harvard University Library, Photographic Service, 1966. References to this set of Peirce's unpublished papers held in the Houghton Library at Harvard employs R. S. Robins's numbering system in *Annotated Catalogue of the Papers of Charles S. Peirce* (Amherst: University of Massachusetts Press, 1967), as emended in "The Peirce papers: A Supplementary Catalogue," *Transactions of the Charles S. Peirce Society*, 7 (1971), 37–57. References are by Robins's manuscript and page numbers.

W *Writings of Charles S. Peirce: A Chronological Edition*, ed. Max H. Fisch et al., 4 vols. to date. Bloomington: Indiana University Press, 1982—. References are given as W followed by volume and page numbers.

FOREWORD

At the time of his death, Father Vincent Potter, in addition to translating Saint Thomas Aquinas's *De malo*, was preparing for publication his essays on the American philosopher Charles S. Peirce. He had virtually completed the task, although there were minor revisions and, in Chapter 1 at least, slight expansions that he wanted to make. He had selected essays ranging from his earliest publications on Peirce to his most recent; for example, "Peirce's Analysis of Normative Science" appeared in the *Transactions of the Charles S. Peirce Society* in 1966, while "Peirce on 'Substance' and 'Foundations'" appeared in *The Monist* in 1992. As a way of rounding off the collection, he had chosen a few of his unpublished papers, though his chief objective was to gather together in one place those interpretive pieces that had been subjected to the critical review of scholarly colleagues.

The two opening sentences of "Peirce on 'Substance' and 'Foundations'" help us put into focus Father Potter's work as an interpreter of Peirce:

> Charles S. Peirce has a great deal to contribute both to understanding and to solving many of the philosophical problems that puzzle contemporary thinkers. In fact, it is probably true that in some ways philosophers of our time are in a better position to understand Peirce's thought than those of his own day.

The opening sentence obviously concerns the contemporary relevance of Peirce's philosophy;[1] the second, the advantages that we—in contrast to *his* contemporaries—have in comprehending that philosophy. Father's deep, abiding conviction was that "Charlie" (as he was wont to call Peirce) can help us think through traditional philosophical issues in a manner that, at once, drives deeper roots into our intellectual tradition and demands critical engagement with contemporary developments.

We can learn much by attending to what is implicit in Father's practice as an interpreter, much about this particular interpreter and, of greater significance, much about the difficult art of philosophical interpretation.[2] The uncritical traditionalist (that is, the thinker so thoroughly immersed in a tradition that he fails ever to attain a critical distance from his own intellectual inheritance) and the deracinated contemporary (the thinker who prides himself for standing apart from any and every intellectual tradition) were, for Father Potter, woefully inadequate models of the intellectual life. In their place the ideal of the critical traditionalist—the thinker engaged in a painstaking, ongoing critical dialogue with ancestors as well as contemporaries—is the one he defended and, indeed, exemplified. The dead weight of tradition is felt as such only by those lacking the intellectual resources to appropriate critically the insights and wisdom inherent in their own tradition; but for thinkers possessing such resources, it would be more suitable to speak of the wings of tradition.

Such, at least, was Father Potter's attitude; in this as in many other matters, we see the influence of Bernard Lonergan, for whom tradition and innovation are a dialectical pair.[3] Properly appreciated, tradition is a source of innovation, and innovation, in turn, is the outgrowth of tradition. The unimaginative repetition of past patterns of thought or conduct is not characteristic of a truly vital tradition; nor is the automatic (in a sense, mechanical) rejection of such patterns the mark of a truly innovative mind. Such rejection is characteristic of a mind excessively anxious about its own originality. The imaginative, critical appropriation of past patterns of thought and conduct marks off the critical traditionalist from both the blind traditionalist and the uprooted contemporary. In opposition to uncritical defenders of an intellectual tradition, the critical traditionalist insists that the vitality of any tradition requires engagement with contemporary developments; in opposition to the deracinated intellectual, s/he stresses that antitraditionalism is itself a tradition (albeit a relatively recent one, at least in its militant contemporary form) and that contemporary thought alone does not provide us with the critical distance needed to address effectively contemporary concerns. In referring to classic literature, Albert Einstein astutely suggested that:

> Somebody who reads only newspapers and at best works of contemporary authors looks to me like an extremely near-sighted person who scorns eyeglasses. He is completely dependent on the preju-

dices and fashions of his times, since he never gets to see or hear anything else.[4]

For Father Potter, Aristotle, Thomas Aquinas, and Peirce were exemplars of a long, rich intellectual tradition; to scorn their texts would be tantamount to scorning powerful lenses by which a sharper, fuller vision of our world might be attained.

Peirce was, for him, a resource, a source he could go to again and again for insight and direction. Father Potter's interpretations of Peirce's texts aimed, above all, at deepening our philosophical comprehension of some important issue (the ontological status of ideals, for example). They were, most certainly, aimed at getting Peirce right, interpreting him in light of his actual assertions and avowed intentions. But the value of getting Peirce right was ultimately subordinated to thinking through some set of issues (the issues to which the texts being interpreted were devoted). If this is perhaps not always so obvious as it might be, that is because Father was convinced that Peirce had gotten some things fundamentally right; so that, in getting Peirce right, we are led to think aright.

Above, I have tried to suggest what manner of interpreter Father Potter was. Below, I will consider what manner of man *C. S. Peirce* himself was and what manner of activity the *philosophical interpreting* of philosophical texts is. Before I do so, however, let me say a word or two more about the status of this manuscript at the time of Father's death. Even though the principal focus of his final weeks was on his translation of Saint Thomas, he had written the first chapter of his essays on Peirce and (even more recently) a note "To the Reader"; moreover, he had compiled a Table of Contents, arranging his essays in an order that made the most sense to him. Hence, this collection of essays owes its content (what has been included) and its arrangement to the author.

At this point, it would be instructive for us to consider carefully the way in which Father Potter proposed (1) to introduce Charles S. Peirce to contemporary readers and (2) to arrange his essays. These provide clear clues for how this important contemporary expositor approached the always challenging, often enigmatic, texts of Peirce.

What Matter of Man Is This?
What Manner of Activity Is Interpreting?

Let us begin, then, at the beginning—with Father Potter's first chapter. First, he introduced the man; then, the realist; and, following this, the pragmaticist. There is warrant in Peirce's own writings for making the acquaintance of the author one is about to read, for, as the youthful Peirce put it:

> Each man has his own peculiar character. It enters into all he does. It is in his consciousness and not a mere mechanical trick, and . . . it enters into all his cognition, it is a cognition of *things in general*. It is therefore the man's philosophy, his way of regarding things; not a philosophy of the head alone—but one which pervades the whole man. (7.595)

The validity and fecundity of the cognitions that a philosopher defends are, of course, not secured by the personality or character of that philosopher. But one of the most admirable forms of personal agency is that involving a resolute will to subject one's own beliefs and judgments to impersonal standards of rational criticism. At its best, reading a philosophical text involves the exercise of such agency: it involves squarely confronting one's thoughts with the assertions and implications encountered in another's text. If the process is to be something more than the clash of the arbitrary wills of reader and author, an appeal to shared and in some respects impersonal standards (the laws of logic, for example, or the facts of experience) is needed. We can, of course, read for the purpose of simply confirming our preconceived opinions (1.2), but reading in this way exhibits a disrespect born of arrogance. Reading for the purpose of evaluating the strength of our opinions reveals, in contrast, a willingness to grant the author the status of interlocutor.

But it would be imprudent to grant any and every author such status, just as it would be foolish to elevate every randomly encountered individual into one's intellectual guide. Peirce is quite explicit about this:

> The reader has a right to know how the author's opinions were formed. Not, of course, that he is expected to accept any conclusions which are not borne out by argument. But in discussions of extreme difficulty . . . when good judgment is a factor, and pure ratiocination

is not everything, it is prudent to take every element into consideration. (1.3)

Immediately after noting this, Peirce offers a brief autobiographical sketch, thereby providing his readers with a sense of not only the process by which he formed his opinions but also the purpose animating his conduct.

In fact, it is for Peirce—quite apart from autobiographical considerations—nothing less than "the primary rule of the ethics of rhetoric that every prose composition should begin by informing the reader what its aim is, with sufficient precision to enable him or [her] to decide whether to read it or not. If the title can do this, all the better."[5] For a pragmatist especially, the notion of aim or purpose is central. For a pragmatic approach to philosophical hermeneutics, purpose is likewise pivotal. As a way of appreciating Father Potter's distinctive approach to the Peircean texts, it will be helpful to highlight some features of this approach, for it is the one he so ably adopted.

A passionate commitment to dispassionate inquiry—a personal espousal of the impersonal criteria on which rational critique is alone possible—may appear paradoxical, but it is not incoherent or contradictory. (Along these same lines, Peirce himself claimed that in order to enjoy science, "it will be needful to have one's heart set on something remote from enjoyment" [2.15]). We ought to appreciate that: "The dry light of intelligence is manifestly not sufficient to determine a great purpose: the whole man [or woman] goes into it" (7.186). Yet, we need to realize that a great purpose defines in its own way the whole person inspired by it. A great purpose such as dispassionate inquiry or compassionate conduct is, for the agents animated by it, something at once constitutive of their identity (it is among the ways they define themselves) *and* transcendent of their accomplishments. It is the way these agents define themselves, but it is simultaneously the way they refine—criticize and correct—themselves. The purpose is not only something to which they are committed but also something by which they are regulated or, more exactly, by which their own efforts at self-regulation are made possible. Apart from a resolute commitment to what Peirce calls a great purpose, there are only meanness and superficiality; resulting from such a commitment are the largeness and depth of spirit that we find so compelling when concretely encountered in, say, the passionate inquirer (Albert Einstein, for example) or the compassionate individual (Mother Teresa).

To make the acquaintance of a person worth knowing, then, involves glimpsing the transcendent purposes animating and inspiring that person. These purposes are, as we have already implied, trans-personal: not private property or so much subjective clay to be molded into whatever form whimsical selves happen to desire, but the beacons by which all too easily misled selves try to chart their course.

Our assessment of any philosopher concerns, in the end, not a purely technical cleverness but a radiantly transcendent purpose. In general, the "great use of a life is," as William James observed, "to spend it for something that outlasts it."[6] But the manner in which one spends one's life, on however exalted a purpose, matters; the nobility of the purpose does not itself secure the nobility of the life. This aspect is brought into sharp focus by James himself when he asserts that: "The solid meaning of life is always the same eternal thing,—the marriage, namely, of some unhabitual ideal, however special, with some fidelity, courage, and endurance; with some man's or woman's pains."[7] Still, James's characteristic stress on the uniqueness of the ideal ought not to distract our attention from what is most relevant for our purposes: what renders life meaningful is admirable service to admirable ideals, be these ideals habitual or not. Ordinarily, these ideals provide means for assessing the manner in which they are being, or have been, served. Hence, fraudulent research marks an *essential* failure, as does wrathful Christianity. The *norms* by which conduct is appraised are generally linked to the *ideals* by which that conduct is animated; thus, the norm of truthful exchange is linked to the ideal of truth itself, just as the norms of charitable conduct are linked to the ideal of self-sacrificial love.

Father Potter's brief biographical sketch of Peirce (a sketch avowedly dependent on Paul Weiss's contribution to the *Dictionary of American Biography*) is intended to illuminate the great purposes animating this singular thinker and, beyond this, the progressively constrained circumstances in which Peirce struggled to serve these purposes. That is, it is intended to convey something of the transcendent ideals and tragic circumstances of Peirce's life. Even from this very brief sketch, one glimpses something of the "fidelity, courage, and endurance" of one who, despite his isolation and poverty, spent his time and energy on pushing further both his first-order investigations into the cosmos and his second-order investigation into the most reliable methods of inquiry.

Very quietly in this first chapter, Father Potter in effect acknowledges the postmodern character of the present moment. He suggests that Peirce can still speak to us "whose world is perhaps even more dramatically different from his than his was from the Middle Ages." In other words, the discontinuity between Peirce's and, for example, Duns Scotus's time is perhaps not so deep as the discontinuity between Peirce's time and our own: the modern epoch might be closer to the medieval period than our own postmodern moment is to later phases of the modern epoch. In general, Father Potter is acutely aware of the ruptures, fragmentations, displacements, etc., which are such prominent features of human history. In particular, he is conscious of the chasm that yawns between those living in the first decades of this century (Peirce died in 1914; James, in 1910) and those living in its last decades.

Though appreciative of the historical ruptures which opened the chasm separating such late-modern thinkers as Peirce and ourselves, Father Potter was skeptical about the currently fashionable forms of postmodern thought. While for Roland Barthes "the birth of the reader must be at the cost of the death of the Author," Father Potter refused to purchase his rights as a reader at the expense of the author's own life! This was especially true in those cases where the author happened to be dead! While for Richard Rorty, in his advocacy of "strong misreading," it is legitimate for readers to beat the text into whatever shape serves their momentary purpose, Father Potter advocated imaginatively re-enacting the enduring purposes embodied in a particular text. He saw the advocacy of strong misreading as a license for textual violence (though the advocates themselves would readily admit this, countering the criticism by charging that it makes a fetish of the text). Fidelity to the text is possible only through imaginative participation in the embodied purposes of some deliberative agent, including the embodiment of these purposes in the text itself.

Authorial intention is not some inaccessible reality. Like every other human purpose, it is in principle something that can be felt as well as understood, however imperfectly or incompletely. If there is always more to any text than an author consciously puts there, it is because the purpose animating the author transcends the control and consciousness of its proximate source. Hence, while the meaning of a text is not reducible to an authorially ascribed significance, the purposes embodied in that text cannot be safely ignored. What is true of texts is true of every other case of human striving: human agents are, at once, competent actors and unwitting playthings of largely hidden forces (for example, the individual unconscious or engulfing currents of historical developments). We are neither completely clueless nor fully competent; in virtually all our exertions, we exhibit a degree of competence, while revealing ourselves as not knowing fully—perhaps even adequately—what we are doing. Authorial agency is a distinctive form of human agency, susceptible to the same limitations and liabilities as other forms (in particular, this pattern of competency and ineptness). If it is always the case (except in the most trivial exercises) that our purposes, especially our great purposes, transcend our performances or productions, then it is the case that the purposes embodied in a text are frustrated as well as fulfilled by that specific textual incarnation. Even so, the presence of purposes in texts as well as other artifacts is, simultaneously, palpable and problematic. The responsible interpreter is thus the responsive reader—responsive, above all, to the tangle of manifest and hidden purposes, of avowed intentions and disclaimed, but nonetheless operative, intentions, of realized and frustrated objectives.

While Father Potter recognized the postmodern character of the present time, he resisted postmodern fashions, especially the fashion of celebrating the so-called death of the author. Texts are not series of traces in which meaning and its comprehension are endlessly deferred, but rather enactments and embodiments of purposes in which those purposes are frustrated as well as fulfilled, concealed as well as revealed. They are not to be beaten into the idiosyncratic shape desired by any and every whimsical interpreter; rather, they are, in some measure, the stable and even stubborn expressions of evolved and evolving purposes. As such, they have the force of invitations to participate in the further articulation of shared purposes.

This, at least, is how Father Potter approached philosophical texts. Above all, he desired to join as a *co-inquirer* Peirce and a handful of other authors (most notably, Thomas Aquinas, Bernard Lonergan, and John E. Smith). A community of purpose makes possible a community of understanding; it also makes possible significant, fruitful *dis*agreement. Both in terms of his own painstaking interpretations of philosophical texts and in terms of his methodological reflections on his interpretive practices, he made a compelling case for what might be called the classical ideal of hermeneutics—understanding the other as other because one, even if only provisionally, imaginatively identifies with that other.

But, in the case of Peirce, the identification was greatly facilitated by the deep intellectual affinities between author and interpreter. The deep distaste for cant and the equally deep desire for rigor proportionate to the subject matter animated both.

CONCRETE FALLIBILISM AND FALLIBILISTIC THEISM

We have considered Father's introductory chapter to this collection as an aid in glimpsing some key features of his hermeneutic approach. It is also illuminating to note how Father Potter organized the chapters of this volume, in particular, how he placed his studies of Peirce's theism as the culmination of this study. One of Peirce's best accounts of human knowing is to be found in "The Neglected Argument for the Reality of God"; in turn, one of his most instructive engagements in the form of self-controlled inquiry he so painstakingly analyzed is precisely this attempt to discern the presence of the divine in the quotidian. No doubt, many followers of Peirce are less than enthusiastic about what some do not hesitate to describe as a failure of nerve—a failure to think through the possibility of a self-propelled universe for which a transcendent Creator is superfluous. But Father Potter insisted upon seeing Peirce's philosophical project as a signal achievement within the grand tradition of Western metaphysics.[8] The thinkers within this tradition were and, indeed, are unembarrassed about the task of articulating a vision inclusive of the divine and, beyond this, a conception of divinity continuous with the major emphases of the traditional notion of a personal God. Not only was Father Potter himself such a thinker, but he took Peirce to be one as well. Of course, it might be insinuated that the interpreter is surreptitiously making the texts of another do the interpreter's own bidding. But the texts of Peirce simply do not allow for such an insinuation to stand. However unpalatable Peirce's theism is to some of his followers, it is—for good or ill—simply an integral part of his philosophical perspective.

So, from the focal question of Chapter 1—What manner of thinker, indeed, what manner of man, is this?—we move ultimately to the focal question of the final chapters: What manner of world is this? Or, alternatively put, what can we responsibly say about the character not only of the reality encompassing us, but also of the reality by which we were generated in the first place and, at every turn, are sustained as well as threatened? For Peirce, it is a world in which the signs of divinity are discernible.

Between these two termini (between the first chapter, on the one hand, and the last three chapters and the Appendix, on the other), there are eight papers. Chapter 2, "The British Connection," takes up an important strand in Peirce's intellectual life and, in effect, continues the task of making Peirce's acquaintance (of specifying just what manner of philosopher he is); it also prepares the way for the following several chapters by highlighting both Peirce's concern for methodology and the roots of his pragmatism. Chapters 3 through 6 form something of a unit, being concerned with either the normative sciences in general (esthetics, ethics, and logic) or the logical maxim for which Peirce is perhaps still best known. The pragmatic maxim is a logical doctrine, and logical inquiry is (for Peirce, at least) one of three normative sciences whose character is ultimately comprehensible only in reference to the two other normative sciences (esthetics, conceived as the investigation of ultimate ends, and ethics, conceived as the investigation of self-controlled conduct). In these chapters (as they have been arranged by their author), we move from a general consideration of the normative sciences to specific questions concerning a particular doctrine in but one of these sciences (questions concerning the pragmatic maxim precisely as a logical doctrine in Peirce's distinctive sense).

From these considerations, we turn to several questions in fundamental ontology, questions concerning substance, continuity, and chance. One novel feature of Father Potter's interpretation of

Peirce is the attribution of a substance ontology to a thinker who is ordinarily supposed to opt for process instead of substance. While *synechism* (the doctrine of continuity) and *tychism* (the doctrine of objective chance) are familiar topics in Peirce scholarship, Father Potter's handling of these doctrines helps us approach these central but difficult topics afresh. From the ontological issues just noted, we turn in Chapters 10 through 12 to another set of such issues, ones bearing directly upon the reality of God.

In this context, an understanding of human experience as a medium of objective disclosure is defended. Drawing upon insights from Bernard Lonergan, Father Potter articulates a notion of *cognitive* experience as an ongoing process in which distinct levels are "interrelated cumulatively and incrementally." Three such levels are presentation, understanding, and judgment. Though dependent on Lonergan's insights, this notion is, at the very least, congruent with Peirce's assertions about experience; Father Potter turns to Lonergan only after explaining experience in terms of Peirce's own categories of Firstness, Secondness, and Thirdness. He does so as a way of making clearer just what is at stake in the fuller recovery of human experience championed by Peirce and, indeed, by the other pragmatists as well. From cognitive experience, he turns to religious experience or, more precisely, experiencing the world religiously. Here Father Potter defends not an *adjectival* model of religious experience, according to which such experience constitutes a clearly demarcatable species of human experiences, but an *adverbial* model (experiencing the world religiously). What emerges from this discussion is a subtle and suggestive account of what John E. Smith calls the religious dimension of human experience. While indebted to Smith no less than to Lonergan for bringing out the religious implications of Peirce's notion of experience, Father Potter is nonetheless not in complete agreement with Smith's own reconstructed understanding. The critical dialogue between the two on this topic is one deserving careful attention, for their differences are illuminating precisely because their agreement is so fundamental.[9]

It would be an understatement to say that Peirce did not think of himself primarily as either a theologian or a philosopher of religions. In fact, he had quite disparaging things to say about both. For Father Potter as well, Peirce's theism was in a sense secondary;

for this expositor, Peirce was first and foremost a realist, but a realist of a distinctive cast. (The very formulation of Peirce's theism is colored by his realism, for rather than speaking of the *existence* of God Peirce insists upon speaking of reality in this *context*.) The cast of Peirce's realism is best conveyed by describing it as scholastic, fallibilist, and pragmaticist. Peirce's robust ontological and methodological commitments (his insistence that generals are real and that inquiry responsibly conducted can disclose the contours and structures of reality) separated him from both William James and John Dewey. Thus, while Father Potter was a quick champion of Peirce's pragmaticism, he was ordinarily never more than a reluctant defender of certain aspects of James's pragmatism or Dewey's instrumentalism.

Against nominalism, Peirce advocated scholastic realism. Against subjective idealism, he advocated commonsensical realism (over against finite human consciousness stands a world not of its own making, resistant to its cognitive no less than its muscular exertions, and yet—in some manner and measure—accessible to that consciousness). Against theoretical skepticism, even (perhaps especially) when it masqueraded as pragmatism, Peirce championed a theoretical fallibilism according to which the possibility of error is ineliminable and ubiquitous, yet the limits of the knowable are never fixed once for all. As conceived by Peirce, this contrite fallibilism is interwoven with a "high faith in the reality of knowledge." Against moral skepticism, he unabashedly championed a "sentimental conservatism" (1.661): "The mental qualities we most admire in all human beings . . . are the maiden's delicacy [or sensitivity], the mother's devotion, manly courage, and other inheritances that have come to us from the biped who did not yet speak; while the characters that are most contemptible take their origin in reasoning" (1.627). At least implicit in such sentimental conservatism is a moral realism: the sensitive person is responding to some actual suffering that but for the blindness of others would be seen as irreducibly real; the courageous person is responding in behalf of a threatened reality in the face of a real threat. The sensitive person does not take herself to be projecting her feelings onto others, but rather to be discerning what others feel, sometimes despite their protestations. The courageous person does not take herself to be projecting her fears upon the world but to be responding to dangers *really* there.

The world is not a blank screen upon which we project our fantasies, though infantile fantasies *do* obstruct even adult perceptions. It is not an amorphous mass out of which we construct a purely human artifact, though human imagination *does* enable us both to discover objective truths and to devise a human habitat. The skeptic and the anti-realist in their own ways fail to give reality its due. In contrast, the strong foundationalist and other defenders of incorrigible knowledge fail to appreciate the extent of our fallibility and the significant degree to which human knowledge is an imaginative construct (a patchwork woven out of abductions).

Reality is directly encountered in our experience and partially disclosed in some of our investigations. Those who deny this conceive of reality as something recondite and, then, deny either our access to that reality or the relevance of any notion of reality for explaining, say, knowledge or some other process or practice. For Peirce and (following him) for Father Potter as well, "the realist is simply one who knows no more recondite reality than that which is represented in a true representation" (5.312). What is truly represented is authentically real; and what is truly represented or, more accurately, represent*able* is what would be ultimately discovered by an infinite community of self-critical investigators. As Father Potter stresses, then, "Peirce's account of truth and reality requires the explicit recognition of the role of the community" (see below, p. 113). Apart from our personal participation in the ongoing efforts of critical inquirers, our claims to know are largely suspect and frequently unreliable. Apart from the ideal of an infinite community, the idea of objective truth is inadequately understood; for while truth can never be simply identified with an actually attained consensus on some question, truth means, for all practical purposes, what unlimited and uncoerced inquirers, given sufficient time and resources, would discover.

In the hands of Peirce, pragmatism was not designed to foreclose theoretical inquiry, or to discredit the very idea of objective truth, or, finally, to preclude the possibility of metaphysics. It was designed to assist theoretical inquirers in approximating objective truth about questions of traditional metaphysics no less than questions of special sciences such as physics, chemistry, and biology. In sum, its function was essentially heuristic: Peirce's methodological reflections on the successful practice of objective inquiry were undertaken for the sake of facilitating such inquiry, for goading it along promising paths and guiding it in effective ways.

> In a letter to James, Peirce himself stressed that: after all pragmatism solves no real problem. It only shows that supposed problems are not real problems. But when one comes to such questions as immortality, the nature of the connection of mind and matter (further than that mind acts on matter not like a *cause* but like a *law*) we are left completely in the dark. The effect of pragmatism is simply to open our minds to receiving any evidence, not to furnish evidence. (8.259)

While it is imperative to appreciate that, regarding such questions, our minds are almost completely in the dark, it is equally crucial to affirm the possibility that, regarding at least some of these theoretical questions, inquiry might progress. The marked tendency of both James and Dewey is to foreclose the possibility of theoretical investigation into ultimate questions. Peirce strenuously resisted this tendency, even though he was acutely aware of the severe limitations of human intelligence.

The first rule of reason is, according to him, that "in order to learn you must desire to learn, and in so desiring not be satisfied with what you already incline to think" (1.135). An important corollary following from the first rule of rational inquiry "deserves to be inscribed upon every wall of the city of philosophy," to wit, "Do not block the way of inquiry." One of the ways in which the path of investigation might be blocked results from "maintaining that this, that, and the other never can be known" (1.138). To suppose that some aspect of reality is forever beyond the reach of inquiry effectively arrests and, in time, will atrophy that reach. But this is just what James and Dewey accomplish in the name of, respectively, pragmatism and instrumentalism. But, for the theoretical investigator, such despair is suicide. Hence, between the extreme of a facile confidence of the human mind's theoretical reach and the extreme of an invincible skepticism, Peirce steered a middle course—one always mindful of human reason's utter puniness, yet ever hopeful of its unpredictable resourcefulness. Some of his most distinctive doctrines—pragmaticism, anthropomorphism, fallibilism, and sentimentalism—need to be interpreted as part of his efforts to steer just such a course. These doctrines provide guidelines for framing our questions more responsibly than we have done so thus far and opening ourselves more fully to the range of potentially relevant evidence than we have considered to date.

Peirce confessed that "out of a contrite fallibilism, combined with a high faith in the reality of knowledge, and an intense desire to find things out, all my philosophy has always seemed to me to grow" (1.14). It grew into a comprehensive vision of the empirical world, understanding empirical in its broad, Peircean sense rather than in its severely circumscribed, "empiricist" sense. Integral to this vision was a conception of God wherein the reality of this Being is depicted "vaguely like a man." The reality of God is not so much established by argumentation as rooted in "sentiment, or obscure perception." This sentiment is nothing less than

> deep recognition of something in the circumambient All, which, if an individual strives to express it, will clothe itself in forms more or less extravagant, more or less accidental, but ever acknowledging the first and last, the A and the O, as well as a relation to that Absolute of the individual's self, as a relative being. (6.428; slightly modified)

From a Peircean perspective, there is no coercive proof for the central doctrine of classical theism or, for that matter, for the contemporary variations of the theistic outlook (in this as well other contexts, the "demonstrations of the metaphysicians are all moonshine" [1.7]). The claims of theists are, like all other substantive claims made by human beings, fallible. Even so, Peirce was convinced that the irreducibly vague utterances by which we give expression to our obscure perception of the divine presence are not utterly vacuous; nor did he suppose that they were completely false. In sum, out of his contrite fallibilism ultimately grew a fallibilistic theism in which the logic of vagueness was enlisted to ensure the meaningfulness of our inescapably vague, anthropomorphic utterances about God. The force and subtlety of this distinctive form of theism are illuminated by Father Potter in the concluding chapters of this book. Like Peirce himself, he was a man with his feet on the ground yet one disposed to muse upon the heavens. He was a critical commonsensist thoroughly committed to the wisdom enshrined in ordinary language and the realities attested by our every experience; yet he refused to be imprisoned in the circle of ordinary usage. He also resisted being deflected from the depth of meaning inherent in what mistakenly we suppose to be *ordinary* experience. For him, mystical experience is not something other than ordinary experience, but rather ordinary experience grasped in its true character as an extraordinary phenomenon. When it is not taken for granted—when it is viewed afresh with the eyes of a child (1.349)—profound depth is intimated, and the divine presence discerned, in our everyday experience. Our task is not to look beyond such experience, but to interpret it with sufficient sensitivity, to read it with adequate resources (rather than the crudest vocabulary of the most narrowly practical terms).

It was the exemplary figure of Charles Peirce as a humble, yet hopeful *theoretical* inquirer to whom Father Vincent Potter was drawn, again and again. "Charlie" was one of his most trusted co-inquirers. The note of familiarity always conveyed to me the sense of rolling up one's sleeves and putting one's hands to the same tasks as the ones to which Peirce devoted himself. For how we ourselves might join Peirce in investigating a staggering array of complex issues, it would be difficult to find a better guide than Father Potter. In a sentence quoted at the outset of this Foreword, we encountered the suggestion that we today are in a better position to understand Peirce's philosophy than were his own contemporaries. One important reason why this is so is because of the work of Vincent G. Potter, s.j. His earlier study, *Charles S. Peirce: On Norms and Ideals*, is still one of the most important contributions to Peirce scholarship, even though it was published almost thirty years ago; and the present collection promises to stand shoulder to shoulder with that earlier study. But, for Father, Peirce scholarship all too quickly degenerates into an inconsequential exercise if it is not animated by philosophical *eros*, the passionate desire to discover what is not yet known. Accordingly, the essays collected in this volume are best conceived as, at once, invitations to join the ongoing work of theoretical inquiry *and* instructions for how such inquiry is responsibly conducted.

Fordham University   VINCENT M. COLAPIETRO

Notes

1. In 1989, there was a sesquicentennial international congress held at Harvard University celebrating Peirce's birth in 1839. Significantly enough, it was called "Charles Sanders Pierce Sesquicentennial International Congress." Father Potter was a speaker at one of the plenary sessions; his paper, a Peircean rejoinder to Charles Hartshorne's process critique of Peirce's theological "musements," appears as an Appendix to the present volume.

2. Though he himself did not write much about either philosophical or theological hermeneutics, two thinkers who influenced him (Bernard Lonergan and John E. Smith) have. His own practice seems closely to accord with the approach to interpretation defended and, indeed, exemplified by these two thinkers, especially Smith.

3. See, for example, Bernard Lonergan, *A Third Collection* (London: Geoffrey Chapman, 1985).

4. *Ideas and Opinions* (New York: Crown Publishers, 1954), p. 72.

5. *Charles Sanders Peirce: Contributions to the Nation*, ed. Kenneth Laine Ketner, Graduate Studies No. 30 (Lubbock: Texas Tech Press, 1987), II, 276

6. R. B. Perry, *The Thought and Character of William James*. II. *Philosophy and Psychology* (Boston: Little, Brown, 1935), p. 289.

7. Ibid.

8. See John E. Smith, *Experience and God* (New York: Oxford University Press, 1968; repr. New York: Fordham University Press, 1995), and *The Analogy of Experience: An Approach to Understanding Religious Truth* (New York: Harper & Row, 1973); and Robert Neville, *The Cosmology of Freedom* (Albany: State University of New York Press, 1995).

9. In *Experience, Reason, and God: John E. Smith in Dialogue*, ed. Vincent M. Colapietro (New York: Fordham University Press, 1996), this specific exchange is sharply focused.

TO THE READER

THE ESSAYS IN THIS COLLECTION were written at different times, for different audiences, and for different occasions. Hence, each stands on its own and can be read independently of the others, provided, of course, the reader have some knowledge of who Charles Peirce was and what in general his philosophical position was. Again, given the circumstances of how each essay came to be written, it is inevitable that there be some repetition, but I have tried to edit out what could be deleted without destroying the sense. I hope the reader will not be too annoyed with any remaining redundancy since it might turn out to be a case of *repetitio, mater studiorum*. Finally, these essays do have a unity: they center on several key Peircean positions (realism, pragmatism, tychism, synechism, and theism) and try to show that these positions are systematically related and internally consistent.

Some may be surprised, or even disappointed, that there is no extensive treatment of semeiotic, admittedly an important and novel contribution of Peirce's to philosophical analysis. But I have explicitly discussed the most basic notions of Peirce's semeiotic in connection with his theory of cognition, both underscoring that he held all human knowing to be mediated by signs and explaining in some detail the meaning and implication of this position. Moreover, my treatment in the later chapters of experience as a medium of disclosure is at least implicitly semeiotic, for disclosure itself is certainly a semeiotic phenomenon *par excellence*. It is true that, in discussing the disclosure of God in and through our experience, I have not drawn extensively upon Peirce's fine-grained analyses and classifications of signs, objects, and interpretants. But it is also true that I have acknowledged in various places the fact that Peirce's philosophical perspective is a semeiotic perspective.

Let us look at the list of essays to show briefly how they are connected. Chapter 1 surveys briefly Peirce's life and philosophy, especially his realism and pragmatism. Chapter 2 adds some material to the biographical material in the first chapter, particularly Peirce's sojourn in England in the 1870s. It also shows the influence on his work of three philosophers from the British Isles—

Scotus, Whewell, and Bain. These three were chosen not only because of their impact on Peirce's pragmatism, but also because their influence on him is less well known than that of Locke, Berkeley, and Hume, not to mention Ockham. Ideally, this chapter should be supplemented by two others, one on his French Connection and the other on his German Connection.

Chapters 3, 4, and 5 deal with how Peirce viewed the relations of normative science, methodology, and pragmatism to one another. Chapters 6 and 7 deal with three key issues in Peirce's ontology and theory of knowledge: realism, the notion of substance, and foundationalism. Chapter 8 deals with "continuity" as a key mathematical notion and a central philosophical category to which Peirce gives much attention, while Chapter 9 deals with the important issues of substantial unity and the foundations of knowledge.

Finally, Chapters 10, 11, 12, and the Appendix take up the issue of Peirce's theism, focusing in 12 on his "Neglected Argument for the Reality of God." Chapter 10, in particular, explores how Peirce viewed the role of experience in religion, and in the course of that discussion attention is again paid to his analysis of human knowing.

I am indebted to so many colleagues and friends who over the years offered criticisms and suggestions to inspire these pieces that I simply cannot enumerate them all here. Let me say simply that I owe a great debt to my professors at Yale, especially John E. Smith; to my colleagues in the Philosophy Department here at Fordham; and to my associates at Indiana University, especially Christian Kloesel and Nathan Houser, and at Texas Tech, especially Kenneth Laine Ketner.

Fordham University   VINCENT G. POTTER

1

Charles Sanders Peirce: An Overview

His Life

CHARLES SANDERS PEIRCE, philosopher, logician, scientist, father of American pragmatism, died of cancer on April 19, 1914, after five years of great suffering.[1] He died an isolated old man of 75, still working on his manuscripts, without a publisher, without students or followers, practically unknown, penniless, and alone. This man, unappreciated in his lifetime, virtually ignored by the academic world of his day, is now recognized as perhaps America's most original philosopher and her greatest logician. Indeed, on the latter score, he is surely one of the logical giants of the nineteenth century, which produced such geniuses as Cantor, Frege, Boole, De Morgan, Russell, and Whitehead. Today, more than eighty years after his death, another generation of scholars is beginning to pay him the attention he deserves.

Who, then, was Charles Peirce? He was born on September 10, 1839, in Cambridge, Massachusetts, the second son of Benjamin and Sarah Hunt Peirce. His father, a professor at Harvard and one of the greatest American mathematicians of his day, played a decisive role in Charles's upbringing and formal education, much in the way the elder Mill influenced his son, John Stuart. Charles's father early introduced him to mathematics, the physical sciences, and logic. At the age of eight Charles took up the study of chemistry on his own, and at twelve had set up his own small laboratory. About the same time he composed a short history of that science. At thirteen, he had read and mastered his elder brother's logic

---

An earlier version of this chapter was given as a lecture at Fairfield University in 1964 on the fiftieth anniversary of Peirce's death.

textbook. At fifteen, he entered Harvard College, and graduated four years later, in 1859, one of the youngest in his class. And yet, for all his genius, his scholastic record was poor. He describes himself as "a very insouciant student."

Peirce's interest in philosophy began during those undergraduate days. He read and expounded as best he could Schiller's *Aesthetische Briefe* to his friend and classmate Horatio Paine. He studied Kant's *Critique of Pure Reason* so thoroughly that he knew whole passages of it almost by heart. Still, due in large measure to his father's influence, he chose to become a scientist. In 1863 he received from Harvard his Bachelor of Science in Chemistry *summa cum laude*. Meanwhile, in 1861, Peirce had joined the United States Coast and Geodetic Survey, with which he was to be associated for thirty years, holding many important posts and doing much original research in photometry and gravitation. In fact, the only book he succeeded in getting published during his lifetime was entitled *Photometric Researches* (1878), and for it he won international recognition. Again, in connection with this research, he received the only official vote of confidence in his entire career when in 1877 he was elected a fellow of the National Academy of Arts and Sciences and a member of the National Academy of Science.

Despite his dedication to science, his interest in philosophy never diminished. In fact, it was strengthened and confirmed by his scientific work. His early efforts were concentrated in the fields of logic and the philosophy of science and in these areas anticipated much of present-day work. The technical papers he published between 1867 and 1885 established him as one of the greatest formal logicians of the day. He lectured at Harvard as an official member of the staff three times between 1864 and 1871, and it was about this time that the "Metaphysical Club," as Peirce later called it, was formed—an informal discussion group which met fortnightly to discuss philosophical problems. It numbered among its members some of the finest minds of the day—Oliver Wendell Holmes, Jr., William James, Chauncey Wright, Francis Abbot, and Nicholas St. John Green, among others—and it was in this imposing intellectual milieu that "pragmatism first saw the light of day." About the same time, too, Peirce's interest in logic led him to read the great scholastics—Aquinas, Scotus, Ockham, Bacon—and to declare unequivocally for "scholastic realism" against nominalism in every form. This exposure to the famous controversy over universals decisively influenced his brand of pragmatism, as we shall see.

Although it is certain that Peirce first discussed and formulated the pragmatic maxim in these informal meetings, the first definite statement of it did not appear until 1878, in a paper originally written in French while he was on his way to Europe in connection with his government employment, and published in *Popular Science Monthly* under the title "How to Make Our Ideas Clear." It read as follows:

> Consider what effects, which might conceivably have practical bearing, we conceive the object to have. Then, our conception of these effects is the whole of our conception of the object. (5.402)

The statement is admittedly crude and led to misunderstanding and misinterpretation by other philosophers who called themselves pragmatists. Peirce would take great pains to clarify his real meaning.

Despite his eagerness to teach, despite his ability and originality, Peirce never had the opportunity to do so for more than eight years of his life. Apart from the early Harvard lectures, his only academic post was at The Johns Hopkins University, and this he held for only five years (1879–1884). After that he never mounted a university podium except to deliver an occasional series of lectures by invitation, despite the direct and personal intervention of William James to the President of Harvard to appoint Peirce to a chair. Yet he was an inspiring lecturer. Too advanced perhaps for the ordinary student, he challenged the more gifted and was respected and highly esteemed by all. He organized a second metaphysical club for his students at John Hopkins, among whom was John Dewey. His rejection by university administrations was due in part to his difficult personality and in part to domestic problems. Paul Weiss sums up his character this way: "he was always somewhat proud of his ancestry and connections, overbearing toward those who stood in his way, indifferent to the consequences of his acts, quick to take affront, highly emotional, easily duped, and with, as he puts it, 'a reputation for not finding things.'"[2] His first marriage in 1862 to Harriet Melusina Fay (granddaughter of the prominent Episcopalian Bishop John Henry Hopkins) ended in divorce in 1883 while Peirce was teaching in Baltimore. His career there ended the next year. He subsequently married Juliette Froissey of Nancy, France, to whom he was devoted the rest of his life, and who survived him. In 1887, having inherited a small legacy, Peirce, now 48, retired to a small farm near Milford, Pennsylvania, where he lived out his life studying and writing. He was continually in financial straits. Once he applied to the Carnegie Foundation for help in publishing a series of books, but he was turned down. He was all but in exile. Near the end, it was only the touching fidelity of his lifelong friend William James that sustained him. Upon his death his widow sold all his papers to Harvard, where they remain to this day.

Such was the brilliant and tragic career of Charles Peirce. Though he never published a book on philosophy, his articles and drafts fill volumes. It has only been since the publication of the *Collected Papers* in the 1930s that the philosophic community has begun to appreciate the scope and depth of his speculations. Peirce is beginning to find his place in American thought: a place in the first rank. A new chronological edition of his works is in progress at the Indianapolis Campus of Indiana University under the general direction of Nathan Houser. Of the projected twenty or twenty-five volumes, five have already appeared.

His Work

Realism vs. *Nominalism*

Why should Peirce be of interest to us? Because, I suggest, he is a very great thinker, and because he is a very great American thinker. But there is another reason why he is of particular interest to me. He knew, respected, and used the great tradition of Western thought, in particular the writings of the great Scholastic Doctors. He had a sense of continuity amid the dramatic changes in Western culture, and that sense saved him from being merely contemporary. It enabled him to address himself to an audience beyond his own time. He can speak to us whose world is perhaps even more dramatically different from his than his was from the Middle Ages. He was able to address himself to the relation of thought and action so much a concern for us today in the areas of social adaptation and politics. I find it remarkable that a great scientist, logician, and philosopher of the nineteenth century not only spent a good deal of time reading the original texts of Aquinas and Scotus but also declared for them on the great issue of our day as well as theirs: nominalism *vs.* realism. He could say at the end of his career that although he had revised his system several times over and changed his mind about many things, he always held himself to be a "scholastic realist."

Peirce certainly was not uncritical of Scholastic thought. Though he was aware that much in it needed updating, he also recognized that much was to be learned from it.

> The works of Duns Scotus have strongly influenced me. If his logic and metaphysics, not slavishly worshipped, but torn away from its medievalism, be adapted to modern culture, under continual wholesome reminders of nominalistic criticisms, I am convinced that it will go far toward supplying the philosophy which is best harmonized with physical science. (1.6)

In one of his early Harvard lectures he paid the Scholastic Doctors the highest compliment of which a man of science is capable. He likened their devotion to that discovering of the truth of the spirit which animates the scientific mind. And he contrasted it with the vanity of "those intellectual nomads, the modern metaphysicians, including the positivists," who seem to be more interested in the brilliant hypothesis than in the humble facts.

> Above all it is the searching thoroughness of the schoolmen which affiliates them with men of science and separates them, world-wide, from modern so-called philosophers. The thoroughness I allude to consists in this, that in adopting any theory, they go about everywhere, they devote their whole energies and lives in putting it to the tests *bona fide*. (1.33)

And again:

> Now this same unwearied interest in testing general propositions is what produced those long rows of folios of the schoolmen, and if the test which they employed is of only limited validity . . . yet the *spirit*, which is the most essential thing—the *motive*, was nearly the same. And how different this spirit is from that of the major part, though not all, of modern philosophers—even those who have

called themselves empirical, no man who is actuated by it can fail to perceive. (1.34)

What, then, was the issue at stake in the nominalist-realist controversy? It was not whether there was an external world, for nominalists and realists alike accepted that as but the requirement of common sense. It was, rather, whether "laws and general types are figments of the mind or are real." If they are figments of the mind, then the world is not in itself intelligible. It does not exhibit any rational structure; it is but a mad puzzle into which man must introduce order. If, on the other hand, they are real, then scientific inquiry seeks to discover the world's structure revealing itself in experience. In a word, because knowledge is always through general categories or universals, if it is to be knowledge of or about the world, the categories or universals must be grounded in that world: the world must exhibit itself as having a rational structure; that is, it must follow some kind of law. For this reason Peirce held that science always has been, and indeed must be, on the side of Scholastic realism, no matter how nominalistic the majority of philosophers who talk about science.

I need not mention that the realism of the scholastics admitted a variety of theories. Nor need I go into the differences between Scotus and Aquinas on this central issue. But I should say a word about why Peirce chose to follow John Duns rather than Thomas. The reason is simply this: Peirce saw in Scotus's plurality of forms and formalities a stronger type of realism than Thomas's stricter Aristotelianism. Thus, he called himself a scholastic realist of a rather extreme stripe. He even criticized Scotus for having been tinged with nominalism because he held onto a theory of the contraction of the universal to the singular through "haecceity" or "thisness." Thomists are fond of criticizing Scotists for a tendency toward extreme realism, while Peirce, oddly, criticizes them for not being extreme enough. Peirce seems to go as far as to make the individual nothing but a bundle of universals (or habits, as he calls them). This is perhaps a serious mistake, and he errs, if indeed he does, in the opposite direction to those nominalists whom he is combating and so, according to some of his critics, never quite satisfactorily accounts for the concrete singular.

If Peirce may have been on the wrong track in his handling of the concrete individual, it seems clear to me that he was on the right one in his insistence on the reality of the general. And it is in this that he made his peculiar contribution to American pragmatism, which, unfortunately, has since developed in a decidedly nominalistic way.

His Pragmaticism

Peirce's pragmatism cannot be adequately discussed without an acquaintance with his general categories: Firstness, Secondness, and Thirdness. Now, the names Peirce gave to the categories are not very informative, and he chose them precisely for that reason. Because they are universal categories, cutting across all reality in much the same way as Scholastic transcendentals do, Peirce felt that no more specific terms would do them justice. He himself likened them to various trios of more familiar categories as a help to his readers, while reminding those readers that the more familiar terms only approximated what he had in mind. For our purposes we can use the more familiar terms. Thus, Firstness approximates the quality peculiar to each thing taken in itself, independent of its relation to anything else. This is close to pure possibility. Secondness approximates the notion of brute, irrational action-reaction, clash, struggle, opposition. This brute aspect characterizes the concrete singular as such. Thirdness approximates the notion of law, rationality, objective thought, real generality or potentiality. Thus, we have: quality, reaction, law; pure possibility, actuality, potentiality; feeling, volition, thought; and so on.

Let us take James's version of pragmatism as typical of the position from which Peirce was to take care to dissociate himself. James once defined his pragmatism as the idea that "the effective meaning of any philosophic proposition can always be brought down to some particular consequence in our future practical experience, whether active or passive; the point lying rather in the fact that the experience must be particular, than in the fact that it must be active." It looks for the "cash-value" of particular concrete experience and makes it the ultimate interpretant of thought.

Thus, when in 1896 William James's *Will to Believe* appeared, Peirce complained that James had pushed the pragmatic maxim "to such extremes as must tend to give us pause." Peirce interpreted his old friend to hold that man's end is action, and, in his article "Pragmatic and Pragmatism," in Baldwin's *Dictionary of Philosophy and Psychology* (1902), criticized him for not seeing that, far from action's being man's end, action itself supposes an end.

> If it be admitted, on the contrary, that action wants an end, and that that end must be something of a general description, then the spirit of the maxim itself, which is that we must look to the upshot of our concepts in order rightly to apprehend them, would direct us towards something different from practical facts, namely, to general ideas, as the true interpreters of our thought. (5.3)

Action cannot be the final logical interpretant of thought because it is not general, but thought is. Thought can be interpreted only in terms of thought; the general can be understood only in terms of the general. The meaning of a conception can be found, not in action, but in the end for which the action (resulting from the conception) is done. The pragmatic maxim should be applied in a thoroughgoing way, Peirce tells us, but,

> when that has been done, and not before, a still higher grade of clearness of thought can be attained by remembering that the only ultimate good which the practical facts to which it directs attention can subserve is to further the development of concrete reasonableness; so that the meaning to the concept does not lie in any individual reactions at all, but in the manner in which those reactions contribute to that development. (5.3)

The meaning of a concept, therefore, is judged in terms of the contribution that the reactions it evokes make toward the realization of the ultimate end of thought. In other words, Peirce introduces a normative function into the pragmatic maxim. The pragmatic maxim, then, seems to be a way of recognizing the reality of the objects of general ideas in their generality. But general ideas "govern" action; they are really laws of growth; they are really final causes; they are really normative.

Peirce himself in his *Dictionary* article admits that his early formulation of the pragmatic maxim might be interpreted in the way in which James, for one, did, but implies that he never meant, even in 1878, his doctrine to be the "stoical axiom" that man's end is action. He explains:

Indeed, in the article of 1878, . . . the writer practised better than he preached; for he applied the stoical maxim most unstoically, in such a sense as to insist upon the reality of the objects of general ideas in their generality. (5.3)

Now, if one rereads carefully "How to Make Our Ideas Clear" in the light of Peirce's subsequent doctrine concerning the nature of habit (as a third or a general), it will become clear that his estimation of his intent and meaning in that article is correct. He did not make action man's end; nor did he make action the end of man's thinking. Action, no doubt, is involved in thinking both in the sense that thinking is a form of action and in the sense that thinking normally results in action and action is a criterion of thought. Peirce does not say that action is the purpose of thinking; he says, rather, that "the establishment of a belief, a rule of action, a habit of action is thought's purpose." But a habit is not an action; it is of an entirely different category. A habit is general; an action is singular. (A habit is a third, while an action is a second.) Still, though this is what Peirce meant and what he strictly said, a superficial reading of the paper could easily lead to misinterpretation.

In any case, in 1903, Peirce decided to make pragmatism the subject of his lectures at Harvard. It would give him an opportunity to compare his doctrine with rivals of the same name. He tells us that he has no particular fault to find with the numerous definitions of pragmatism he had lately come across, yet "to say exactly what pragmatism is describes pretty well what you and I have to puzzle out together" (5.16). Then in a playful and ironic passage Peirce teases the "new pragmatists" for not acknowledging their source.

> To speak plainly, a considerable number of philosophers have lately written as they might have written in case they had been reading either what I wrote but were ashamed to confess it, or had been reading something that some reader of mine had read. For they seem quite disposed to adopt my term *pragmatism*. I shouldn't wonder if they were ashamed of me. What could be more humiliating than to confess that one had learned anything of a logician? (5.17)

Peirce is delighted to share the opinions of such a brilliant company and has no complaint to make against them except that they are "lively."

> The new pragmatists seem to be distinguished for their terse, vivid and concrete style of expression together with a certain buoyancy of tone as if they were conscious of carrying about them the master key to all the secrets of metaphysics. (5.17)

No doubt, Peirce has in mind this "cocksureness," not merely qualities of literary style, when he chides the pragmatists for being too "lively." One thing that he could not tolerate was "cocksureness." This was for him the very antithesis of the scientific attitude or humble "fallibilism." It is clear that Peirce had in mind James (among others), who enthusiastically pushed the maxim to extremes. The pragmatic maxim was not intended to be an open-sesame for all metaphysical problems or a panacea for all intellectual ills. Peirce meant it merely to be an aid toward "making our ideas clear." (It is a method, not a *Weltanschauung*; cf. 5.13, note 1, ca. 1902.) It was put forward not as a principle of speculative philosophy, but as a logical maxim, or, better, a semantical maxim that would help guide logical and, finally, metaphysical investigation. No doubt, the maxim involves a great deal of the speculative, but it itself is not a "sublime principle of speculative philosophy."

Therefore, around 1903, due to the sudden popularity of "pragmatism," Peirce was very much preoccupied with dissociating his views from those circulating at the time and with making his own very clear and unequivocal. More than once he demanded, directly and indirectly, that he be given credit for having introduced the term into philosophy and for having laid the groundwork on which others had built (however, so badly). Again, in 1905, Peirce felt that he ought to try once more to explain what his conception of pragmatism entailed and he even went so far as to coin a new word for it:

> So, then, the writer, finding his bantling "pragmatism" so promoted, feels that it is time to kiss his child good-by and relinquish it to its higher destiny; while to serve the precise purpose of expressing the original definition, he begs to announce the birth of the word "pragmaticism" which is ugly enough to be safe from kidnappers. (5.414)

This series of three articles appeared in *The Monist*.

The pragmatic in Peirce's sense is not to be confused with the practical. It is not the practical consequences of a notion which make it true, and meaningful, but its truth and meaningfulness which make it have consequences. An idea's consequences may be criteria for, but do not constitute in some crude sense, its truth and meaningfulness. Thus, we are back to Peirce's repudiation of the crude notion that action is man's end and what makes ideas true and significant. The key to an idea's truth and significance is its relation "to some definite human purpose," to some end which governs action, as law governs cases. Rational cognition is an instance of Thirdness and so must be interpreted in terms of some other third. For Peirce this can be nothing else but rational purpose. The pragmatic maxim, then, is but a way of expressing this relation. Once again, therefore, we see that Peirce intends meaning to be identical with rational purpose, not with action alone.

In the same 1905 article, Peirce tries to answer certain objections, indicating as clearly as one could wish the connection he saw between pragmaticism and normative science. It is objected, first, that according to the pragmatic position nothing enters into the meaning of a concept but an experiment; but an experiment, in itself, cannot reveal anything more than a constant conjunction of antecedent and consequent (5.424). This typical Humean objection, Peirce observes, betrays a misunderstanding of the fundamental point of pragmaticism. In the first place, the objection misrepresents what is involved in an "experiment." An experiment is not an isolated, "atomic" event, but one always situated in a connected series forming a system. An experiment essentially involves the following ingredients: (1) an experimenter, (2) a verifiable hypothesis concerning the experimenter's environment, and (3) a sincere doubt in the experimenter's mind concerning the truth of that hypothesis. The experimenter, by an act of choice, must single out certain identifiable objects to be operated upon. Then, by an external (or quasi-external) act, he modifies those objects. Next comes a subsequent reaction of the world upon the experimenter through perception. Finally, he recognizes the teaching of the experiment.

> While the two chief parts of the event itself are the action and the reaction, yet the *unity of essence of the experiment lies in its purpose and plan*, the ingredients passed over in the enumeration. (5.424; emphasis added)

In the second place, this sort of objection fails to catch the pragmaticist's attitude of mind. Rational meaning does not consist in an experiment, but in *experimental phenomena*. The phenomena to which the pragmaticist refers are not particular events which have already happened to someone or to something in the past, but "what *surely will* happen to everybody in the living future who shall fulfill certain conditions" (5.425). The essence of experimental phenomena, then, is that they have been predicated.

> The phenomenon consists in the fact that when an experimentalist shall come to *act* according to certain schemes that he has in mind, then will something else happen, and shatter the doubts of sceptics, like the celestial fire upon the altar of Elijah. (5.425)

In the third place, this sort of objection overlooks, in a very nominalistic way, the fact that the experimenter is not interested in this or that single experimental phenomenon. He is interested in their *general kinds*, for what is conditionally true *in futuro* can only be general. In other words, experimental method implicitly at least affirms the reality of generals (5.426).

It is just at this point that the connection between pragmaticism and the normative sciences becomes unmistakable. Peirce asks how it is that the rational meaning of a proposition lies in the future. According to his theory a proposition has meaning precisely to the extent to which, by its form, it becomes applicable to human conduct, "not in these or those special circumstances, nor when one entertains this or that special design, but that form which is most directly applicable to self-control under every situation, and to every purpose" (5.427). Now, only future conduct is subject to self-control, and for the proposition's form to apply to every situation and purpose upon which it has any bearing, "it must be simply the general description of all the experimental phenomena which the assertion of the proposition virtually predicts" (5.427). According to pragmaticism, therefore, a proposition's meaning is capacity for governing future action through the knower's exercise of self-control. That is its "rational purport."

The next objection is that pragmaticism is a thoroughgoing phenomenalism. Peirce denies the allegation in the light of what had just been said about "rational purport." We pass over that in order to get to the answer to the next objection more directly connected with the point we have been trying to make. This is the crucial objection, in Peirce's view, and it involves the fundamental mistake of James.

> QUESTIONER: Well, if you choose so to make Doing the Be-all and the End-all of human life, why do you not make meaning to consist simply in doing? Doing has to be done at a certain time upon a certain object. Individual objects and single events cover all reality, as everybody knows, and as a practicalist ought to be the first to insist. Yet, your meaning, as you have described it, is *general*. Thus, it is of the nature of a mere word and not a reality. . . . (5.429)

The objection is put about as forcibly and clearly as it can be. For Peirce it touches the very heart of the matter, because it illustrates the fundamental option between nominalism and realism. The objection is powerful because it involves so many things that have to be admitted, and Peirce clears away the ground by immediately conceding what he must:

> It must be admitted, in the first place, that if pragmaticism really made Doing to be the Be-all and the End-all of life, that would be its death. For to say that we live for the mere sake of action, as action, regardless of the thought it carries out, would be to say that there is no such thing as rational purport. Secondly, it must be admitted that every proposition professes to be true of a certain real individual object, often the environing universe. Thirdly, it must be admitted that pragmaticism fails to furnish any translation or meaning of a proper name, or other designation of an individual object. Fourthly, the pragmaticistic meaning is undoubtedly general; and it is equally indisputable that the general is of the nature of a word or sign. Fifthly, it must be admitted that individuals alone exist; and sixthly, it may be admitted that the very meaning of a word or significant object ought to be the very essence of reality of what it signifies. (5.429)

These admissions come down to this: pragmaticism holds that meaning or rational purport, because it is necessarily general, can only belong to the category of Thirdness, and, consequently, as has so often been observed, cannot be reduced to action-reaction or to individual existence, which belongs to the category of Secondness. Of course, a general is of the nature of a word or sign, precisely because it cannot be exhausted by a singular individual instance, just as a word or sign can stand for many different individuals. Though it is true that generals do not *exist*, it does not follow that they are not *real*. They have the reality of *types* or *forms* to which objects may conform but which none of them can exactly be (5.429). In other words, those generals which are real have a *normative function* ("scholastic realism," cf. 1.16ff., Lowell Lectures, 1903).

Some generals, then, are real. Furthermore, they may have a real efficacy in just the same way as common sense acknowledges an efficiency in human purposes. Human actions are controlled in terms of human purposes; they are specified and determined by certain ends and goals. So, too, real generals specify and determine human knowledge. Real generals are what constitute the cosmos as ordered and intelligible and so are both the conditions of possibility that there be any rationality whatsoever and the normative principles of a rationality (human) continually dependent upon the shock of experience. Peirce puts it this way: "individual existence or actuality without any regularity whatever is a nullity. Chaos is pure nothing" (5.431).

According to Peirce, if this "scholastic realism" be put in the form of a general conditional proposition as to the future calculated to influence human conduct, one has the pragmatic maxim. True pragmatism, therefore, or, as Peirce preferred, "pragmaticism," does not make action the *summum bonum*, but rather the growth of concrete reasonableness in the world of existents. As evolution progresses, human intelligence plays a greater and greater role in that development through its characteristic power of self-control. There is an interaction between human intelligence and the evolutionary process. In the beginning human intelligence emerged from that process, but once emerged, it influences the course of evolution through deliberate conduct. Human intelligence becomes one of nature's agents in that process. Nature's objective regularity specifies man's knowledge (final cause) accordingly. Even if, through some perversity, some men, even over long periods of time, should choose to counteract Nature's directives, in the long run experience will force man to recognize her as growing in rationality in spite of him and as guiding him in the development of his own quest for reason.

Accordingly, the pragmaticist does not make the *summum bonum* to consist in action, but makes it to consist in that process of evolution whereby the existent comes more and more to embody those generals which were just now said to be *destined*, which is what we strive to express in calling them *reasonable*. In its higher stages, evolution takes place more and more largely through self-control, and this gives the pragmatist a sort of justification for making the rational purport to be general. (5.433)

After having remarked the close parallelism between the pragmatic maxim and Aristotle's *dictum de omni* (5.435), Peirce concludes this extremely informative article by insisting upon the utter inadequacy of action (Secondness in general) to account for the generality (Thirdness) involved in meaning (5.436). To understand fully all that is involved in this contention, one would have to undertake a serious study of continuity, which "is simply what generality becomes in the logic of relatives, and thus, like generality, is an affair of thought, and is the essence of thought." The motive for alluding to this theory, says Peirce, is to emphasize what is absolutely essential to the doctrine of pragmaticism: namely, that

> the third category—the category of thought, representation, triadic relations, mediation, genuine thirdness, thirdness as such—is an essential ingredient of reality, yet does not by itself constitute reality, since this category can have no concrete being without action, as a separate object on which to work its government, just as action cannot exist without the immediate being of feeling on which to act. (5.436)

Almost fifteen years earlier (ca. 1892) Peirce had said, "My philosophy resuscitates Hegel in a strange costume" (1.42). Indeed, the "Secret of Hegel" was just that he had discovered that the universe is everywhere permeated with continuous growth (1.40–41). Peirce tells us again that pragmaticism is "closely allied to Hegelian absolute idealism," with this important difference: Thirdness alone is not enough to make the world. Hegel's fundamental mistake was to dismiss Firstness and Secondness (5.436; cf. 5.79, 5.37ff.).

In 1906 Peirce added a long note to the original statement of the pragmatic maxim as it appeared in "How to Make Our Ideas Clear." The first thing he remarks is that he used, contrary to his wont, five derivates of the word *concipere* in the maxim's formulation. He did so for two reasons: (1) to show that he was speaking of meaning "in no other sense than that of <u>intellectual purport</u>," and (2) "to avoid all danger of being understood as attempting to explain a concept by percepts, images, schemata, or by anything but concepts." Action is like the finale of a symphony of thought. Nobody would say that the finale was the purpose of the symphony; it is, rather, its upshot.

Of course, pragmatism recognizes a connection between thought and action. It ultimately makes thought apply to action, but to conceived action. This is quite a different matter from saying either that thought (that is, the purport of symbols) consists in action or that thought's ultimate purpose is action.

> Pragmaticism makes thinking to consist in the living inferential metaboly of symbols whose purport lies in conditional general resolutions to act. As for the ultimate purpose of thought, which must be the purpose of everything, it is beyond human comprehension; but according to the stage of approach which my thought has made to it—with aid from many persons, among whom I may mention Royce (in his *World and Individual*), Schiller (in his *Riddles of the Sphinx*), as well, by the way, as the famous poet [Friedrich Schiller] (in his *Aesthetische Briefe*), Henry James the elder (in his *Substance and Shadow* and in his conversations), together with Swedenborg himself—it is by the indefinite replication of self-control upon self-control that the *vir* is begotten, and by action, through thought, he grows an esthetic ideal, not for the behoof of his own poor noodle merely, but as the share which God permits him to have in the work of creation. (5.403, n. 3)

Notes

1. The biographical material comes from Paul Weiss's article, "CSP," in the *Dictionary of American Biography,* 1934, 14, 398–403.

2. Ibid., p. 399.

2
Peirce's British Connection

ALTHOUGH CHARLES PEIRCE is perhaps most often remembered as the father of the philosophical movement known as pragmatism, he was also, and perhaps especially, a logician, a working scientist, and a mathematician.[1] During his lifetime Peirce most often referred to himself, and was referred to by his colleagues, as a logician. Furthermore, Peirce spent thirty years actively engaged in scientific research for the United States Coast and Geodetic Survey. The National Archives in Washington, D.C., hold some five thousand pages of his reports on this work. Finally, the four volumes of his mathematical papers edited by Professor Carolyn Eisele eloquently testify to his contributions to that field as well.

These facts are important background to what I have to say in this essay. I will talk about Peirce's philosophy, but what I have to say can be properly appreciated only when Peirce's philosophy is understood as growing out of his firsthand experience with experimental science and its methodology. Peirce's pragmatism, I contend, is significantly, even radically, different from that of James or Dewey, because it is the result of his reflections upon his own life in the laboratory and of his thorough, even painstaking, study of logic. Neither James nor Dewey had quite this combination of experiences. James was a physician and experimental psychologist, but not a logician. Dewey was a logician, but not a working scientist. But Peirce, from his boyhood, lived science, logic, and philosophy. From this passionate interest, from this consuming desire to understand the world and our understanding of it, his pragmatism was born.

The British scientific and philosophical tradition played a major

---

An earlier version of this chapter appeared as "Charles Sanders Peirce: 1839–1914," in *American Philosophy*, ed. Marcus G. Singer (Cambridge: Cambridge University Press, 1985), pp. 21–41.

role in shaping Peirce's thought. I am convinced that his distinctive view of pragmatism is in continuity with an authentic British philosophical tradition which antedates the classical empiricism-triumvirate of Locke, Berkeley, and Hume. We might call this Peirce's "British Connection."

Even so, Peirce is not simply a British philosopher who happened to grow up in the Colonies. His pragmatism has a distinctively American spirit about it, although that spirit may be difficult to state succinctly. The so-called "classical" period of American philosophy is usually said to extend from the end of the American Civil War to just before World War II. During that time, according to some, philosophy in America became American Philosophy.[2] Under the umbrella term "pragmatism," philosophers in America developed a distinctively American "spirit," if not a philosophical doctrine. That spirit, put roughly, was that ideas, if they are to merit serious attention, must be practical. They must not remain mere abstractions, but must have some payoff or relevance to the problems of men.

Prior to this classical period, however, philosophy in America was largely a repetition of European thought—mostly British Empiricism but with generous doses of Scottish Commonsensism and a dash of French Enlightenment. After the Civil War, German thought began to have a major impact on American thinkers. Kant and Hegel gained influence largely through the St. Louis Hegelians.[3] About that time, too, increasing numbers of Americans were going to Germany to study. Among them, for example, was William James. These students returned marked by that experience and enthusiastic to take the German university as the model for the fledgling American graduate education. Although Peirce never studied in Germany, he traveled there extensively on scientific business, and knew German philosophical thought through his close study of Kant. Peirce's pragmatism, we might say, was born of British and of German stock. Yet his "bantling," as he once called it (5.14), has a definite resemblance to its British ancestry in its concern for the empirical. Late in his life, reminiscing about the meetings in Cambridge, Massachusetts, of the "Metaphysical Club" in the early 1870s, Peirce remarked:

> The type of our thought was decidedly British. I, alone of our number, had come upon the threshing floor of philosophy through the

doorway of Kant, and even my ideas were acquiring the English accent. (5.12)

Only recently has Peirce's work received recognition within the scientific and academic communities in America and Europe.[4] In fact, there have been testimonials to his genius which, to some, might seem extravagant. Let me cite just one example. In a paper on Peirce's existential graphs read to the Institute of Mathematics and Its Application on January 20, 1981, Professor J. A. Faris, formerly of the Queen's University of Belfast, gave this appraisal of Peirce: "He was a polymath, and because of the extraordinary range of his knowledge and interests, and the great strength and originality of his intellect, I think of him as deserving to be classed along with, for example, Aristotle and Leibniz."[5] This is to put Pierce in no mean company. If such an appraisal is correct, philosophers, at least, ought not to neglect his views, even if only to criticize them.

Recently, the German side of pragmatism's family has recognized its descendant. Contemporary German thinkers have taken a more than passing interest in Peirce's semeiotic theory and in his understanding of the relation of theory and praxis. I have in mind, of course, among others, the Frankfurt school.[6]

While Peirce's recognition by scholarly professionals is perhaps finally assured, still his works are not likely to be read by the general public. William James, Peirce's lifelong friend, once described him as full of flashes of brilliance amid Cimmerian darkness.[7] Anyone who has struggled with Peirce's texts knows what James meant. This obscure quality to much of Peirce's writing explains in part the fact that he was in eclipse until relatively recently. Besides, his published papers were few. His voluminous unpublished writings were for many years virtually unavailable. When in the 1930s Charles Hartshorne and Paul Weiss edited the *Collected Papers*, their choice of materials represented only a small part of the manuscripts. A new chronological edition, currently in preparation at the Indianapolis campus of Indiana University, will make available a great deal more of the manuscript material. At present at least twenty volumes are projected. Still, Peirce's obscure style and the inherent difficulty of his subject matter will most likely keep him off the best-seller list.

Now that Peirce's papers are being more thoroughly examined

by a growing number of scholars, the close connection between his personal experience of science and his pragmatic philosophy is becoming ever more evident. Let us consider, then, how that connection grew strong and assumed a definite character through his ties, formed by personal acquaintance and by study of their work, to Britain's philosophers and men of science.

Peirce visited England five times between 1870 and 1883 and while there got to know many of the most prominent British scientists, mathematicians, and logicians. He also won their esteem for his scientific, mathematical, and logical acumen. W. K. Clifford called him the greatest living logician[8] and this high opinion was concretely attested to by his election in 1880 to the London Mathematical Society.

Peirce's five journeys to Europe were all connected with his scientific work with the United States Coast and Geodetic Survey. His first visit to London was in 1870 when he was sent by the Survey as an advance party to check sites for the observation of the solar eclipse due to occur on December 22, 1870. On his second visit in 1875–1876 he visited the newly built Cavendish Laboratory at Cambridge University and consulted with Maxwell concerning the flexure of the pendulum. In 1877 he traveled to Europe a third time to deliver a paper to the International Geodetic Association in Stuttgart. It was during this ocean crossing that Peirce wrote his best-known article, "How to Make Our Ideas Clear," in which he formulated the so-called pragmatic maxim. To practice his French, Peirce composed the article in that language and later translated it into English. The English version was published first, in *Popular Science Monthly*, and about a year later the French version appeared in *Revue philosophique*. This essay was the second in a series of six that appeared in *Popular Science Monthly* under the general title "Illustration of the Logic of Science." It seems that Peirce had hoped to publish all six articles in French and in German as well as in English, but only the first two articles appeared in French, and none appeared in German.

In 1880 and 1883 Peirce made his final voyages to Europe. Not only was he then elected to the London Mathematical Society, but he was also a frequent guest of Clifford, Jevons, Spencer, and other friends at the Royal Society, the Athenaeum Club, and the Metaphysical Society.

Peirce thought that to do philosophy well it was absolutely essential to get logic straight. We know from any number of his papers that he greatly esteemed the work of British logicians. One such paper, "Why Study Logic?" (2.119–216), was intended to be part of a book he never published, "Minute Logic." In it Peirce contrasts what he calls "the English position" on reasoning (for example, Boole, De Morgan, Whewell, J. S. Mill, Jevons, Venn, et al.) with the "German position" (Sigwart, Wundt, Schuppe, Erdmann, Bergmann, Husserl, et al.) and comes down unequivocally on the side of the English. As Peirce sees it, the English consider logic to be objective, while the Germans consider it to be subjective. The English come to logic with their characteristic frame of mind. The "English position" opposes any doctrine that bases the soundness of reasoning on a sense of, or feeling for, rationality. For Peirce, there is not a logical taste or a logical instinct or a logical *Gefühl* in terms of which we recognize an argument as sound.[9] He rejects any attempt to reduce logic to intuition or to psychology. In effect, Peirce sees logic as the science of how one *ought* to think, not of how one *must* think. Logic, then, is a normative science, and reasoning is reasoning only if it is subject to critical control. Such critical control is exercised in terms of the purpose of any reasoning, namely, to avoid disappointments and disasters. The hard facts are what we want to know, he writes. The whole motive of one's reasoning is to prepare for them. Reasoning is to be judged sound, therefore, insofar as those hard facts will not and cannot disappoint what reason promises. How one feels about any mode of reasoning has nothing to do with it. "That is the *rationale* of the English doctrine. It is as perfect as it is simple" (2.173).

I think it worth noting that Peirce's preference for the "English position" makes the norm for logical validity *empirical* in two ways: (1) it makes reasoning to consist in the observation and manipulation of diagrams or "graphs"; and (2) it makes reasoning the means of attaining truth, that is, of discovering what is the case independently of what anyone might think or wish or hope. I am convinced that this objectivist view of logic led to two of Peirce's most important and original contributions to the field, namely, his system of existential graphs to diagram his logic of relatives[10] and his broadening of the notion of logic to include methodology (or a logic of discovery) by distinguishing inference into adduction, deduction, and induction.

Peirce was influenced in his thinking about science and its methodology not only by Britain's men of science and logicians but also by her philosophers. Since it would be impossible in a brief essay to treat all the British philosophers Peirce studied, I have selected three, each one of whom made a direct and positive contribution to his pragmatism. Two of them, Alexander Bain and William Whewell, were his contemporaries; the third, John Duns Scotus, flourished more than five hundred years earlier. Scotus inspired Peirce's version of realism; Whewell confirmed his interpretation of scientific method; and Bain furnished his logic with a psychological framework. We begin with Scotus.

Peirce considered the nominalist-realist controversy the most important philosophical issue on the solution of which just about everything else depended. In a long letter to Victoria Lady Welby in 1909, after recounting to her his early training, he writes:

> By this time the inexactitude of the Germans, and their tottering logic utterly disgusted me. I more and more admired British thought. Its one great and terrible fault, which my severe studies in the schoolmen rescued me from,—or rather, it was because I suspected they were right about this that I took to the study of them & found that they didn't go far enough to satisfy me,—was their extreme Nominalism. To be sure *all* modern philosophers were nominalists, even Hegel. But I was quite convinced they were absolutely wrong. Modern science, especially physics, is and must be . . . essentially on the side of scholastic realism.[11]

Scotus defended realism; Ockham championed nominalism. Peirce's account of how the nominalists assumed ascendancy in the universities, casting out the Dunces, as they were called, makes it a political rather than an intellectual matter. However that may have been, the important thing is to recall what was at stake, what the issue was between these two British thinkers. Peirce puts it this way in one place:

> Roughly speaking, the nominalists conceived the *general* element of cognition to be merely a convenience for understanding this and that fact and to amount to nothing except for cognition, while the realists, still more roughly speaking, looked upon the general, not

only as the end and aim of knowledge, but also as the most important element of being. Such was and is the question. (4.1)

The earliest published statement of Peirce's siding with the realists in this controversy is the 1868 paper "Some Consequences of Four Incapacities" in the *Journal of Speculative Philosophy*. There he develops his notion of Truth and of Reality which, so far as I can tell, he never retracted. Again in 1871 in his critical review of Fraser's edition of the works of Berkeley in the *North American Review*, he reiterates and develops his convictions about "scholastic realism." When I say that Peirce opted for "scholastic realism," I am using his own expression. Whether he thought that his realism was indeed that of Scotus, I am not sure. I rather think, however, that he realized that his version was significantly different, for he says that even Scotus was tinged with nominalism (1.560) in his insistence that *haecceitas* contracts the universal to the particular (8.208). Furthermore, Peirce characterizes his own realism as "extreme" over against Scotus's more moderate view (5.77, 5.470). Finally, he frequently identifies his realism with that proposed by his friend and colleague Francis E. Abbot in *Scientific Theism*; in that book Abbot consciously modified the realism of the scholastics along the lines of modern scientific systems, calling his view "Relationalism."[12] Other commentators, such as John Boler, have suggested other differences.[13] All that the phrase need mean is that Peirce was inspired by the Scholastic realists and developed a position something like theirs. They and he held that some general conceptions are real, that is, some are not mere figments of the mind.

According to Peirce, the nominalist would reason something like this. Nothing is immediately present to us but thoughts. Those thoughts are caused by sensations which in turn are constrained by something outside the mind. Because this something is outside the mind, it is independent of how we think, and is, therefore, the real. Whatever these external things be, they produce sensations which can be embraced under some conception. One can say, for example, that one man is like another, but there is no way in which one can justly claim that two real men have anything in common. One knows only the mental term or thought-sign "man" standing indifferently for the sets of sensations caused by the two external realities. Strictly speaking, the sets of sensations do not have anything at all in common either. Such a view makes reality to consist exclusively in bare particulars which, because they are outside consciousness, are unknowable things-in-themselves.

Peirce, the realist, looks at it in quite another way. Although all human thought contains an arbitrary and accidental element which limits it according to the circumstances and powers of the individuals, still human opinion tends, in the long run, to a definite form. If inquiry is pursued long enough, and information enough is available to the inquirers, no matter how different (or even erroneous) their initial opinion, and no matter how idiosyncratic their initial circumstances, their final conclusions will be identical. A deaf man and a blind man may witness the same event in very different ways but conclude that they witnessed the *same* event. The realist thinks that there is an answer to every genuine question which is arrived at in the long run, that is, at the *end* of inquiry. Such an answer consists, not in the particular sensations of singular men, but in the truths about objects expressed in and through general terms. What those truths express is independent, not of thought in general, but of all that is arbitrary and individual in thought. It is quite independent of how you, or I, or any number of men think. This—and nothing else—according to Peirce, is the real.

Peirce opines that such a conception of reality is fatal to the idea of the thing-in-itself. There is no reality that is incognizable, although there may be much that is not yet actually known by you or me or any number of men. Since the thing-in-itself, according to Peirce, is literally unthinkable, Kant must be corrected.

Peirce's realism is to be understood in terms of his categories, and he arrived at his categorical scheme through logic. He was convinced that all predicates are relations and that those relations are monadic, dyadic, or triadic. Any higher polyadic relation can be analyzed into some combination of those three. Yet those three cannot be resolved into simpler components. Hence, monad, dyad, triad are both necessary and sufficient to account for any more complex predicate (that is, one with more relatives). But this suggests that the fundamental categories of being are also three and only three, which Peirce denominates, respectively, Firstness, Secondness, and Thirdness. Firstness is the category of sheer possibility, a "may-be" or "might-be." Secondness is the category of actuality, an "is" or "are." Thirdness is the category of the necessary (in the sense of the destined), a "would-be" or "would-do." Each category is really distinct from and irreducible to every other even though they cannot be separated in our experience. We can distinguish them in thought by precisive abstraction in a definite, non-reversible order. Thus, one can prescind Secondness (actuality) from Thirdness (the destined), and Firstness (mere possibility) from Secondness, but one cannot experience either Firstness or Secondness without Thirdness. The third category, then, mediates between the airy shadows of mere possibility and the brute force of actuality. It is properly the category of thought, of regularity, or law-likeness, and so is the category of the Real *par excellence*. Peirce's realism, then, means at least this: "would-be's" are neither a collection of actuals (no matter how large) nor a mere figment of one's mind (no matter how convenient). The Real is what would be or what would happen if certain conditions are fulfilled—and that independently of what you or I or anyone else might happen to think.

Finally, then, Peirce distinguishes the real from the existent. General conceptions are real (they are not figments dependent upon anyone's thinking), but they do not exist. Existence is a distinct category from that of Reality. The former designates brute force, mere action-reaction, while the latter designates regularity, continuity, law. In short, the real is what is destined, that is, what would be in the long run under certain conditions.[14]

I have dwelt upon Peirce's realism at length because he considered it essential to his pragmatism. It is pragmatism's realism which allows it to be empirical but not positivist. Peirce was convinced that the realist interpretation of pragmatism was the only one that would recommend itself to a working scientist familiar with the history of science who had carefully studied logic as method. James, for example, was a working scientist but had steadfastly avoided logic. Mill, on the other hand, had studied logic but was not a working scientist. Both, according to Peirce, were nominalists.

James dedicated his book *Pragmatism* to John Stuart Mill. "To the memory of John Stuart Mill," he writes, "from whom I first learned the pragmatic openness of mind and whom my fancy likes to picture as our leader were he alive to-day."[15] Peirce would certainly not fancy Mill as leader of his kind of pragmatism. Were he to have chosen such a leader, it would have been another British scientist and logician, William Whewell. In the 1840s a lively controversy arose between Mill and Whewell precisely on the nature of scientific inquiry and discovery. Peirce definitely sided with Whewell and always thought of him as the one who pointed the way to a correct understanding of the nature of scientific investigation. Max Fisch has summed up the matter well:

> Apart from its [Peirce's Harvard lectures on "British logicians" in the academic year 1868–1869] including Peirce's first public exposition of the logic of relations, and showing the fruits of a deeper study of Duns Scotus and of Ockham, the course inaugurates Peirce's lifelong championship of Whewell against Mill in the 'logic of science'. Whewell was himself a scientist (indeed he coined the word); Mill is not. Whewell was also a historian of science; Mill is not. Whewell followed Kant; Mill does not. Whewell was a realist; Mill is a nominalist.[16]

The precise point at issue in this celebrated controversy was the nature of induction. Mill contended that induction is simply the tying together of observed facts, while Whewell maintained that such colligation required the introduction of a new Idea. Mill seemed to think that facts are quite independent of theory, while Whewell insisted that fact and theory are relative to each other. Mill contended, for example, that in the case of Kepler's discovering planetary motion to be elliptical, it was simply a matter of Kepler's reporting an observed fact without adding anything to it. Mill asserted that this fact, found in the motion of Mars, was just the sum of the observations. Whewell held that the elliptical orbit was not simply the sum of observations but rather that the very hypothesis of the orbit's being an ellipse suggested how the observations might be accounted for. The introduction by Kepler of a new idea provided a new perspective from which to interpret the observations. Whewell did not think that Kepler simply imposed an idea on reality. On the contrary, he suggested that Kepler *discovered* the fact that Mars's orbit was elliptical in and through an hypothesis. The point is that Whewell realized that science does not discover facts simply by "reading them off." Fact in science is more often than not confirmed theory.[17]

Whewell was accused of being a "mere Kantist" (by Professor Bowen, according to Peirce; W 2: 341) dragging "*a priori*'s" into science in a very rationalistic way. In his Harvard lecture on Whewell, Peirce defended him against this charge (made, he says, out of ignorance). While Whewell's point may fit in with Kant's analysis, it did not arise *from* Kant's analysis. It arose, rather, from the history of scientific discoveries. The fact is that scientists do their research in this way. Peirce would have been better satisfied if Whewell had explicitly rejected Kant's noumenon, for then the allegation of his being a "mere Kantist" would not have been made.

That James should have adopted Mill, and Peirce, Whewell, as their respective patrons should lead us to suspect that the differences between their understanding of pragmatism involve the difference between a nominalist and a realist understanding of human cognition as inquiry. Below I will try to show that this is indeed the case, but first let us consider Alexander Bain's contribution to Peirce's pragmatic theory.

In the latter half of the nineteenth century Bain's works on psychology were standard treatises.[18] Peirce and James knew them well. Peirce once remarked that pragmatism "is scarce more than a corollary" of Bain's definition of belief (5.12). According to Bain, belief is that upon which one is prepared to act. Peirce adopted Bain's view of belief in his 1878 version of pragmatism. In fact, it served as the psychological framework for Peirce's logic throughout his career. But in the late 1860s and the early 1870s Bain's position was disputed by John Stuart Mill. In 1869 Mill published a new edition of his father's (James Mill's) *Analysis of the Phenomena of the Human Mind* to which he and Bain added essays critical of the elder Mill's theory of belief and of each other's. The details of this controversy need not detain us except to say that James Mill thought belief to consist in indissoluble associative bonds, and John Stuart, in some other mysterious residuum.

Bain's own theory of belief underwent several revisions. These revisions reveal an uncertainty as to whether belief is essentially intellectual or volitional. This waffling is important because it helps to explain, I think, not only the difference Peirce thought he saw between his pragmatism and James's but also some ambiguity in Peirce's own 1878 version of pragmatism.

Bain's problem was to decide whether belief is essentially a fact of intellect or of will. In his 1869 essay for the James Mill re-edition of *Analysis*, he calls it an error to think of belief as "mainly a fact of the Intellect, with a certain participation of feelings." There he insists that belief is essentially a development of the active nature of our will. Elsewhere around this time he admits that belief always contains intellectual elements, but they do not constitute the attitude of believing, because nothing in mere intellect makes us act or contemplate action, and hence nothing in it makes us believe. In 1872, however, in an appendix to the second edition of his *Mental Science*, Bain admits it to be an error to make the fundamental nature of belief "The Spontaneous Activity of the System." Now belief is "a primitive disposition to follow out any sequence that has been once experienced, and to expect the result." He now calls belief a fact of our intellectual nature and claims only its energy comes from emotions and will. Again in 1875 in the third edition of *The Emotions and the Will*, Bain makes the same move toward intellect, even though the chapter on belief contains expressions like these: belief is "essentially relation to Act, that is, volition . . . ; Action is the basis, and ultimate criterion, of belief. . . ." Peirce criticized James and other pragmatists for making action the be-all and end-all of thought (5.429, 8.256). Without doubt the expressions which gave rise to that criticism are traceable to Bain.

I suspect that Bain's indecision concerning the essence of belief comes from a failure sharply to distinguish the act of believing from what is believed. Belief as an act of adherence to some opinion can plausibly be understood as consisting in one's readiness to act. And it seems unobjectionable to hold that actually acting in a way appropriate to the circumstances is the test of whether one truly believes something or not. But this does not immediately and directly yield a criterion for deciding the meaning of what is believed (or not believed). It is with this second, the meaning of what is believed, that the pragmatic maxim is concerned. The maxim, then, is not simply a restatement of Bain's definition of belief but, as Peirce thought, a conclusion to be drawn from that definition. That conclusion once drawn, however, will be differently understood depending on whether one thinks the act of believing is volitional (James, perhaps) or intellectual (Peirce, for certain).

But just how did Peirce draw the pragmatic maxim as a corollary from Bain's definition of belief in his 1878 article (5.394–402)? He argues as follows: thinking is stimulated by the irritation of doubt and ceases when that irritation is removed by the fixation of belief. Belief is a conscious appeasement of doubt establishing in us a habit or rule of action. Beliefs are distinguished from one another by the modes of action to which they give rise. To determine *what* we believe (not *that* we believe) is to determine what habits the thought in question involves. To determine what habits a thought involves is to determine what sensible result would follow from the action so dictated by the thought under certain specifiable sensible conditions. Hence, Peirce concludes:

> Thus our action has exclusive reference to what affects the senses, our habit has the same bearing as our action, our belief the same as our habit, our conception the same as our belief. . . . Our idea of anything *is* our idea of its sensible effects. . . . (5.401)

But this is the pragmatic maxim.

One final note before bidding Bain farewell. By adopting the doubt-belief framework Peirce shifts the emphasis from thought taken as an isolated cognitive incident, to thought taken as an ongoing process of discovery. In the series of articles published in the *Journal of Speculative Philosophy* in 1868–1869, Peirce argues that there is no intuitive cognition and that all thought is in signs (5.213–357; W 2: 193–272). It follows that there is no first cognition and that a thought is interpreted only by another thought. Peirce never abandoned this position, but after he had adopted Bain's psychology of belief, the cognitive continuum was understood as a continuum of inquiry, that is, a continuum of doubt-inquiry-belief.[19]

We have considered the influence on Peirce's pragmatism of Scotus's "scholastic realism," Whewell's logic of discovery, and Bain's analysis of belief. But just how is Peirce's understanding of pragmatism different from other versions which proliferated after James had made the maxim popular? That Peirce thought his was significantly different is clear from the fact that he adopted another term for it, namely, "pragmaticism," a term he says is ugly enough to be safe from kidnappers (5.414).

There are at least three points of difference between James's and Peirce's formulation of the pragmatic maxim: (1) perfect clarity in contrast to relative clarity of conceptions, (2) sensations and particulars in contrast to conceptions and generals as interpretants of thought, and (3) practicalism in contrast to pragmatism or pragmaticism. The significance of these differences seems to me to be the following. James's supposition that there is "perfect" clarity of conceptions entails that they be perfectly definite and determinate. If an idea's definiteness and determinateness were *perfect*, the idea would have no generality and, hence, would be reduced to a sensation. For Peirce, every general conception, as general, is intrinsically vague, that is, in some respect indefinite and indeterminate.[20] A *perfectly* clear and distinct *general* idea is a contradiction in terms. To think that an idea's meaning is nothing but the sum total of the particulars for which it actually stands is, according to Peirce, a nominalistic error, because no number of actual particulars exhaust a concept's meaning. If there are general ideas, therefore, they must be to some degree indeterminate and indefinite. Furthermore, what those ideas represent must be real (not mere mental figments); otherwise, Peirce argues, scientific prediction could not be explained.

James's insistence on "what sensations we are to expect" and on "some particular turn to our experience" also implies a nominalistic view. In his article on pragmatism in Baldwin's *Dictionary of Philosophy and Psychology* (1902), Pierce remarks that James pushed the pragmatic method "to such extremes as must tend to give us pause." He continues:

> The doctrine appears to assume that the end of man is action. . . .
> If it be admitted, on the contrary, that action wants an end, and that that end must be something of a general description, then the spirit of the maxim itself, which is that we must look to the upshot of our concepts in order rightly to apprehend them, would direct us toward something different from practical facts, namely, to general ideas, as the true interpreters of our thought. . . . the meaning of the concept does not lie in any individual reactions at all, but in the manner in which those reactions contribute to that development [of concrete reasonableness]. (5.3)

For Peirce, action cannot be an interpretant of thought, because action, that is, the acting itself, is concrete and singular. No one acts in general; one performs this or that action. Thought, on the other hand, always has an element of generality. Hence, thought and action cannot be identified; nor can thought be interpreted by action.[21] Thought and action are certainly intimately related. Thought no doubt *applies* to action, in the sense that it is to be interpreted in terms of the *habits* or behavior or action which call for certain kinds of action under certain conditions. But then this is action as conceived, or thought about, and so generalized.

Finally, the significance of Peirce's insistence on the term "pragmatism" over against James's interchanging it with "practicalism" is to be found in Peirce's efforts to eliminate an ambiguity in the whole notion of practical bearings or effects.[22] Certainly, the term "practical" has several meanings. In one sense it simply means action or behavior, and in that sense all human action is practical. In a second sense it means the immediate relevance of means to ends—in effect "what works." In a third sense it refers to some purpose we have in mind, some end we wish to achieve, which specifies the kind of behavior that is appropriate. If two thoughts make no practical difference to the purpose one has in mind, then they can be considered to mean the same thing with respect to that purpose. Thus, a carpenter can consider two boards to be of equal length if whatever small difference there is between them makes no difference to what he intends to make. Peirce seems to think that James slides from the second to the third sense and back again. Peirce wants to make it clear that he means the third sense and so uses Kant's term "pragmatic." The sum total of all the conceivable practical bearings upon conduct is what a conception means. Hence, Peirce thinks it essential to consider what ends or purposes are general and to interpret our thought insofar as they become in use dispositions to act (habits or beliefs). If, as James suggests, we must anticipate the sensations we would experience or the particular turn our experience would take if certain thoughts were acted upon, this anticipation would be of *kinds* of sensations and of *kinds* of experience and, hence, general ideas about those sensations and experiences. Action, and so the sensations which constitute the particular experience as particular, are the upshot of thought, not its interpretant or its purpose.

Consider these restatements of the maxim. In 1903 in his Harvard lectures on pragmatism, Peirce puts it this way (perhaps with tongue in cheek);

> Pragmatism is the principle that every theoretical judgment expressible in a sentence in the indicative mood is a confused form of

thought whose only meaning, if it has any, lies in its tendency to enforce a corresponding practical maxim expressible as a conditional sentence having its apodosis in the imperative mood. (5.18)

In 1905 in a *Monist* article, "Issues of Pragmaticism," Peirce restates his maxim in a way he hopes would make clear once for all what he means:

> The entire intellectual purport of any symbol consists in the total of all general modes of rational conduct which, conditionally upon all the possible different circumstances and desires, would ensue upon the acceptance of the symbol. (5.438)

Pierce, then, thought James to be nominalistic in that he made action the purpose of thought, not merely its outcome or upshot. In that case James implicitly makes some non-thought the ultimate logical interpretant of thought and, hence, implicitly subscribes to an incognizable (the sensuous flux of experience as proposed in his "radical empiricism"). For Peirce, this is the one great sin against logic as method, because it blocks the road to inquiry (6.171, 6.273).[23]

To be fair to James, however, I must say that in 1906, Peirce, while still insisting on the differences between his understanding of pragmatism and James's, writes in a more irenic vein:

> The most prominent of all our school and the most respected, William James, defines pragmatism as the doctrine that the whole "meaning" of a concept expresses itself either in the shape of conduct to be recommended or of experience to be expected. Between this definition and mine there certainly appears to be no slight theoretical divergence, which, for the most part, becomes evanescent in practice. (5.466)

Much more could and, no doubt, should be said both about British influences on Peirce and about his pragmatism. I have not said a word about the influence of Herbert Spencer, negative though it was, on Peirce's evolutionary cosmology. I have passed over in silence the positive influence of Charles Darwin whose scientific work Peirce more than admired. I have not touched Peirce's doctrine of the normative sciences and their essential role in understanding pragmaticism. Finally, I have no more than hinted at Peirce's system of categories, which he considered to be his one lasting contribution to philosophy and as the correction of Kant which a serious study of logic, as understood by the English, demands. Oddly enough, Peirce thought that his corrections of Kant made his own views a resuscitation of Hegel "in a strange costume" (1.42).[24] Such considerations would bring us to Peirce's tychistic views of cosmology and to the synechistic ontology which grounds his "scholastic realism." But all of this will have to wait for another occasion.

Notes

1. See Max H. Fisch, "Peirce as Scientist, Mathematician, Historian, Logician, and Philosopher," *Proceedings of the C. S. Peirce Bicentennial International Congress*, Graduate Studies No. 23 (Lubbock: Texas Tech Press, 1981), pp. 13–34. I want to thank Professor Fisch for his help in preparing this essay. His suggestions and leads to material, historical and philosophical, were invaluable. See Carolyn Eisele, *Studies in the Scientific and Mathematical Philosophy of Charles S. Peirce*, ed. Richard M. Martin (The Hague: Mouton Publishers, 1979). See *The New Elements of Mathematics by Charles S. Peirce*, ed. Carolyn Eisele, 4 vols. in 5 (The Hague: Mouton Publishers, 1976), for Pierce's works on mathematics.

2. See John E. Smith, *The Spirit of American Philosophy* (New York: Oxford University Press, 1963), pp. vii–xi.

3. See Woodbridge Riley, *American Thought: From Puritanism to Pragmatism and Beyond* (New York: Peter Smith, 1941), pp. 240–53.

4. See Max H. Fisch, "The Range of Peirce's Relevance," *The Relevance of Charles Peirce*, ed. Eugene Freeman, The Monist Library of Philosophy. (La Salle, Ill.: The Hegeler Institute, 1983), pp. 11–37.

5. "C. S. Peirce's Existential Graphs," *Bulletin of the Institute of Mathematics and Its Application*, 17 (1981), 232.

6. Thus, for example, in 1976 a two-volume German translation of Peirce by Gerd Wartenberg appeared in Frankfurt. Karl-Otto Apel edited that edition and wrote extensive introductory material. In 1981 an English translation of Apel's book on Peirce, *From Pragmatism to Pragmaticism*, appeared in the United States. Finally, it may be surprising that the President of the C. S. Peirce Society for the year 1982–1983 was Klaus Oehler of Hamburg University, himself a translator of Peirce. No doubt there are many and varied reasons why Peirce has attracted the attention of German thinkers. Apel's reason I find fascinating. He sees Peirce's pragmatism, as distinct from James's and Dewey's, as a dialogue partner

for Marxism and from which Marxism has something important to learn. He uses the unusual term "logical Socialism" to characterize Peirce's theory of inquiry, emphasizing as it does the community of investigators. One wonders whether Apel is searching for an alternative to Marxist "dogmatic" and unconditioned predictions about the course of history. It might surprise some Americans, I dare say, to think that some aspects of their indigenous philosophy are close enough to Marxism to be an interesting alternative for "a public, emancipatory mediation of theory and praxis." Hegel, through Kant, however, is pragmatism's and Marxism's common ancestor. See *Charles Sanders Peirce: Schriften zum Pragmatismus und Pragmatizismus*, trans. Gerd Wartenberg, ed. Karl-Otto Apel, 2nd ed. (Frankfurt: Suhrkamp, 1976); Karl-Otto Apel, *Charles S. Peirce: From Pragmatism to Pragmaticism*, trans. M. Krois (Amherst: University of Massachusetts Press, 1981); *Charles S. Peirce: Über die Klarheit unserer Gedanken*, ed. and trans. Klaus Oehler (Frankfurt: Vittorio Klostermann, 1968).

7. *Pragmatism: A New Name for Some Old Ways of Thinking* (Cambridge, Mass.: Harvard University Press, 1975), p. 10.

8. Edward L. Youmans, editor of the *Popular Science Monthly,* writing from London to his sister in the United States on October 29, 1877, reports Clifford's remark. Cited by Max H. Fisch in "Supplement: A Chronicle of Pragmaticism, 1865–1879," *The Monist*, 48 (1964), 461.

9. One would infer that Peirce would not have much sympathy with James's "Sentiment of Rationality."

10. See Faris, "C. S. Peirce's Existential Graphs," and Don Roberts, *The Existential Graphs of Charles S. Peirce* (The Hague: Mouton, 1973).

11. *Semiotic and Significs: The Correspondence Between Charles S. Peirce and Victoria Lady Welby,* ed. Charles S. Hardwick (Bloomington: Indiana University Press, 1977), pp. 114–15.

12. (Boston: Little, Brown, 1885).

13. See his "Peirce, Ockham, and Scholastic Realism," in *The Relevance of Charles Peirce*, ed. Eugene Freeman The Monist Library of Philosophy (La Salle, Ill.: The Hegeler Institute, 1983), pp. 93–106; *Charles Peirce and Scholastic Realism* (Seattle: University of Washington Press, 1963). See also Michael L. Raposa, "Habits and Essences," *Transactions of the Charles S. Peirce Society,* 20 (1984), 147–67.

14. See my *Charles S. Peirce: On Norms and Ideals* (Amherst: University of Massachusetts Press, 1968), pp. 8–24, for a discussion of Peirce's categories.

15. P. 14.

16. "Supplement," 450.

17. Whewell's major works on inductive method were *History of the*

Inductive Sciences, first published in 1837, and *The Philosophy of the Inductive Sciences Founded upon Their History*, first published in 1840. Both went through several editions. For good accounts of Whewell's controversy with Mill, see E. W. Strong, "William Whewell and John Stuart Mill: Their Controversy about Scientific Knowledge," *Journal of the History of Ideas*, 16 (1955), 209–31; C. J. Ducasse, "Whewell's Philosophy of Scientific Discovery," *Philosophical Review*, 60 (1951), 56–69, 213–34.

18. Those treatises are *The Senses and the Intellect* (1855) and *The Emotions and the Will* (1859). A one-volume abridgment appeared in 1868 under the title *Mental Science*. For a careful historical study of what and how the members of the "Metaphysical Club" at Cambridge, at whose meetings Pierce first formulated pragmatism, knew about Bain's definition of Belief, see Max H. Fisch, "Alexander Bain and the Genealogy of Pragmatism," *Journal of the History of Ideas*, 13 (1954), 413–44, on which I heavily depend for my presentation.

19. Fisch, "Alexander Bain," pp. 438–42, for discussion of Peirce's pre- and post-Bain approach to knowing.

20. I discuss vagueness in chapter 12 of the present collection and in *On Norms and Ideals*, pp. 89–90. See 5.505–509, 5.447–448; 3.93–94; 2.357.

21. See 5.475–493. Peirce gives here a long explanation of what he means by "interpretant." He distinguishes three interpretants: emotional, energetic, and logical. The emotional is the feeling produced by the sign; the energetic is the effort, mental or physical, elicited by the sign; and the logical is the sign's rational purport. The pragmatic maxim is meant to clarify a sign's rational purport. Peirce concludes that the final logical interpretant of a concept can only be a habit (not another concept, not a desire, not an expectation). Action is not a logical interpretant either. It is thought's energetic interpretant (hence, there is a connection between thought and action) but it is not thought's rational purport precisely because it lacks generality.

22. See Smith, *Spirit of American Philosophy*, pp. 13–17.

23. Even if we suppose this assessment is correct, to be fair to James we should admit that Peirce's first exposition of pragmatism in the 1878 article "How to Make Our Ideas Clear" was open to such an interpretation. There he analyzed "hardness" according to the pragmatic maxim (5.403ff.) The results were misleading and later rejected. Imagine a diamond crystallized within soft cotton where it remains until completely burned up. No other substance is ever rubbed against it. Would it be false to say that the diamond was soft? Pierce answers that it would not be incorrect or even false to call it soft, because nothing prevents us from saying that all bodies remain soft until they are touched, when their

hardness increases with the pressure until they are scratched. Such modes of speech "would involve a modification of our present usage of speech with respect to the words 'hard' and 'soft', but not their meanings. For they represent no fact to be different from what it is" (5.403). This passage might be understood in a nominalist or even positivist sense. Again writing to Calderoni, Peirce admits: "I myself went too far in the direction of nominalism when I said that it was a mere question of the convenience of speech whether we say that a diamond is hard when it is not pressed upon, or whether we say that it is soft until it is pressed upon. I *now* say that experiment will provide that the diamond is hard, as a positive fact. That is, it is a real fact that it *would* resist pressure, which amounts to extreme scholastic realism. I deny that pragmatism as originally defined by me made the intellectual purport of symbols to consist in our conduct. On the contrary, I was most careful to say that it consists in our *concept* of what our conduct *would* be upon *conceivable* occasions" (8.208). The passage is nominalistic, then, because it tends to identify the real with the actual. The meaning of "hardness" is in the actual resistance of the diamond to pressure. Potentiality in the diamond to resist pressure is only a linguistic usage, not a matter of a real fact where "real" means not a figment of mind. Peirce would later (after 1903) put the matter this way, that "would-be's" are real even though they cannot be reesse in futuro, as Peirce would say) and as such are general. and no number of actual cases exhausts their meaning. Even though Peirce maintains in his letter to Calderoni that he did not intend to fall back into nominalism, nonetheless the example was unfortunate and could easily have been so understood. And if, mind you, James was in fact a nominalist already, it is understandable why he attributed to Peirce his own interpretation, which Peirce found unacceptable.

24. Yet see 5.38 for a passage in which Peirce denies any conscious influence of Hegel upon his thought.

3

Peirce on Normative Science

EVEN AS A BOY Pierce was interested in the normative sciences. He recounts that he picked up his elder brother's textbook in logic and worked right through it on his own. Undoubtedly, his mathematician father encouraged and directed his interest. But logic was not the only normative science to which he early applied himself. He tells us that as an undergraduate at Harvard (ca. 1855) he expounded as best he could Schiller's *Aesthetische Briefe* to his friend Horatio Paine (2.197). Almost fifty years later he expressed regret that he had not followed up this study in a serious way, because he then saw how fundamental it is to a theory of knowledge (2.120, 2.197, 5.129ff.).

Although logic received most of Peirce's attention throughout his long career, still he was always interested in ethical systems (2.198). Until the 1880s, however, he considered ethics to be nothing more than an art or a practical science which relied little upon theoretical principles. It should be remembered that the first formulation of the pragmatic maxim—which he later called "a rough approximation" (5.16)—and his analysis of belief in terms of what one is willing to act upon appeared in the 1870s. Pierce says that he began to see the importance of ethical *theory* around 1882 (2.198). At that time he started to distinguish morality from "pure" ethics. As a result of this illumination he undertook a serious study of the great moralists (5.111, 5.129) and began to suspect that there was some important connection between ethics and logic (5.111). It was only some ten years later (ca. 1894) that this suspicion became a firm conviction (2.198) and only in about 1899 was he ready to say

---

An earlier version of this chapter appeared as "Peirce's Analysis of Normative Science," in *Transactions of the Charles S. Peirce Society*, 2 (1966), 5–32.

that ethics is truly a normative science (5.129). Peirce's judgment in this matter, therefore, was not hasty. It was the result of long reflection during the height of his intellectual powers (in 1899 Peirce was only 58 years old). Finally, in 1903 he made public his conclusions in the Lowell Lectures of that year (5.533), but even then he was not prepared to say apodictically that esthetics is a normative science, indeed the science upon which both ethics and logic ultimately rest. He was content with the modest proposal of an opinion and an hypothesis (5.129, 2.197).

Even though Peirce came to undertake a serious study of the normative sciences only late in his career, he did not consider them an appendix to pragmaticism or a mere afterthought. He was convinced of the fundamental importance of the normative sciences for a correct understanding of his system. It would be a basic mistake, therefore, to assume that because his exposition of their role is short and unsatisfactory, it is not an integral part of what he conceived to be his "architectonic system." It would perhaps be more correct to say that Peirce's realization of the place of these sciences put in his hands the capstone that unified all that he had been trying to do more or less successfully for some forty years. At least Peirce himself seems to have looked at it in this way.

In a letter to William James, dated November 25, 1902, Peirce remarks that many philosophers who call themselves pragmatists "miss the very point of it."

> But I seem to myself to be the sole depositary at present of the completely developed system, which all hangs together and cannot receive any proper presentation in fragments. My own view in 1877 was crude. Even when I gave my Cambridge lectures I had not really got to the bottom of it or seen the unity of the whole thing. It was not until after that that I obtained the proof that logic must be founded on ethics, of which it is a higher development. Even then, I was for some time so stupid as not to see that ethics rests in the same manner on a foundation of esthetics,—by which, it is needless to say, I don't mean milk and water and sugar. (8.255)

Other pragmatic positions, then, are only fragmentary. They lack the unity provided by a theory of the normative sciences, and this deficiency has led those positions into error—the error of making action the be-all and the end-all of thought (see, for example, 8.211–212, 1.343).

For Peirce, then, normative science is the study of what ought to be (1.218), of norms or rules which need not but ought to be followed (2.156). "Ought," then, excludes uncontrollable compulsion and rigid determinism, because it is always possible to act contrary to the "ought." The "ought" implies ideals, ends, purposes which attract and guide (1.575) deliberate conduct. Peirce sometimes refers to it as the science "which investigates the universal and necessary laws of the relation of Phenomena to *Ends* . . ." (5.121). Still, he looks upon normative science as positive science, that is, as an inquiry which seeks for positive knowledge expressible in categorical propositions.

> By a *positive* science I mean an inquiry which seeks for positive knowledge; that is, for such knowledge as may conveniently be expressed in a *categorical proposition*. Logic and the other normative sciences, although they ask, not what *is* but what *ought to be*, nevertheless are positive sciences since it is by asserting positive, categorical truth that they are able to show that what they call good really is so; and the right reason, right effort, and right being, of which they treat, derive that character from positive categorical fact. (5.39)

The statements of normative science, then, make a truth claim. They are founded in experience—that same experience upon which philosophy in general is founded, namely, "which presses in upon every one of us daily and hourly" (5.120).[1]

It is understandable, therefore, why Peirce sometimes describes normative science as that which treats of phenomena in their Secondness (see 5.123, 5.125, 5.110, 5.111). As a positive science, it deals with fact, and fact is in the category of Secondness. Again, its proper and peculiar appreciations of the facts relate to the conformity of phenomena to ends (themselves not immanent in those phenomena), and this is another dyadic relation, or Secondness (5.126). In terms of the relation of phenomena to ends, normative science enables one deliberately to approve or disapprove certain lines of conduct. Thus, it is the science which separates the sheep from the goats, makes the dichotomy of good and bad (see 5.37, 5.110, 5.111). From every viewpoint, normative science involves an "emphatic dualism" (5.551).

Because normative science deals with "ought," that is, with deliberate conduct, and because it allows one to make value judgments concerning such conduct, one might be tempted to look upon it as an art or a practical science. We have seen that for many years Peirce himself so considered ethics (cf. 5.111). Yet Peirce insists again and again that normative science is purely theoretical, indeed, "the very most purely theoretical of purely theoretical sciences" (1.282; cf. 1.575, 5.125). To say that knowledge of normative science would directly and in itself help one to think more correctly, or live more decently, or create more artistically, would be like saying that a knowledge of the mechanics involved in a game of billiards would allow us to become master-players (see, for example, 2.3). A vast knowledge of physics does not make a good mechanic; nor is it so intended. Normative science looks primarily to an understanding of certain sets of conditions. Of course, Peirce sees and explicitly says that normative science is closely related to art (1.575), and that there are "practical sciences of reasoning and investigation, of the conduct of life, and of the production of works of art" (5.125) which correspond to the normative sciences "and may be probably expected to receive aid from them" (5.125).

> But they are not integrant parts of these sciences; and the reason that they are not so, thank you, is no mere formalism, but is this, that it will be in general quite different men—two knots of men not apt to consort the one with the other—who will conduct the two kinds of inquiry. (5.125)

Normative science, then, is theoretical, and according to Peirce this is precisely why it is and must be called "normative" (1.281). Its business is analysis or definition (1.575).

Peirce feels obliged to emphasize that normative science is not a special science. It is a subdivision of philosophy and as such relies upon data available at any time to anyone through reflection upon experience. It does not require specialized techniques or apparatus for its observations, as physics or chemistry or psychology does. Furthermore, he insists that, although philosophy may make use of such special data now and then, it is not significantly aided thereby—not even by the results of psychology (5.125, 3.428). Thus, he frequently argues, the science of logic, contrary to the opinion of the German School,[2] cannot be reduced to a matter of feeling. Ultimately, an argument cannot be judged valid because of some instinctive feeling that it is so, or by a compulsion so to judge, or by appeal to an intuition (see 2.155ff., 2.19, 2.39–52, 3.432). In general, the psychological fact that men for the most part show a natural tendency to approve the same arguments as logic approves, the same acts as ethics approves, and the same works of art as esthetics approves is insignificant support for the conclusions of those sciences. And if one were to urge in a particular case, let us say, that something is logically sound simply because men have a strong and imperious tendency to think so, one would be arguing fallaciously (5.125). It would be much like arguing for the truth of a proposition from the certitude that one has about it, instead of justifying one's certitude by establishing the truth of the proposition. In a paper written ca. 1906 Pierce makes exactly the same observations and adds a distinction that is quite to the purpose. He says that those logicians who make logic rest on psychology confound *physical* truths with *psychological* truths (5.485). Of course, logic rests upon the former since they are observational data ("of the rudest kind") with which speculative grammar deals. It is such psychical truths Peirce has in mind when he explicitly admits that there is in a sense a compulsion at the base of logic, a compulsion arising from positive observation of a faulty situation, not a compulsion of mere feeling, or a compulsion based on the principles of another theoretical science (3.428). The mistake of the psychologizing logicians is not so much in recognizing the presence of a compulsion of some sort as in making logical consequentiality consist of "*compulsion of thought*" (3.432).[3]

Peirce warns that if the reader does not see that normative science deals with phenomena in their Secondness, the reason lies in a too narrow conception of that branch of philosophy (5.125). He takes care to point out two ways in which modern philosophy generally misconstrues the nature of normative science. In the passages we are about to consider, his references to these errors are exceedingly brief, and thus enigmatic. A certain amount of explanation is necessary to understand why he considers these views so important, and to realize in what way they differ radically from his own.

The first mistake, according to Peirce, is to think that the chief and only concern of normative science is to differentiate goodness and badness and to say to what degree a given phenomenon is good or bad. The error here is to think of normative sciences mathematically or quantitatively, instead of qualitatively. The distinctions that are of interest in normative science are those of kind, not of degree. Thus, Peirce says that logic, in classifying arguments, recognizes different *kinds* of truth; ethics admits of *qualities* of good; and esthetics is so concerned with qualitative differences "that, abstracted from, it is impossible to say that there is any appearance which is not esthetically good" (5.127). In a word, the important question for normative science is not how good something is, but whether it is good at all. Peirce calls this "negative goodness" or "freedom from fault."

> I hardly need remind you that goodness, whether esthetic, moral or logical, may either be *negative*—consisting in freedom from fault—or *quantitative*—consisting in the degree to which it attains. But in an inquiry, such as we are now engaged upon, negative goodness is the important thing. (5.127)

In other words, a quantitative treatment of goodness would suppose that it comes in discrete packages, whereas in reality goodness is a continuum. In a certain sense, goodness does not admit of degrees. It is of the nature of a quality—of a Firstness—and is what it is without reference to anything else. To be sure, goodness involves a complex relation (for example, in the case of moral goodness, between end, means, intention, and circumstances), but goodness *qua* goodness is an undifferentiated quality. Thus, the old scholastic maxim: *bonum ex integra causa, malum ex quocumque defectu.* Nor does this insight into the continuity of goodness conflict with our use of comparative and superlative degrees of the adjective "good," because they refer to a concrete subject participating or sharing in goodness, not to the quality itself. Again, Peirce would not deny that one might be able to set up a quantitative scale of measurement to indicate the degree in which a certain set of concrete subjects share in goodness, but he would insist that such a scale is, to some extent at least, arbitrary and can never claim exactitude.

The second mistake of modern philosophy in this matter is to think that normative science relates exclusively to the human mind. "The beautiful is conceived to be relative to human taste, right and wrong concern human conduct alone, logic deals with human reasoning" (5.128). Pierce tells us that in the truest sense these sciences *are* sciences of mind, but that the mistake is to think of mind in the narrow Cartesian way as something that "resides" in the pineal gland.

> Everybody laughs at this nowadays, and yet everybody continues to think of mind in this same general way, as something within this person or that, belonging to him and correlative to the real world. A whole course of lectures would be required to expose this error. I can only hint that if you reflect upon it, without being dominated by preconceived ideas, you will soon begin to perceive that it is a very narrow view of mind. I should think it must appear so to anybody who was sufficiently soaked in the *Critic of the Pure Reason*. (5.128)

Indeed, it would take "a whole course of lectures" to present Peirce's theory of mind. But, clearly, Peirce is making the same point here as he made in his letter to James (8.256) where he labeled as nominalistic (and hence erroneous) the notion that thought is in consciousness rather than consciousness in thought. Mind is thought, and thought is Thirdness, and Thirdness is ubiquitous. The human mind is only one manifestation of Mind, the highest perhaps because it has the greatest capacity for self-control, but not unique. Here again Peirce is insisting upon the continuity of reality. If mind is anywhere, it is everywhere in one form or another.

Peirce divided normative science into three disciplines: esthetics, ethics, and logic. This division was, in his eyes, by no means arbitrary. It had an inner logic dictated by the very process of reasoning itself. To appreciate fully the great importance Peirce attached to these three disciplines it is necessary to examine their close interrelation. It will become evident that what Peirce means by esthetics, ethics, and logic is not exactly what has been traditionally meant. He tended to keep the terminology because it was close enough to his own conception to introduce the reader and direct his attention to the general area he was to discuss.[4] I think that it will become clear as we proceed that Peirce's early hesitation to call ethics a theoretical science and his persistent doubts about the nature of esthetics can be traced to a confusion in his own mind and in the literature he read as to what these subjects treat.

Let us begin, then, by examining at length one of Peirce's earliest presentations of the divisions of normative science and their interrelation. In his text on "Minute Logic" (ca. 1902), he explains that after a study of phenomenology one must undertake "the logic of the normative sciences, of which logic itself is only the third, being preceded by Esthetics and Ethics" (2.197). He tells us that he had only recently come to realize the importance of esthetics in logical theory and that he is not completely clear about the matter yet himself. He goes on to say, as we have seen, that for a long time he had looked upon ethics as an art and that, again, only recently he had come to appreciate both its role as a theoretical science and its connection with logic (2.198). He had until then not clearly distinguished ethics from morality. His mistake was to think ethics was correctly defined as the science of right and wrong. Only when he realized that these are themselves *ethical* conceptions did he see that they could not be used to define ethics.

> We are too apt to define ethics to ourselves as the science of right and wrong. That cannot be correct, for the reason that right and wrong are ethical conceptions which it is the business of that science to develop and to justify. A science cannot have for its fundamental problem to distribute objects among categories of its own creation: for underlying that problem must be the task of establishing those categories. (2.198)

Ethics, then, is not concerned directly with pronouncing this course of action right and that wrong, but with determining what makes right right and wrong wrong. It has to do with norms or ideals in terms of which those categories have meaning. Peirce therefore came to see ethics as the science of ends.

> The fundamental problem of ethics is not, therefore, what is right, but, what am I prepared deliberately to accept as the statement of what I want to do, what am I to aim at, what am I after? . . . It is Ethics which defines that end. (2.198)

Now it becomes clear just what the relation of ethics to logic is. Logic deals with thinking, and thinking is a kind of deliberate activity. It, therefore, has an end. But if ethics is the science that defines the end of any deliberate activity, it also defines the end of thinking. Logic is a study of the means of attaining that end, that is, the study of sound and valid reasoning.[5] The dependence of logic on ethics, therefore, is apparent. Thus, Peirce concludes, "it is, therefore, impossible to be thoroughly and rationally logical except upon an ethical basis" (2.198).

A similar line of reasoning holds good for esthetics. Peirce began to appreciate its importance as a theoretical science and as the foundation of ethics only when he began to realize that esthetics should no more be defined in terms of beauty than ethics should be defined in terms of right. The reason is the same: the beautiful and the ugly are categories within esthetics. It is precisely these categories that esthetics must establish and justify. Again, esthetics, as a theoretical discipline, does not judge this or that to be beautiful, or this or that to be ugly. It has to do with the norms and ideals in terms of which we can define, and ultimately apply to, these categories. And so it is closely allied with ethics. Peirce reasons this way:

> Ethics asks to what end all effort shall be directed. That question obviously depends upon the question what it would be that, independently of the effort, we should like to experience. But in order to state the question of esthetics in its purity, we should eliminate from it, not merely all consideration of effort, but all consideration of action and reaction, including all consideration of our receiving pleasure, everything in short, belonging to the opposition of the *ego* and the *non-ego*. (2.199)

Esthetics, then, deals with ends (or more properly *the* end) in themselves. It studies the admirable per se, regardless of any other consideration. This is the ideal of ideals, the *summum bonum*.[6] As such it needs no justification; it is what it is and gives meaning to the rest. As such it belongs to the category of Firstness. English has no suitable word for it, Peirce observes, but the Greek *kalos* comes close. "Beautiful" will not do, because *kalos* must include the unbeautiful as well. Whatever term may be chosen to express it, the question of esthetics is to determine what is admirable, and therefore desirable, in and for itself (2.199).

> Upon this question ethics must depend, just as logic must depend upon ethics. Esthetics, therefore, although I have terribly neglected it, appears to be possibly the first indispensable propedeutic to logic. . . . (2.199)

Peirce's position in this section of the "Minute Logic" is clear enough and makes good sense in terms of his revised notions of ethics and esthetics. Human action is reasoned action, but reasoned action is deliberate and controlled. Deliberate and controlled action is action governed by ends, but ends themselves may be chosen, and that choice, to be rational, must be deliberate and controlled. This ultimately requires the recognition of something admirable in itself. Logic, as the study of correct reasoning, is the science of the means of acting reasonably. Ethics aids and guides logic by analyzing the ends to which those means should be directed. Finally, esthetics guides ethics by defining what is an end in itself, and therefore admirable and desirable in any and all circumstances regardless of any other consideration whatsoever. As we shall see, Peirce concludes that this *summum bonum* is nothing else than reasoned and reasonable conduct. Ethics and logic are specifications of esthetics. Ethics proposes what goals man may reasonably choose in various circumstances, while logic proposes what means are available to pursue those ends.

A problem arises, however, as we read on in the "Minute Logic." The fourth chapter deals specifically with normative science, and in it Pierce seems to contradict what he has said previously. There he seems to deny that pure ethics and esthetics are normative sciences at all. He seems to say that only logic is truly normative. Is there any way around the apparent inconsistency?

Peirce begins the chapter by enumerating various general positions concerning the number and nature of divisions of normative science. Everyone is agreed that logic is normative. The majority of writers also include esthetics and ethics, so that the division corresponds to the ancient triad of ideals: the true, the beautiful, and the good. Others, however, admit only two normative sciences, namely, logic and ethics. The former would consider the conformity of being to thought. According to the latter, logic and ethics are normative precisely because nothing can be logically true or morally good without a purpose to be so. Thus, the conformity therein involved is controlled and deliberate. But such control seems to be conspicuously lacking when it is a question of something's being beautiful or ugly. It simply is beautiful or is ugly without any purpose so to be. Consequently, they exclude esthetics from the trio (1.575).

Finally, there seems to be some doubt as to whether ethics is truly normative. The subject matter of pure ethics is not "right and wrong" or "duties and rights." These are practical matters that make "heavy drafts upon wisdom" (1.577). No, these questions are a superstructure raised upon the foundations of pure ethics. The question at the center of pure ethics is "What is good?" and this is not normative, but prenormative. The reason, Peirce explains, is that:

> It does not ask for the conditions of fulfillment of a definitely accepted purpose, but asks what is to be sought, *not* for a reason, but back of every reason. Logic as a true normative science, supposes the question of what is to be aimed at to be already answered before it could itself have been called into being. Pure ethics, philosophical ethics, is not normative, but prenormative. (1.577)

It certainly seems that here Peirce makes logic the only "true normative science." This is not to deny, however, that it depends on the answer that ethics gives to the prenormative question "What is good?" And there is no use objecting that logic already has its own object, truth, because in the final analysis logic must face the question "What is truth?" In other words, just what is it that logic seeks? And, of course, this involves the question of ethics in a particular context: truth is a good (cf. 1.578–579). "Truth is nothing but a phase of the *summum bonum*, the subject of pure ethics" (1.575).

There is a real difficulty in reconciling this chapter with the earlier one. The problem stems from Peirce's inability to decide clearly, once for all, just what is to be included in the discipline called "ethics." He is searching in this work and will continue to search until almost the end of his career when he will discard that terminology altogether. The same is true of his presentation of esthetics, but his difficulty is more acute. The reader will have perhaps already remarked that, in the passages just discussed, what Peirce deems pure, prenormative, ethics in the fourth chapter sounds very much like the esthetics he discussed in an earlier chapter. Nevertheless, the inconsistencies that one would expect to find in an original theory (at least in the first stages of articulation) are not destructive of the essential insight that Peirce is trying to express. Some clear gains have been made, and the line of thought is beginning to emerge. Furthermore, some remarks can be made that diminish somewhat the confusion these inconsistencies may cause.

In the first place, when reading the "Minute Logic," one must remember that it is a text on *logic*. Consequently, logic will be the center of attention and the main perspective from which the entire work will be developed. Thus, for example, in the section entitled "Why Study Logic?" Peirce says that he is to treat, not precisely the normative sciences, but "the logic of the normative sciences" (2.198). So, too, when he points out the importance of esthetics as "propedeutic to logic," he concludes that "the logic of esthetics" ought not be omitted from the science of logic (2.199). This fact may help us to understand in part why Peirce in the fourth chapter makes esthetics and ethics prenormative. His main interest is logical; logic certainly is a "true normative science"; esthetics and ethics are necessary "propedeutics." Hence, from that point of view one could think of them as in a sense prenormative—that is, prelogical. There is some textual evidence that Peirce was thinking of the topic in this way. Thus, after he has reviewed the current opinions as to the number of normative sciences, he remarks:

> Those writers, however, who stand out for the trinity of normative sciences do so upon the ground that they correspond to three fundamental categories of objects of desire. As to that, the logician may be exempted from inquiring whether the beautiful is a distinct ideal or not; but he is bound to say how it may be with the true. . . . (1.575)

Peirce, then, writing as a logician, explicitly disclaims any responsibility for settling the question of the number of normative sciences. The only point he feels obligated to make is that the true is an aspect of the good and that, therefore, logic can be satisfactorily studied only once it has taken into consideration its purpose and end.

In the second place, Peirce identifies the usual tripartite division of normative science in his chapter on ethics with positions he had criticized earlier. This is clearly the case in his discussion of esthetics, and a case, less strong perhaps, might also be made for what he says about ethics. It will be remembered that here in Chapter Four he says that the usual division of the normative sciences into logic, esthetics, and ethics makes their objects the true, the beautiful, and the good. Yet earlier he had said that esthetics had been seriously handicapped by its definition as the science of the beautiful. Now this apparent inconsistency might be diminished if we look at it this way: those who (like Schleiermacher) would exclude esthetics from the normative sciences are correct if esthetics has as its subject matter, or object of study, the beautiful. The reason would be simply this: if the beautiful is the object about which esthetics concerns itself, not merely a category within that science, it must be an ultimate. There could be no argument about it; it could not be subjected to any criticism; there could be no legitimate and resolvable difference of opinion as to what is beautiful and what is not. One would see that "X" is beautiful or one would not. In other words, esthetics could not be a science that would allow one to decide and to judge that something is beautiful or not. It would not be normative at all in this regard, but at most phenomenological. The beautiful would be a "non-natural quality," and any attempt to analyze it would be to fall into the "naturalistic fallacy." On this view, then, it would be correct to say that esthetics is not normative with regard to questions of beauty, but perhaps prenormative. On the other hand, if esthetics is defined, as it was in the earlier section of the "Minute Logic," as the science of the admirable per se, it may be considered normative in this respect precisely because it investigates the ideal in terms of which one might separate the sheep from the goats, the beautiful from the ugly, and defend and justify that discriminatory judgment in terms of a norm. It is doubtful whether Peirce saw this distinction clearly here, because in a later discussion he was still struggling with the question of whether there can be such a thing as esthetic goodness and badness. Yet if it is admitted that this analysis could have been lurking just behind the clarity of consciousness, then all that would have been necessary for Peirce to avoid his apparent inconsistency would have been to state that he was discussing two different conceptions of esthetics.

A similar, though perhaps less convincing, case might be made for what he says about ethics. The difficulty here, however, is that the former mistake to which he objected was not in defining ethics as concerned with the good, but with right and wrong, duties and rights. Still, although he is not so explicit about it as in the case of esthetics, we suspect his thinking is the same. For if one takes the good as the *object* of ethical study and not as a category within the science, again it becomes an ultimate, which cannot be judged but merely recognized. Such a study cannot be normative, but only prenormative. It cannot justify the distinction of good and bad; it can only accept it as a primitive given. Again, we have something like G. E. Moore's familiar notion. If Pierce had this in mind as the paradigm of theoretical ethics when he wrote the fourth chapter of the "Minute Logic," it is understandable why he looked upon it as prenormative. On the other hand, if in the earlier section he was objecting to the indescribability of goodness, and rejecting at least implicitly the "naturalistic fallacy" as no fallacy at all, then he would be justified in making ethics a theoretical, normative science, a science of ends, in terms of which one might judge goodness and badness, insofar as goodness and badness were not "non-natural" properties but qualities arising from the complex relation of conformity and disconformity to ends.[7]

In any case, Peirce has made this significant gain: he has seen that truth and goodness are intimately connected. He will exploit this insight in his Pragmatism Lectures of 1903. There he will strive to show that logic, ethics, and esthetics deal with three kinds of goodness, and that this goodness is ultimately reasonableness manifesting itself in three different ways. Let us consider in some detail what he has to say in these famous lectures.

In the first lecture, "Pragmatism: The Normative Sciences," Peirce again tells us that traditionally the normative sciences have been numbered as three: logic, ethics, and esthetics, and that he will continue to employ these terms. He characterizes these sciences as those which distinguish good and bad in the representation of truth, in the efforts of the will, and in objects regarded simply in their presentation, respectively (5.36). Thus he begins to develop explicitly the notion that the sciences in question all deal with kinds of goodness.

The purpose of this first lecture is to sketch the connection between his form of pragmatism and the normative sciences. After expounding his maxim, he makes this important inference:

> For if, as pragmatism teaches us, what we think is to be interpreted in terms of what we are prepared to do, then surely *logic*, or the

doctrine of what we ought to think, must be an application of the doctrine of what we deliberately choose to do, which is Ethics. (5.35)

Pragmatism is a doctrine of logic. It is a logical method helping us to know just what we think and believe. The meaning of our thought is to be interpreted in terms of our willingness to act upon that thought; it is to be interpreted in terms of its conceived consequences. Peirce, then, sees a connection between thinking and doing, and therefore a connection between good thinking and good doing. What we are prepared to accept as proper conduct, good conduct, approvable conduct, as the interpretant of our thinking, must be the measure of proper, good, acceptable—in a word, *logical* thinking. Thus, logic depends upon ethics. But in its turn ethics must depend upon something else. Conduct is approved or disapproved to the degree that it conforms or fails to conform to some purpose, but the question remains as to what purposes are to be adopted in the first place.

> But we cannot get any clue to the secret of Ethics . . . until we have first made up our formula for what it is that we are prepared to admire. I do not care what doctrine of ethics be embraced, it will always be so. (5.36)

To determine what we are prepared to admire, what is admirable per se, is the task of esthetics.

> It [ethics] supposes that there is some ideal state of things which, regardless of how it should be brought about and independently of any ulterior reason whatsoever, is held to be good or fine. In short, ethics must rest upon a doctrine which, without at all considering what our conduct is to be, divides ideally possible states of things into two classes, those that would be admirable and those that would be unadmirable, and undertakes to define what it is that constitutes the admirableness of an ideal. (5.36)

Esthetics, then, attempts to analyze the *summum bonum*, the absolutely ideal state of things which is desirable in and for itself regardless of any other consideration whatsoever. Esthetics, then, studies the ideal in itself; ethics, the relation of conduct to the ideal; and logic, the relation of thinking to approved conduct.[8]

In the following lectures in the series, Peirce continues to hammer home the key insight into the normative sciences: they all have to do with goodness and badness, with approval and disapproval. Thus, the essence of logic is to criticize arguments, that is, to pronounce them acceptable or not, good or bad (5.108). But to say that certain arguments are good or bad implies that they are subject to control. It supposes that in the future we can avoid using bad arguments and strive to use good ones. Indeed, the very notion of criticism implies the ability to control, and to correct.

> Any operation which cannot be controlled, any conclusion which is not abandoned, not merely as *criticism* has pronounced against it, but in the very act of pronouncing that decree, is not the nature of rational inference—is not reasoning. Reasoning as deliberate is essentially critical, and it is idle to criticize as good or bad that which cannot be controlled. Reasoning essentially involves *self-control*; so that the *logica utens* is a particular species of morality. (5.108)

The distinction of logical truth and falsity, then, is nothing but the distinction of logical goodness and badness, which in turn is only a special case of moral goodness and badness.

This is the very heart of the matter. It is the very heart of Peirce's logic and of his entire philosophical outlook. To make a normative judgment is to criticize; to criticize is to attempt to correct; to attempt to correct supposes a measure of control over what is criticized in the first place. Any other kind of criticism, any other conception of goodness and badness, is idle (see 2.26). In this Peirce was directly opposed to almost all other schools of thought of his day.[9] Two of these positions he considered to be of particular importance because their objections to his own position are serious and not easily answered. The first objection says that Peirce's position makes logic a question of psychology (5.110). Now, this is John Stuart Mill's view and one that Pierce criticized at length again and again (see, for example, 2.47–51). The principle on which Mill based his opinion is that to say how a man *ought* to think has to be based ultimately on how he *must* think. In the passage we are now examining Peirce does not take up a detailed reply. In like measure, we will content ourselves with his simple denial of the allegation.

> The first [objection] is that this [Peirce's position] is making logic a question of psychology. But this I deny. Logic does rest on certain

facts of experience among which are facts about men, but not upon any theory about the human mind or any theory to explain the facts. (5.110)

Psychology, like any science, theorizes about facts. In Peirce's view, logic itself theorizes about facts, not about another theory. The second objection is more serious and, on Peirce's own admission, deceived him for many years (5.111). It argues that by making logic dependent upon ethics, and ethics dependent upon esthetics, he in effect has fallen into the error of hedonism. What is more, such a hierarchical arrangement of the normative sciences involves a basic confusion of the categories of Firstness and Secondness (5.110). Clearly, this objection is a difficulty that Peirce proposed to himself and that prevented him for a long time from seeing the importance of normative science for his own thought. On the one hand, he had been convinced from early in his career of the error of hedonism, and on the other, he did not clearly see how to avoid an inconsistency in his doctrine of the categories if he accepted the traditional triple division of normative science.[10] Let us consider in some detail, then, how Peirce resolved this problem.

The answer came to him through a more penetrating analysis of his categories. He began to realize that one can and does have a representation of a second or a first as well as of a third. With this new light it was clear to him that, "To say that morality, in the last resort, comes to an esthetic judgment is *not* hedonism—but is directly opposed to hedonism" (5.111). How is this so? Well, consider the phenomena of pleasure and pain to which the hedonist appeals as the ultimate factors in a man's choice. They are *not* mainly phenomena of feeling at all (5.112). Peirce says that, despite his special training in recognizing qualities of feeling, he cannot discover any such quality common to all *pains* (5.112). All that careful observation reveals is that "there are certain states of mind, especially among states of mind in which Feeling has a large share, which we have an impulse to get rid of" (5.112). To add that such an impulse is excited by a common quality of feeling is a *theory*, not a fact. Therefore, hedonism cannot claim to be a giver of experience, although, like any other theory, it appeals to experience for confirmation. Furthermore, granting that the phenomena of pleasure and of pain are prominent only in those states of mind in which feeling is predominant, they do not consist in any common feeling-quality of pleasure or of pain (even supposing that there are such qualities (5.113). If one analyzes the phenomenon of pain, one will see that it consists in "a Struggle to give a state of mind its *quietus*" (5.113). It is, therefore, in essence an event, an actuality, not just a mere quality of feeling; or, in terms of the categories, pain is essentially a second, not a first, although undoubtedly it is accompanied by a first. A similar analysis of pleasure will reveal that it consists in "a peculiar mode of consciousness allied to the consciousness of *making a generalization*, in which not Feeling, but rather Cognition is the principle constituent" (5.113). In other words, Pierce analyzes pleasure as a sort of third—an affair of mind, not of mere conscious feeling:[11]

> it seems to me that while in esthetic enjoyment we attend to the totality of Feeling—and especially to the total resultant Quality of Feeling presented in the work of art we are contemplating—yet it is a sort of intellectual sympathy, a sense that here is a Feeling that one can comprehend, a reasonable Feeling. I do not succeed in saying exactly *what* it is, but it is a consciousness belonging to the category of Representation, though representing something in the Category of Quality of Feeling. (5.113)

Thus, to make esthetics the science upon which the other two normative sciences depend is not to subscribe to hedonism and is not to confuse the categories. The categories are not confused, because esthetics deals with the representation (a third) of a quality of feeling (a first), just as ethics deals with a representation (a third) of an action (a second), and logic with a representation of thought (a third). Again hedonism is avoided, because on this view pleasure consists in something intellectual—it is not the case that something is deliberately approved because it is pleasurable; rather, something is pleasurable (esthetically pleasing) because it is approved of. Perhaps it would be more accurate to say that Peirce is saying that something is pleasurable because it is reasonable, not vice versa.[12]

In the Pragmatism Lectures, therefore, Peirce has once for all linked logical truth and falsity to moral goodness and badness. He is still not absolutely sure that there is a science of esthetics (so that moral goodness and badness would be a species of esthetic goodness and badness), but he is inclined to think so, and for the sake of developing his line of thought assumes that there is one (5.129). It is essential to notice that Peirce at this point has made an important connection between goodness and badness and conformity or disconformity to an end or ideal. Normative science in general is the science of the laws of conformity of things to ends; normative sciences in particular are distinguished in terms of what sort of "things" one is considering in relation to their ends:

> Esthetics considers those things whose ends are to embody qualities of feeling, ethics those things whose ends lie in action, and logic those things whose end is to represent something. (5.129; see also 3.340ff.)

The "things" he is talking about are more precisely aspects or modes of things corresponding to the three universal categories of Firstness, Secondness, and Thirdness. In Scholastic terms we might say that Peirce distinguishes these sciences by their "formal objects." *Qua* sciences, however, each normative science employs *representations* of its formal object, and these representations are of course thirds. *Qua* normative, each of these sciences treats its object in its Secondness, precisely because it is engaged in judging good and bad within the phenomena considered.

In the remainder of the section we have been considering (5.130), Peirce argues in much the same way as he did before. Logic criticizes and classifies arguments. This criticism and classification implies *quantitative approval* (or disapproval) of the arguments so analyzed. In turn, approval supposes control of what we approve. Hence, inference is a voluntary act. But the approval of a voluntary act is a moral approval. Hence, logic is a kind of moral conduct and so is subject to ethical norms. At this point, however, Peirce again manifests some lingering doubts about esthetics.

> Ethics—the genuine normative science of ethics, as contradistinguished from the branch of anthropology which in our day often passes under the name of ethics—this genuine ethics is the normative science *par excellence*, because an end—the essential object of normative science—is germane to a voluntary act in a primary way in which it is germane to nothing else. For that reason I have some lingering doubt as to there being any true normative science of the beautiful. (5.130)

The emphasis has shifted from that of the "Minute Logic." We have seen that there logic upstages all other considerations to the point that Peirce calls pure ethics "prenormative." Here he stresses the dependence of logic on ethics, and he has come to see that because reasoning in the last analysis is a *voluntary* act, ethics, not logic, is *the* normative science. But precisely because of this insight he finds difficulty fitting esthetics into the scheme. The problem is always the same: things seem to be beautiful or ugly independently of any purpose so to be (see above and my remarks about "the beautiful" being the object of esthetics). Still, if by the "beautiful" we mean what is *kalos*, what is admirable in itself, Peirce feels that the only kind of goodness such an ideal can have is esthetic, and so the morally good is a species of the esthetically good after all.

> On the other hand, an ultimate end of action *deliberately* adopted—that is to say, *reasonably* adopted—must be a state of things that *reasonably* recommends itself in itself aside from any ulterior consideration. It must be an *admirable ideal*, having the only kind of goodness that such an ideal *can* have; namely, esthetic goodness. From this point of view the morally good appears as a particular species of the esthetically good. (5.130)

But just what is the esthetically good? What is the admirable in itself? In the first place, according to the doctrine of the categories, it must be of the nature of a first. It must be some positive, simple, immediate quality pervading a multitude of parts. It makes no difference what subjective effect that quality may produce in us; it is esthetically good.

> In the light of the doctrine of the categories I should say that an object, to be esthetically good, must have a multitude of parts so related to one another as to impart a positive simple immediate quality to their totality; and whatever does this is, insofar, esthetically good, no matter what the particular quality of the total may be. If that quality be such as to nauseate us, to scare us, or otherwise disturb us to the point of throwing us out of the mood of esthetic enjoyment . . . then the object remains none the less esthetically good, although people in our condition are incapacitated from a calm esthetic contemplation of it. (5.132)

But from this account follow a number of startling and paradoxical conclusions. In the first place, there is no such thing as positive esthetic badness. Everything is what it is, and as such has some quality pervading its totality. Everything, then, to this extent is esthetically good. (The Scholastics called this ontological goodness.) In the second place, if one considers goodness and badness as relative terms, then one might also correctly say that there is no such thing as esthetic goodness. This is the very conclusion that Peirce draws (5.132). All that one has is various esthetic qualities, which are what they are.

> All there will be will be various esthetic qualities; that is, simply qualities of totalities not capable of full embodiment in the part, which qualities may be more decided and strong in one case than in another. But the very reduction of the intensity may be an esthetic quality; nay, it *will* be so; and I am seriously inclined to doubt there being any distinction of pure esthetic betterness and worseness. My notion would be that there are innumerable varieties of esthetic quality, but no purely esthetic grade of excellence. (5.132)

What is behind Peirce's continual hesitation about esthetics is perhaps becoming clearer. It seems to be this: normative science supposes criticism and control; but esthetic qualities seem to be just what they are regardless of anything else and so are beyond criticism and beyond control. The distinction of good and bad implies approval and disapproval. But in what sense can one approve or disapprove of something that is ultimate? In a way one can only recognize it for what it is, unless one's approval of an aim makes it ultimate. Peirce, however, cannot subscribe to that without reservation, since that would make that ultimate subjective and arbitrary.

Thus Peirce, in the following paragraph, considers another moment in the process of adopting ideals, namely, the instant when an esthetic ideal is proposed as an ultimate end of action. Now it is no longer simply a question of considering the ideal itself, but of my adopting or rejecting that ideal. Peirce talks in terms of Kant's categorical imperative pronouncing for or against the ideal, but with this important difference: while for Kant the imperative is itself beyond control, for Peirce it is not. The imperative itself is open to criticism, and this is what makes it rational (5.133). At this point, then, there is room for a distinction between good and bad aims: a good aim is one that can be consistently pursued; a bad aim is one that cannot. It follows, then, that a bad aim cannot be ultimate.[13] A good aim, Peirce tells us, becomes ultimate once it is *unfalteringly* adopted, because then it is beyond criticism (5.133).

The question, then, is to ascertain what end or ends are possible, that is, what end or ends can be consistently pursued under all possible circumstances. This is the problem of the *summum bonum*. The difficulty, however, is that here Peirce makes this inquiry a problem of ethics rather than of esthetics. Nevertheless, the general line of his thinking in the matter is clear enough, though he is having a great deal of trouble classifying the steps according to the traditional triad of the normative sciences. Perhaps at this point it would be well to consider his final formulation of the normative sciences to see how he recognized and attempted to meet these difficulties.

In the "Basis of Pragmaticism" (1905–1906) Peirce shows in his usual way that "the control of thinking with a view to its conformity to a standard or ideal is a special case of the control of action" (1.573). Thus, the theory of controlling thinking, "Logic," must be a special determination of the theory of controlled action—what he has up to now called "Ethics." The theory of the control of conduct and action in general is the second of the trio of normative sciences and the one "in which the distinctive characters of normative science are most strongly marked." What should this science be called?

> Since the normative sciences are usually held to be three, Logic, Ethics, and [Esthetics], and since he [Peirce], too, makes them three, he would term the mid-normative science ethics if this did not seem to be forbidden by the received acception of that term. (1.573)

At least Peirce seems to have become aware of one of the obstacles in his earlier attempts to classify the "mid-portion of coenoscopy"— the usual way in which the term "ethics" had been used. Traditional treatises on ethics included much more than he wanted to include in the mid-normative science. Thus, for instance, they included analyses of the idea of *summum bonum* to which action was to conform. But Peirce wishes to make the mid-normative science only a theory of the conformity of action to an ideal, reserving the study of the ideal itself for another science, esthetics. This throws a good deal of light on the apparent confusion in his lectures on pragmatism discussed in the preceding paragraphs. There he was using the term "ethics" in its traditional sense and applying it to the mid-normative science. Hence, what he includes under "ethics" and "esthetics" overlapped. To make the distinction sharper he proposes new terminology.

> He [Peirce] accordingly proposes to name the mid-normative science, as such (whatever its content may be) *antethics*, that is, that which is put in place by ethics, the usual second member of the trio. It is the writer's opinion that this antethics should be the theory of the conformity of action to an ideal. Its name, as such, will naturally be *practics*. Ethics is not practics. . . . (1.573)

Peirce's problem with esthetics had always been to make sense of goodness and badness applied to esthetic qualities since they seemed to be entirely beyond criticism and control. By the time he wrote the "Basis of Pragmaticism," a number of considerations had helped him come to a satisfactory solution. The line of reasoning which would offer an answer seems evident to us. What is required is a distinction between esthetic qualities in themselves, that is, in their own intrinsic reality, and the conscious adoption of them as ideals to be pursued—similarly, in the case of the ultimate aim, the *summum bonum*, a distinction between its own objective reality and its conscious acceptance and approval. Armed with this sort of distinction one could argue that the business of esthetics is to seek out through reflective analysis (see 1.580) what end is ultimate (can be consistently pursued in any and all circumstances) and to use this as a norm in adopting any particular esthetic quality as an ideal. According to this account of esthetics there would be the necessary element of criticism and control even with respect to the *summum bonum*—not in the sense that the objective reality of that *bonum* would be affected, but in the sense that one would accept it and conform to it willingly and deliberately.[14] The only question is whether or not Peirce had such an explanation in mind.

There can be little real doubt that Peirce did come to this sort of solution, although a detailed proof would require many more pages of analysis than I have available.[15] There is sufficient evidence for my immediate purpose in the following paragraph from the 1906 "Basis of Pragmatism":

> Every action has a motive; but an ideal only belongs to a line of conduct which is deliberate. To say that conduct is deliberate implies that each action, or each important action, is reviewed by the actor and that his judgment is passed upon it, as to whether he wishes his future conduct to be like that or not. His ideal is the kind of conduct which attracts him upon review. His self-criticism, followed by a more or less conscious resolution that in its turn excites a determination of his habit, will, with the aid of the sequelae, *modify* a future action; but it will not generally be a moving cause to action. It is an almost purely passive liking for a way of doing whatever he may be moved to do. Although it affects his own conduct, and nobody else's, yet the quality of feeling (for it is merely a quality of feeling) is just the same, whether his own conduct or that of another person, real or imaginary, is the object of the feeling; or whether it be connected with the thought of any action or not. If conduct is to be thoroughly deliberate, the ideal must be a habit of feeling which has grown up under the influence of a course of self-criticisms and of hetero-criticisms; and the theory of the deliberate formation of such habits of feeling is what ought to be meant by *esthetics*. (1.574)

The first thing to notice is that in this passage it is not a question of the ideal in itself, but rather of the ideals as the agent's. It is a question of what attracts him upon review. Thus, Peirce has shifted the emphasis from the "admirable *per se*" to a consideration of the habit of feeling in the agent in the presence of certain ends proposed as ideals. An end is made the agent's ideal through the mediation of habit, and, in its turn, habit, by its aspect of efficacious determination, will modify action in terms of the ideal so adopted. The second thing to remark is that the habits of feeling through which one makes an ideal one's own are subject to criticism and control. They develop; they are modified; they are corrected. Consequently, the ideals that one adopts are subject to criticism and control—or, better, the adoption of this or that ideal is subject to control. In the case of the ultimate ideal or *summum bonum*, of course, its deliberate adoption is conditioned only by its recognition, since refusal to make it one's own would involve the living contradiction of a rational man's using his reason in order to be irrational. To put it another way: rejection of an ideal recognized as ultimate would be a refusal to accept the inevitable finality of human activity. The recognition of the *summum bonum* is a question of comparing experience with the transcendental condition of such an ultimate, namely, that it is such that it can be pursued in any and every circumstance. Thus, when the pursuit of an ideal is rendered impossible, it cannot be ultimate (see 1.599ff.). According to Peirce, then, habits of feeling and the adoption of ideals are subject to criticism and control, and indeed must be if they are to be called reasonable. Thus, *esthetics* is truly a normative science if it be thought of as the science of the deliberate formation of such habits of feeling.

Notes

1. Yet in "Minute Logic," written shortly before the 1903 Harvard lectures which I have been quoting (that is, about 1902), Peirce writes: "The science which Berkeley, Kant, and others have developed, and which goes by the name of the theory of cognition, is an experimental, or positive science. It learns and teaches that certain things exist. It even makes special observations. But the experimental element in logic is all but nil. No doubt it is an observational science, in some sense; every science is that. Even pure mathematics observes its diagrams. But logic contents itself almost entirely, like mathematics, with considering what would be the case in hypothetical states of things. Unlike the special sciences, it is not obliged to resort to experience for the support of the laws it discovers and enunciates, for the reason that *those laws are merely conditional, not categorical*. The normative character of the science consists, precisely, in that condition attached to its laws" (2.65; emphasis added).

It certainly seems that Peirce is inconsistent here. Perhaps he merely changed his mind. In any case I have been hard put to reconcile these passages. In conversations with colleagues, however, a number of things have been suggested to diminish the conflict. (1) In the passage quoted in this note Peirce is interested in distinguishing logic from any *Erkenntnislehre* which makes psychology its basis. Psychology might tell us how we must think—what are the uncontrollable processes involved—but logic as a normative science must deal with reasoning precisely from the point where it can be controlled. Logic, then, is not a positive science in the same way as psychology is, and in this respect it is closer to mathematics. (See 5.126 for Peirce's attempt to distinguish normative science from mathematics on three scores, the first of which is precisely that the deductions of normative science are intended to conform to positive truth of fact, while mathematics deals only with hypotheses.) (2) When Peirce says that the conditional character of the laws of logic is precisely what makes logic normative, he means to stress that logic lays down rules for right thinking, and rules, because they refer to ends to be achieved, are more appropriately expressed in conditional, not categorical, propositions. He certainly has in mind formal rules of thinking which would be valid in any universe of rational creatures, but does not necessarily restrict normative logic to formal considerations. Thus, he admits that logic does need at least that experience necessary to motivate its research, and in another place tells us that all true laws, true generals, formal as well as material, are characterized by conditional necessity only. While logic is like mathematics, it is still distinguished from it in that it also must take into consideration the processes of thinking and the nature of the object of thought as they actually are, not just as they might be. (3) Peirce makes the laws of logic the laws of being. Normative logic looked at in this way might conceivably be thought of as making categorical statements of positive fact about reality, and still hold that the norms, rules, or laws which it enunciates are to be put in the form of conditional, not categorical, propositions. Considered precisely as norms or laws for right thinking, they ought to take the form: "If you want X, do Y." Considered as laws of being, general facts about reality, they might be expressed in categorical form, perhaps something like this: "It is a general fact or law of nature that if you want X, do Y." These suggestions are offered for what they are worth. At least we are working on the principle that before a man's thinking is pronounced inconsistent every effort to save it ought to be made. Cf. R. S. Robin, "Peirce's Doctrine of the Normative Science," *Studies in the Philosophy of Charles Sanders Peirce, Second Series*, ed. E. C. Moore and R. S. Robin (Amherst: University of Massachusetts Press, 1965), pp. 275ff., for a perceptive discussion of this difficulty.

2. For example, Schroder, Sigwart, Wundt, Schuppe, Erdmann, Bergmann, Glogau, Husserl. Peirce opposes to this group the "English logicians" Boole, De Morgan, J. S. Mill, Venn (see "Why Study Logic"); and yet he is very critical of J. S. Mill for "psychologizing" (see 2.39–51).

3. Cf. 2.47–48 and Richard J. Bernstein's "Peirce's Theory of Perception" in *Studies in the Philosophy of Charles Sanders Peirce, Second Series*, pp. 165–89 for a thorough analysis of the role of "compulsion" in authenticating perceptual judgments. Certitude is not a sign of or a guarantee of truth.

4. Peirce ultimately substituted the term "practics" for "ethics" and

warned the reader repeatedly that his use of the terms "logic" and "esthetics" was peculiar. Evidently he simply could not think of better designations.

5. Peirce later defines normative science as the science of ends. Here he says logic is a science of means. The inconsistency is only apparent, because means are themselves subordinate or partial ends. Thus, reasoning has its own end, attaining truth, yet relative to action it is a means.

6. The *summum bonum* ought not to be thought of as simply another member in a series of goods, not even the least member. Peirce is not always as clear as might be desired in the way he uses the term, but as we shall see as we continue our analysis, he did not fall into that mistake. Cf. H. W. Schneider, "Fourthness," *Studies in the Philosophy of Charles Sanders Peirce*, ed. R. P. Wiener and F. H. Young (Cambridge: Harvard University Press, 1952), p. 211.

7. I suspect that what Pierce is trying to express is something akin to the Scholastic distinction between transcendental and predicamental categories. Traditionally the Scholastics looked upon Oneness, Truth, and Goodness (some included Beauty) as the absolutely universal categories which attached to being as being independent of and thus cutting across all genera and species. These transcendental categories are not really distinct from being itself, but are merely three aspects of it, three ways in which man can consider it. When these transcendentals are predicted of this or that being they are so by analogy. Because these categories are transcendental, they can be discovered only by phenomenological analysis. The Scholastics distinguished from these ultimate and absolutely universal categories, particular categories related to the former. Thus, for example, they distinguished logical and ontological truth. Again, they distinguished moral or ethical goodness from ontological goodness. The normative sciences of logic and ethics, in terms of the transcendental categories of truth and goodness, set up norms for deciding the logical truth or falsity of propositions and arguments, and for deciding the moral goodness or badness of such and such deliberate conduct. Perhaps Peirce was unconsciously sliding from one type of category to the other, and thus at one time saw ethics as prenormative and at another as normative.

8. It must not be imagined that esthetics and ethics do not involve logic. They do because they are theoretical sciences. Therefore, it would be incorrect to think that Peirce held for a purely emotive conception of ethics, or for a purely subjective conception of esthetics (not to be confused with mere taste). All three normative sciences involve deliberate approval, and hence are based on reasoning. The distinction to be kept in mind is that between *logica utens* and *logica docens* which Peirce himself never tires of making. Logic as a normative science is *docens*—a

thinking about thinking wherever it may occur. That Peirce was aware of the possibility of confusion on this point is evidenced by his constant rebuttal of any type of hedonism as illogical and hence unreasonable.

9. For Peirce's survey of opinions, thirteen in all, see 2.19–78.

10. The difficulty he felt was something like this: the three universal categories are irreducible; but logic clearly deals with thirds, ethics with seconds, and esthetics with firsts. How, then, can one consistently seek the source of a third in a second and the source of a second in a first?

11. For Peirce, consciousness is merely a collection of qualities of feeling, or, better, qualities of feeling are the contents of consciousness. "My taste must doubtless be excessively crude, because I have no esthetic education; but as I am at present advised the esthetic Quality appears to me to be the total unanalyzable impression of a reasonableness that has expressed itself in a creation. It is a pure Feeling but a feeling that is the impress of a Reasonableness that Creates. It is the Firstness that truly belongs to a Thirdness in its achievement of Secondness" (from the first draft of Lecture V of the Lectures on Pragmatism, Peirce Papers, Houghton Library, Harvard University, #310).

12. Perhaps the reader sees in what direction this line of thinking will take Peirce: the admirable in itself is the growth of reasonableness in the world. Peirce develops this theme at length in a paper called "Ideals of Conduct," part of his Lowell Lectures of 1903 (1.591–615).

13. An ultimate aim is what would be pursued under all possible circumstances (5.134) and hence would not be disturbed by one's subsequent experiences (5.136).

14. One might refuse to recognize or to accept the ultimate good, but then that would be to act unreasonably and so to act without true liberty. See 1.602: "My account of the facts, you will observe, leaves a man at full liberty, no matter if we grant all that the necessitarians ask. That is, the man *can*, or if you please is *compelled*, to *make his life more reasonable*. What other distinct idea than that, I should be glad to know, can be attached to the word liberty?" See also 5.339, note.

15. I think that such a proof would have to consider at least the following: (1) Peirce's distinction between motive and ideal, (2) his realization that ideals can influence man's actions in different ways and in different degrees of awareness, and (3) the role of habit in deliberate conduct.

4

Action Through Thought: The Ethics of Inquiry

CHARLES S. PEIRCE is credited with being the father of the pragmatic movement, to date America's only indigenous philosophy. Yet I suspect that his thought might be judged by some to be "un-American" because it does not live up to the stereotype of "American" fairly widespread both here and abroad. According to this popular view Americans are the great technicians; they have the know-how; they are successful in the practical world of business, commerce, and industry. But as speculative thinkers, as men of cosmic vision, Americans are a sorry lot! Not a Kant, not a Hegel among them! I hope this consideration of Peirce will challenge such a view by showing that Peirce's pragmaticism is as sophisticated and serious as any philosophical movement abroad, and indeed more so than some. The "American Mind," to use Emerson's phrase, is speculative, complex, and rich, and we ought not sell it short.

Permit me to mention some of Peirce's philosophical views which, according to the popular stereotype, might be considered quite "un-American." Peirce held a version of "scholastic" realism against nominalism in all its forms. Further, he was convinced that metaphysics is a genuine theoretical science and that physical science receives its principles of investigation from philosophy. He held that theory and practice should have nothing immediately to do with each other; that higher education is not primarily for teaching but for research (the principle way of learning); that action is not the end-all and be-all of thought; that pleasure, success, better

---

An earlier version of this chapter appeared as "Charles S. Peirce: Action Through Thought—The Ethics of Experience," in *Doctrine and Experience,* ed. Vincent G. Potter (New York: Fordham University Press, 1988).

living are not properly and specifically human goals at all. In short, Peirce, the pragmatist, in the name of that very method, had to foreswear the practical, the immediate, the useful as of any real consequence for either science or philosophy. I dare say that this will come as a surprise to many abroad and is already an embarrassment to some American thinkers who pride themselves on being in the mainstream of America's philosophical tradition.

Peirce had a great deal to say about experience, a great deal to say about beliefs. Beliefs are to be brought to the test of experience, and at the same time, insofar as they shape our conduct, beliefs influence what our future experience is likely to be. In a word, Peirce was much concerned about the relation between theory and practice.

I would like, therefore, to take up the following issues: (1) Peirce's separation of theory from practice; (2) the meaning of the pragmatic maxim in terms of "practical consequences"; and (3) Peirce's understanding of the relation between Instinct and Reason as the ground of the ultimate continuity between theory and practice expressed in the maxim.

To begin, then, Peirce consistently and repeatedly maintained not only that theory had nothing whatever to do with practice but also that it ought not have anything to do with it. Peirce makes his most sustained case in this matter in a series of lectures delivered at Harvard in 1898. Let me give some background to those lectures.[1]

During the spring and summer of 1897 Peirce worked on eight lectures to be given at Cambridge as a result of William James's efforts to bring him to the Harvard campus in some capacity or other. Two years earlier James had unsuccessfully intervened on Peirce's behalf, asking President Eliot to appoint him to a permanent chair in the Philosophy of Nature. Eliot flatly refused even to have Peirce considered, and so James had to settle for inviting him to give a lecture series. In December 1897, Peirce sent James an outline of the eight lectures—all of them on logic. James wrote back lamenting the choice of topic since "'there are only three men who could possibly follow your graphs and relatives.'" In a most friendly way, and out of the sole motive of having Peirce's series be a success, James advised Peirce to "'be a good boy and think a more popular plan out'"—one that would hold the audience's interest. James remarks, "'Separate topics of a vitally important character would do perfectly well.'"

Peirce's reaction was predictable. He was deeply hurt and disappointed. He wrote back accepting the conditions without enthusiasm and without holding out any hope that he could thus give his hearers any idea or account of his philosophy since it reposed "'entirely upon the theory of logic.'" He remarks that no doubt James has gauged the capacity of his students correctly and that "'it agrees with all I hear and the little I have seen of Cambridge.'" He cannot resist comparing the Harvard students with those whom he tutored in New York City for whom, he tells James, the method of graphs proved quite easy because their minds were stimulated by New York life. "'Your Harvard students of philosophy find it too arduous a matter to reason exactly. Soon your engineers will find it better to leave great works unbuilt rather than go through the necessary calculations.'"

Peirce set to work redoing the entire series. He entitled this revision "Detached Ideas on Topics of Vital Importance," but it was advertised in Cambridge under the inoffensive title "Reasoning and the Logic of Things." Despite James's suggestions a great deal of logic found its way into those lectures. Royce wrote to James that they put him on a completely new direction.[2] It was also the occasion for some of Peirce's most ironic remarks on "the practical" in education.

Consider the title Peirce suggested for the series. Nothing could be more foreign to his view of philosophy than a set of "detached ideas," and nothing could be less promising a subject for philosophical discourse than "vitally important topics." If one thing is clear, it is that Peirce thought philosophy must be done systematically. Further, philosophy had little or no immediate relevance for "life" and its vital concerns. According to Peirce:

> Philosophy is that branch of positive science (i.e., an investigating theoretical science which inquires what is the fact, in contradistinction to mathematics which merely seeks to know what follows from certain hypotheses) which makes no (special) observations but which contents itself with so much of experience as pours in upon every man during every hour of his waking life. (5.13, note)[3]

Philosophy has three branches: Phenomenology, Normative Science, and Metaphysics. These are related to each other as first, second, and third. Metaphysics involves the other two and is the science of the Real *par excellence*.[4] Yet Peirce is fond of saying that metaphysics is gibberish, and meaningless, not intrinsically but because of its backward state. That backward state is due fundamentally to the neglect of Kant's advice to build metaphysics architectonically, that is, in the manner in which a house is constructed—on a broad and solid base and out of materials tested for the purpose (see, for example, 1.176–179, 5.5, 6.7–34). This architectonic structure must be put together with exact logical care.

> What is needed above all, for metaphysics, is thorough and mature thinking; and the particular requisite for success in the critic of arguments is exact and diagrammatic thinking. (3.406)

In a word, there can be no sound metaphysics unless it be systematic and based on logic. Finally, metaphysics can advance if and only if it is done by "laboratory men" whose sole motivation is the pursuit of truth wherever it may be found (see, for example, 5.412, 1.618–620). Furthermore, the purpose of any theory is "to furnish a rational account of its object" (2.1), and so theory aims directly at nothing but knowledge.

Here Peirce is combatting two rather common views of theoretical investigation. The first we might call the "doctrinaire view" and the second the "utilitarian view." According to the first, science and philosophy are looked upon as a body of acquired truth to be taught and to be learned in the interest of instructing and of bettering mankind. The possession of this truth is expected to have immediate beneficial effects upon individuals and society. According to the second, frequently held in conjunction with the first, the sole legitimate motive for scientific or philosophical inquiry is the application of the results for the immediate personal or social benefit of mankind. Technology becomes science's ultimate motive and justification; ideology becomes philosophy's.

According to Peirce, the doctrinaire view simply misses science as a "living historic entity."

> As such it [science] does not consist so much in *knowing*, nor even in "organized" knowledge, as it does in diligent inquiry into truth for truth's sake, without any axe to grind, nor for the sake of the

delight of contemplating it, but from an impulse to penetrate into the reason of things. (1.44)

The second view, he contends, corrupts the scientific enterprise from the beginning, because it prejudices the outcome and restricts the extent and scope of research. Such a view might be called "logical hedonism" inasmuch as it falls victim to the same mistake as moral hedonism does. Just as moral hedonism mistakes some form of "pleasure" for the moral good, so logical hedonism mistakes some form of "utility" for the truth. Such an error, in Peirce's view, generally results in achieving neither genuine satisfaction nor authentic utility (see 1.619).

Peirce once said that the pragmatic maxim was nothing but Jesus' recommendation "By their fruits you shall know them" (Matt. 7:20). He might also have justly pointed out that the ethical principle of investigation proposed here is also anticipated by the New Testament, in the parable of the lilies of the field (Matt. 6:28–33; Luke 12:27–31). Peirce might have paraphrased it something like this: "Seek first the truth, and all these things will be added to you."

Let us consider Peirce's "topics of vital importance" in some detail. In the first lecture of the Cambridge series, "Philosophy and the Conduct of Life," Peirce remarks that the Greeks

> expected philosophy to affect life—not by any slow process of percolation of forms, as *we* may expect that researches into differential equations, stellar photometry, the taxonomy of echinoderms and the like will ultimately affect the conduct of life—but forthwith in the person and soul of the philosopher himself, rendering him different from ordinary men in his views of right conduct. (1.618)

This I would call the "Immediate Relevance" thesis.[5] Peirce exempts Aristotle, however, from this mentality because he was not altogether Greek. Peirce continues:

> Now, Gentlemen, it behooves me, at the outset of this course, to confess to you that in this respect I stand before you an Aristotelian and a scientific man, condemning with the whole strength of conviction the Hellenic tendency to mingle philosophy with practice. (1.619)

Practice, the conduct of life, utility, what would forthwith make one a better or a more successful person—none of this has or should have anything to do with science or philosophy since such an attitude would undermine those disciplines and endanger the moral integrity of their practitioners. The backward state of metaphysics, Peirce thinks, is directly attributable to the fact that it is largely in the hands of "seminary men" who

> have been inflamed with a desire to amend the lives of themselves and others, a spirit no doubt more important than the love of science, for men in average situations, but radically unfitting them for the task of scientific investigation. (1.620)

According to Peirce, all men might be put into one of three categories depending on what they considered to be the highest good in life.

> If we endeavor to form our conceptions upon history and life, we remark three classes of men. The first consists of those for whom the chief thing is the quality of feelings. These men create art. The second consists in the practical men, who carry on the business of the world. They respect nothing but power, and respect power only so far as it is exercised. The third class consists of men to whom nothing seems great but reason. If force interests them, it is not in its exertion, but in that it has a reason and a law. For men of the first class, nature is a picture; for men of the second class, it is an opportunity; for men of the third class, it is a cosmos, so admirable, that to penetrate to its ways seems to them the only thing that makes life worth living. These are the men whom we see possessed by the passion to learn, just as other men have a passion to teach and to disseminate their influence. If they do not give themselves over completely to their passion to learn, it is because they exercise self-control. Those are the natural scientific men; and they are the only men that have any real success in scientific research. (1.43)

"Vital importance" has two senses, and Peirce's irony depends on the play between them. In the literal sense "vitally important topics" refers to questions of physical life and to well-being in the common course of things. In the extended sense it refers to those questions of ultimate significance which make life worth living at all. If one should think that the literal sense is the only meaning, then neither philosophy nor science need play any role in that person's life. Attention to one's natural sentiments and instincts in these matters will afford one a much better chance of success. On the other hand, if one is convinced that coming to know the truth about oneself and about the universe is what makes human life specifically human and thus affords man his only genuine fulfillment, then the pursuit of philosophy and science becomes a way of life and questions of everyday business take a secondary and relatively modest place of importance.

Practice in the sense of "the conduct of life" Peirce would divorce from theory. This includes the entire area of practical affairs, whether such decisions concern ordinary business or great crises.

> In the great decisions, I do not believe it is safe to trust to individual reason. In everyday business, reasoning is tolerably successful but I am inclined to think that it is done as well without the aid of theory as with it. A *logica utens*, like the analytical mechanics resident in the billiard player's nerves, best fulfills familiar uses. (1.623)

> But in practical affairs, in matters of vital importance, it is very easy to exaggerate the importance of ratiocination. Man is so vain of his power of reason! . . . It is the instincts, the sentiments, that make the substance of the soul. Cognition is only its surface, its locus of contact with what is external to it. (1.626, 1.628)

Peirce claimed that he could strictly prove all this, "but only by assuming a logical principle . . ." (1.629). According to Peirce, then, Reason itself recommends this attitude toward theory and practice.

> Were I willing to make a single exception to the proposition I thus enunciate that theory and practice be kept separate and to admit that there was one study which was at once vitally important and scientific, I should make that exception in favor of logic; for the reason that if we fall into the error of believing that vitally important questions are to be decided by reasoning, the only hope of salvation lies in formal logic, which demonstrates in the clearest manner that reasoning itself testifies to its own ultimate subordination to sentiment. (1.672)

At the same time Peirce observes that if one accept this "conservative sentimentalism" and so modestly rate one's reasoning powers in matters of vital importance, then one would find that the very first command of instinct is that one recognize a higher business than one's own. Thus reason recommends reliance on instinct in practical matters, while instinct itself commands that one look beyond the practical.

> Thus while reason and the sciences of reasoning strenuously proclaim the subordination of reasoning to sentiment, the very supreme command of sentiment is that man should generalize. . . . (1.673)

I will return to this point.

In 1896 William James's *The Will to Believe* appeared with its touching dedication to Peirce. In these Cambridge lectures Peirce substitutes the "will to learn" for "the will to believe," at least in matters of theoretical investigation.

> I hold that what is properly and usually called *belief* . . . has no place in science at all. We *believe* the proposition we are ready to act upon. . . . But pure science has nothing at all to do with action. . . . (1.635)

This brings me to the second issue: the meaning of "practical consequences" in the pragmatic maxim. There is something paradoxical about Peirce's remark excluding all belief from science. The pragmatic maxim after all was formulated in the context of the fixation of belief. In those early papers Peirce argued that the whole point of inquiry is to fix belief and that scientific method is the best way to do it. How then can he now claim that belief has no place at all in science? As a first step toward making some sense out of this, I think it will help to recall the distinction between science as a lived experience and science as an established body of "truths," that is, of "theoretical beliefs." Genuine doubt, not mere "paper doubt," is the stimulus of scientific inquiry. When the irritation of such doubt is removed, inquiry ceases. Fixation of belief in that sense may be the upshot or outcome of inquiry, but it cannot be its immediate motive. Only the Will to Learn, to pursue genuine doubt wherever it may lead, can play a role in science. To fix belief is to cut off investigation and so is to bring science as a lived enterprise to an end.

Furthermore, Peirce considered the notion of "theoretical belief" to be odd. At best it could mean only that certain scientific laws and theories are provisionally accepted by the scientific community. Only in this sense is there a body of "scientific truths" and so of "theoretical beliefs."

A practical belief is a habit of deliberate behavior, that upon which we are prepared to act. A theoretical "belief" is an expectation concerning future experience, either actual or merely possible. While it is true that "every proposition that is not pure metaphysical jargon and chatter must have some possible bearing upon practice" (5.539), as the pragmatic maxim says, still it must have some "possible bearing," that is, it must have some conceivable practical consequences. This is true even of pure theoretical propositions. Conceivable practical consequences or possible bearing in practice is quite distinct from practical consequences in the sense of practice—action here and now. In Peirce's words, while every theoretical belief is at least indirectly a practical belief, this is not the *whole* meaning of a theoretical belief. It is further an expectation or anticipation of future experience, actual or merely possible, not in the sense that it anticipates some muscular sensation (as in a practical belief) but in the sense that it is

> the stamp of approval, the act of recognition as one's own, being placed by a deed of the soul upon an imaginary anticipation of experience, so that, if it be fulfilled, . . . the person will claim the event as his due, his triumphant "I told you so" implying a right to expect as much from a justly regulated world. (5.540)

Since all beliefs essentially involve expectation (5.542) and so look to the future, so must the theoretical beliefs of science. What is expected from them *directly*, however, is not some bodily reaction. *Indirectly* and *ultimately*, through the mediation of thought, such "muscular sensation" may be anticipated. What is *directly* anticipated by theoretical belief can only be another *thought*. Consider some of Peirce's examples.

> To say that a quadratic equation that has no real root has two different imaginary roots does not sound as if it could have any relation to experience. Yet it is strictly expectative. It states what would be expectable if we had to deal with quantities expressing the relations between objects, related to one another like the points of the plane of imaginary quantity. So a belief about the incommensurability of the diagonal relates to what is expectable for a person dealing with fractions; although it means nothing at all in regard to what could be expected in physical measurement. . . . Riemann declared that infinity has nothing to do with the absence of a limit but relates solely to measure. This means that if a bounded surface be meas-

ured in a suitable way it will be found infinite, and that if an unbounded surface be measured in a suitable way, it will be found finite. It relates to what is expectable for a person dealing with different systems of measurement. (5.541)

Similar examples might be drawn from history and theology.

Consequently, even if every proposition must have a reference to some conceivable application to practice in order for it to have any definite meaning at all, still, when the pragmatic maxim is applied to "theoretical beliefs," the "practical consequences" are purely matters of thought. Even in practical life, insofar as they have been articulated and critically scrutinized, practical consequences have been transformed through thought into rules for deliberate (rational) conduct.

It would be too long to repeat here what I have said elsewhere concerning the efforts of Peirce to dissociate himself from other pragmatists whom he thought pushed the maxim too far so as to make action the be-all and end-all of thought.[6] It is enough to note that Peirce argued to the contrary.

> If it be admitted . . . that action wants an end, and that that end must be something of a general description, then the spirit of the maxim itself, which is that we must look to the upshot of our concepts in order rightly to apprehend them, would direct us toward something different from practical facts, namely, to general ideas, as the true interpreters of our thought. (5.3)[7]

Peirce's pragmatism recognizes a fundamental connection between thought and action, between theory and practice, but without confusing the two and without inverting the order of the relation. Thought *ultimately* applies to action and theory ultimately applies to practice, at least in the sense of referring to conceivable action and to conceivable practice. But this is quite different either from making thought to consist in action and theory to consist in practice, or from making thought's ultimate purpose action and theory's ultimate purpose practice. Action through thought is only the upshot of inquiry; it is neither its purpose nor its legitimate motive.

I would like now to touch briefly on the final theme: the relation between instinct and reason as the ground of the pragmatic maxim and as the explanation of the continuity between theory and practice. In Peirce's opinion all scientific inquiry supposes a Realism, in the sense that the Real is co-extensive with the Knowable. There is no Kantian noumenon. If this is so, the Real constitutes a network of relations such that everything is connected with everything else or, to put it another way, the Real is everywhere continuous. *Natura non facit saltus.* This continuous Real is systematically explored through abduction, deduction, and induction. But since neither deduction nor induction yields any new knowledge about the Real, abduction is at the heart of all discovery. But, according to Peirce, abduction is nothing but instinctive reason. It is the power nature provided man in the course of evolution for survival in the evolving cosmos by enabling him to meet and to help bring about radically new situations. While it is true that Peirce, on the one hand, rejects as improbable any instinct for logicality in the sense of a feeling of logical connection which guarantees the correctness of any inference, still, on the other hand, he admits instinctive reason which, while it may be wrong more often than it is right, nonetheless is right often enough to allow us to discover some of Nature's Laws.

> Galileo appeals to *il lume naturale* at the most critical stages of his reasoning. Kepler, Gilbert and Harvey—not to speak of Copernicus—substantially rely upon an inward power, not sufficient to reach the truth by itself, but yet supplying an essential factor to the influences carrying their minds. It is certain that the only hope of retroductive reasoning ever reaching the truth is that there may be some natural tendency toward an agreement between the ideas which suggest themselves to the human mind and those who are concerned in the laws of nature. (1.80–81)

Peirce, perhaps under the influence of Chauncey Wright, accepted a thoroughgoing evolutionism. He held that human reason must be an evolutionary development of animal instinct.

> Side by side, then, with the well-established proposition that all knowledge is based on experience . . . we have to place this other equally important truth, that all human knowledge, up to the highest flights of science, is but the development of our inborn animal instincts. (2.754)

Peirce bases this opinion precisely on *il lume naturale*, the faculty for guessing right, without which scientific knowledge would have been impossible.

For Peirce, then, reason is itself in continuity with instinct, and so might be considered to be man's specific instinctive power. It is an evolutionary development of the instinct of feeding and breeding. This led him to identify his pragmaticism with a position which he called Critical Commonsensism. As the name suggests, it is sympathetic to the Scottish School and yet is critical of some details. There are some beliefs which are indubitable because they are instinctive. Such beliefs are acritical and essentially vague. Nonetheless they are at the very heart of the power of reason itself and function as a necessary counterbalance to scientific fallibilism. That there is order in the world is one such belief. That God is real is another (see 5.508, 8.262).[8]

Instinctive reason with its vague instinctive beliefs inserts man into an evolving world not merely as a product of that creative process but also as an active cooperative agent. Since through reason he has the power of reflection and a high degree of self-control, man holds the unique and privileged position of co-creator (5.403, note 3).

Peirce describes the highest end which man can pursue, the admirable in itself, in terms of "concrete reasonableness":

> I do not see how one can have a more satisfying ideal of the admirable than the development of Reason so understood. The one thing whose admirableness is not due to an ulterior reason is Reason itself comprehended in all its fullness, so far as we can comprehend it. Under this conception, the ideal of conduct will be to execute our little function in the operation of creation by giving a hand toward rendering the world more reasonable, whenever, as the slang is, it is "up-to-us to do so." (1.615)

NOTES

1. For an account of this episode in Peirce's life and for the correspondence between Peirce and James, see R. B. Perry, *The Thought and Character of William James*. II. *Philosophy and Psychology* (Boston: Little, Brown, 1935), pp. 417–21.

2. Royce's letter to James in 1901 is cited by Perry, ibid., p. 421.

3. "By a positive science I mean an inquiry which seeks for positive knowledge; that is, for such knowledge as may conveniently be expressed in a categorical proposition" (5.39).

4. For the relation of philosophy's branches to the categories, see my *Charles S. Peirce: On Norms and Ideals* (Amherst: University of Massachusetts Press, 1967), pp. 18–24.

5. For a treatment of "immediate relevance" in philosophy, see my "The Irrelevance of Philosophy," *Thought*, 49, No. 193 (June 1974), 145–55.

6. See my *Norms and Ideals*, pp. 3–7, and chaps. 5 and 6 below.

7. Peirce went so far as to revise the maxim several times to make his meaning clear. See, for example, 5.18.

8. For an extended development of Peirce's views on God, see chap. 12 below.

5

Normative Science and the Pragmatic Maxim

ALTHOUGH PEIRCE CAME TO RECOGNIZE the nature and role of the normative sciences only late in his career, he was nonetheless convinced that his account of the hierarchical dependence of logic on ethics and of ethics on esthetics was a discovery of fundamental importance for a correct understanding of his thought, and one that distinguished his "pragmaticism" from other, more familiar, interpretations of his own famous maxim. It would be a mistake to think that because this was a late development in Peirce's thought, it was an afterthought. It would also be a mistake to think that because Peirce's exposition of that role was short and unsatisfactory, it was not an integral part of what he conceived to be his "architectonic" system. More correctly, Peirce thought that his realization of the place of these sciences put in his hands the capstone that unified all that he had been trying to do for some forty years.

In a letter to William James, dated November 25, 1902, Peirce remarks that many philosophers who call themselves pragmatists "miss the very point of it," and he tells us why:

> But I seem to myself to be the sole depositary at present of the completely developed system, which all hangs together and cannot receive any proper presentation in fragments. My own view in 1877 was crude. Even when I gave my Cambridge lectures I had not really got to the bottom of it or seen the unity of the whole thing. It was not until after that that I obtained the proof that logic must be founded on ethics, of which it is a higher development. Even then, I was for some time so stupid as not to see that ethics rests in the same manner on a foundation of esthetics,—by which, it is needless to say, I don't mean milk and water and sugar. (8.255)

An earlier version of this chapter appeared in the *Journal of the History of Philosophy*, 5 (1967), 41–53.

Other pragmatic positions, then, are only fragmentary.[1] They lack the unity provided by a theory of the normative sciences, and this deficiency has led them into a serious error: the error of making action the be-all and the end-all of thought.[2] If other pragmatists had a correct view of the normative sciences, they would see how intimately these sciences are connected with his categories.

> These three normative sciences correspond to my three categories, which in their psychological aspect, appear as Feeling, Reaction, Thought. I have advanced my understanding of these categories much since Cambridge days; and can now put them in a much clearer light and more convincingly. The true nature of pragmatism cannot be understood without them. It does not, as I seem to have thought at first, take Reaction as the be-all, but it takes the end-all as the be-all, and the End is something that gives its sanction to action. It is of the third category. (8.256)

I will not examine in detail here the connection between the categories and the normative sciences. I will simply note Peirce's insistence thereupon.[3] When he did see it, he realized how crude his first presentation of the maxim was. In the 1878 papers ("How to Make Our Ideas Clear" and "The Fixation of Belief") he seemed to identify meaning with action-reaction,[4] because he had not yet seen that action-reaction is to be understood only in terms of purpose, and that purpose is essentially thought. Thought may well involve action, but it cannot be identified with it since Secondness and Thirdness are irreducible.[5] The acknowledgment of the role of ends in action is the insight into the role of the normative sciences, and this acknowledgment brought about Peirce's successive attempts to formulate the pragmatic maxim in a more sophisticated and adequate way. Meaning is the rational *purport* of a concept.[6] It is essentially a third, not a second, even though a second may be involved in its recognition.

Peirce goes on to explain to James how the correct and systematic understanding of pragmatism involves synechism, that is, the doctrine of law in the cosmos:

> one must not take a nominalistic view of Thought as if it were something that a man had in his consciousness. Consciousness may mean any one of the three categories. But if it is to mean Thought it is more without us than within. It is we that are in it, rather than it in any of us. . . .

This then leads to synechism, which is the keystone of the
arch. (8.256–257)

The line of thought begins to become clearer: All action supposes ends, but ends are in the mode of being of thought because they are general. Thought, however, is not merely in consciousness; thought, rather, pervades everything so that consciousness is in thought. Generals, then, are real, and so authentic pragmatism is realistic. In the lectures on pragmatism given at Harvard in 1903 Peirce explicitly suggests that the normative sciences get us "upon the trail of the secret of pragmatism" (5.129). Consequently, we may say that for Peirce the categories, the normative sciences, pragmatism, synechism, and "scholastic realism" are of a piece.[7]

The conclusion to be drawn is that despite the relatively short time he spent working out his conception of the normative sciences, despite his many hesitations as to what ought to be included under that rubric, and despite the promissory character of the development which he left us, Peirce was convinced that he had seen how and where they fitted into his view of philosophy, uniting the whole thing and molding his earlier attempts to formulate the pragmatic maxim into a comprehensive and highly subtle analysis of meaning.

Even as a boy Peirce was interested in the normative sciences. He recounts how he picked up his elder brother's textbook in logic and worked right through it on his own. Undoubtedly, his mathematician father encouraged and directed this interest. But logic was not the only normative science to which he early applied himself. He tells us that as an undergraduate at Harvard (ca. 1855) he expounded as best he could Schiller's *Aesthetische Briefe* to his friend Horatio Paine (2.197). Almost fifty years later he expressed regret that he had not followed up this study in a serious way, because he then saw how fundamental it is to a theory of knowledge (2.120, 2.197, 5.129ff.).

Although logic received most of Peirce's attention throughout his long career, still he tells us that he was always interested in ethical systems (2.198). But until the 1880s he considered ethics to be nothing more than an art or practical science that relied little upon theoretical principles. It should be remembered that the first formulation of the pragmatic maxim—which he later called "a rough approximation" (5.16)—and his analysis of belief in terms of what one is willing to act upon appear in the 1870s. Peirce says that he first began to see the importance of ethical *theory* around 1882 (2.198). At that time he started to distinguish morality from "pure" ethics. As a result of this illumination he took up serious study of the great moralists (5.111, 5.129) and began to suspect that there was some important connection between ethics and logic (5.111). It was only some ten years later (ca. 1894) that this suspicion became a firm conviction (2.198), and only in about 1899 was he ready to say that ethics is truly a normative science (5.129). Peirce's judgment in this matter, therefore, was certainly not hasty. Rather, it was the result of long reflection during the height of his intellectual powers (in 1899 Peirce was only 58 years old). Finally, in 1903, in the Lowell Lectures of that year, Peirce made his conclusions public for the first time (5.533); but even then he was not prepared to say apodictically that esthetics is a normative science and indeed the science upon which both ethics and logic ultimately rest. He was content with the modest proposal of an opinion and an hypothesis (5.129, 2.197).

In the Cambridge lectures of 1903, Peirce explicitly related his doctrine about the normative sciences to the correct understanding of pragmatism as he first used the term. He tells us that once one sees that the normative sciences in general examine the laws of conformity of things to ends, one begins "to get upon the trail of the secret of pragmaticism" (5.130). What, then, was the development of the "pragmatic maxim" from about 1893 onward? Just how did Peirce's speculation concerning the normative sciences modify his thinking about the meaning of his 1878 statement (5.402)?

Peirce considered the first formulation of the maxim "crude" (8.255) and only approximate (5.16). His first emendation (5.402, note 2) was made in 1893 at approximately the time he began to see a connection between logic and ethics. This note was meant to meet the objection that the maxim is "skeptical and materialistic."[8] Peirce defends himself with an appeal to a collective finality governing the "realization of ideas in man's consciousness and in his works." We must be on our guard, he warns us, against understanding the maxim in too individualistic a sense. The fruit born of an individual is not limited just to what he aims his endeavors at;

whether he knows it or not, his efforts contribute to a collective result: a growth of reasonableness in the world.

> Individual action is a means and not our end. Individual pleasure is not our end; we are all putting our shoulders to the wheel for an end that none of us can catch more than a glimpse at—that which the generations are working out. But we can see that the development of embodied ideas is what it will consist in. (5.402, note 2)

Three years later, William James's *Will to Believe* pushed the pragmatic maxim "to such extremes as must tend to give us pause." Peirce interpreted his old friend's position to be that man's end is action, and, in an article for Baldwin's *Dictionary of Philosophy and Psychology* (1902),[9] criticized him for not seeing that, far from action's being man's end, action itself supposes an end.[10]

> If it be admitted, on the contrary, that action wants an end, and that that end must be something of a general description, then the spirit of the maxim itself, which is that we must look to the upshot of our concepts in order rightly to apprehend them, would direct us towards something different from practical facts, namely, to general ideas, as the true interpreters of our thought. (5.3)

Action, then, cannot be the final logical interpretant of thought, because it is not general, while thought is.[11] Thought can be interpreted only in terms of thirds; the general can be understood only in terms of the general. The meaning of a conception can be found, not in action, but in the end for which the action (resulting from the conception) is done (cf. 1.343-344). Of course, the practical facts must not be overlooked or ignored. And if one chooses to call the attention that must be paid to them the "pragmatic maxim," then it should be applied in a thoroughgoing way indeed. But:

> when that has been done, and not before, a still higher grade of clearness of thought can be attained by remembering that the only ultimate good which the practical facts to which it directs attention can subserve is to further the development of concrete reasonableness; so that the meaning of the concept does not lie in any individual reactions at all, but in the manner in which those reactions contribute to that development. (5.3)

The meaning of a concept, therefore, is judged in terms of the contribution which the reactions it evokes make toward the realization of thought's ultimate end. In other words, Peirce introduces in the pragmatic maxim itself a normative function. The pragmatic maxim is a way of recognizing the reality of the objects of general ideas in their generality. But general ideas "govern" action; they are really laws of growth; they are really final causes; they are really normative.

In this *Dictionary* article Peirce himself admits that his early formulation of the maxim did lend itself to the sort of interpretation given it by James and others, but he implies that he never meant it to be the "stoical maxim" that man's end is action. He explains:

> Indeed, in the article of 1878 referred to above, the writer practised better than he preached; for he applied the stoical maxim most unstoically, in such a sense as to insist upon the reality of the objects of general ideas in their generality. (5.3)

Now, if one rereads carefully "How to Make Our Ideas Clear" in the light of subsequent clarification by Peirce, it will become clear that, in truth, he did not make action man's end; nor did he make action the end of man's thinking. Action, no doubt, is involved in thinking both in the sense that thinking is a form of action and in the sense that thinking normally results in action. Action is, therefore, certainly a criterion of thought. But he does not say that action is the purpose of thinking. Its purpose is the establishment of "a belief, a rule of action, a habit of thought."[12] A habit is not an action. It is in an entirely different category. A habit is general; an action, singular. A habit is a third; an action, a second. Still, although this is what Peirce meant and what, strictly, he said, a superficial reading of the paper could lead to misunderstanding, especially if one were not acquainted with Peirce's subsequent development of the nature of habit as general. Then, too, his examples of how the maxim is to be applied are misleading and betray perhaps a certain hesitation and unclarity in the new doctrine he was trying to work out. For example, he applies the maxim to elucidate the meaning of the term "hard":

> Suppose, then, that a diamond could be crystalized in the midst of a cushion of soft cotton, and should remain there until it was finally burned up. Would it be false to say that that diamond was soft? . . . We may, in the present case, modify our question, and ask what prevents us from saying that all hard bodies remain perfectly soft

> until they are touched, when their hardness increases with the pressure until they are scratched. . . . there would be no *falsity* in such modes of speech. They would involve a modification of our present usage of speech with regard to the word "hard" and "soft," but not their meanings. (5.403)

This certainly seems to be a rather strong expression of the very sort of operationalism that Peirce branded nominalistic and hence erroneous because it reduces potentiality to actuality. In another place and at a later date (ca. 1905) he criticized and modified the misleading character of his illustration (cf. 5.403, note 3; 1.615; 8.208). He regretted the infelicitous example because it tended to obscure rather than to clarify what he intended to say.

In any case, in 1903, Peirce decided to make pragmatism the subject of a series of lectures at Harvard. This gave him the opportunity of comparing his doctrine with others of the same name but of a different spirit. In those lectures he tells us that he has no particular fault to find with the numerous definitions of pragmatism he had lately come across, but "to say exactly what pragmatism is describes pretty well what you and I have to puzzle out together" (5.16). Then, in a playfully ironic passage, he teases the "new pragmatists" for not acknowledging their debt to him:

> To speak plainly, a considerable number of philosophers have lately written as they might have written in case they had been reading either what I wrote but were ashamed to confess it, or had been reading something that some reader of mine had read. For they seem quite disposed to adopt my term *pragmatism*. I shouldn't wonder if they were ashamed of me. What could be more humiliating than to confess that one had learned anything of a logician? (5.17)

Peirce is delighted to share the opinions of such a brilliant company and has no complaint to make against them except that they are *"lively"*:

> The new pragmatists seem to be distinguished for their terse, vivid and concrete style of expression together with a certain buoyancy of tone as if they were conscious of carrying about them the master key to all the secrets of metaphysics. (5.17)

No doubt, Peirce has in mind "cocksuredness," not merely quality of literary style, when he chides this liveliness. One thing he could not tolerate was a cocksure attitude. For him this was the very antithesis of the scientific attitude, humble "fallibilism" or willingness to learn (cf. 1.9ff., 1.55, 1.141). Peirce clearly had in mind those who enthusiastically pushed the pragmatic maxim "to extremes." The maxim was not intended to be an open-sesame to all metaphysical problems or a panacea for all intellectual ills. It was proposed, not as a principle of speculative philosophy, but as a logical, or, perhaps better, a semantic maxim that would guide all types of investigation.[13] Indeed, Peirce recognized that

> one of the faults that I think they [the new pragmatists] might find with me is that I make pragmatism to be a mere maxim of logic instead of a sublime principle of speculative philosophy. (5.18)

And, with tongue in cheek, he continues:

> In order to be admitted to better philosophical standing I have endeavored to put pragmatism as I understand it into the same form of a philosophical theorem. I have not succeeded any better than this:
> Pragmatism is the principle that every theoretical judgment expressible in a sentence in the indicative mood is a confused form of thought whose only meaning, if it has any, lies in its tendency to enforce a corresponding practical maxim expressible as a conditional sentence having its apodosis in the imperative mood. (5.18)

Peirce managed to get his logical principle into the form of a philosophical theorem, but he immediately appends his original statement of the maxim, thereby leaving his audience to judge whether the new form is really an improvement. In any case, he never uses that form again. Still, there is one important point made in it, that is, that the pragmatic maxim must be interpreted in terms of conditionals. Indeed, the burden of the Harvard lectures is to show that meaning is intimately bound up with real laws of nature, that is, with real potentialities in things expressible in conditional sentences. The conditional necessity of law is expressed not only by a "will be," but also by a "would be," because law deals with the realm of the possible—what *would be* the case whenever certain conditions are fulfilled. What the conditional expresses is not merely the juxtaposition of an antecedent and a consequent, but also the *consequence* or connection between them. "If such and such *were* the case (or were done), then such and such *would* follow." When Peirce came to see this more clearly, he corrected what he had said about the relationship between the hardness of a diamond and scratching with carborundum. A diamond never scratched is nevertheless hard, because if it *were* brought into contact with carborundum it *would be* scratched. Thus the meaning of hardness is not in an action but in an intention or "intellectual purport."

During this whole period (ca. 1896–1903), then, due to the sudden popularity of "pragmatism," Peirce was very much preoccupied with dissociating his views from those circulating. Again, in 1905, he felt that he ought to try once more to explain what his notion of pragmatism entailed and even went so far as to coin a new word for it, "pragmaticism," which was "ugly enough to be safe from kidnappers" (5.414). So he published a series of three articles in *The Monist,* which contains perhaps the clearest presentation of his case he ever wrote.

In the first of these essays ("What Pragmatism Is") he re-expressed the maxim like this:

> Endeavoring, as a man of that type [a "laboratory-man"] naturally would, to formulate what he so approved, he framed the theory that a *conception,* that is, the rational purport of a word or other expression, lies exclusively in its conceivable bearing upon the conduct of life; so that, since obviously nothing that might not result from experiment can have any direct bearing upon conduct, if one can define accurately all the conceivable experimental phenomena which the affirmation or denial of a concept would imply, one will have therein a complete definition of the concept, and *there is absolutely nothing more in it.* (5.412)

This formulation makes it clear that the maxim has very little, indeed, to do with the practical. And Peirce explains that his awareness of this fact determined his choice of the name "pragmatism" or "pragmaticism" rather than "practicism" or "practicalism."

> But for one who had learned philosophy out of Kant, as the writer, along with nineteen out of every twenty experimentalists who have turned to philosophy, had done, and who still thought in Kantian terms most readily, *praktisch* and *pragmatisch* were as far apart as the two poles, the former belonging to the region of thought where no mind of the experimentalist type can ever make sure of solid ground under his feet, the latter expressing relation to some definite

human purpose. Now quite the most striking feature of the new theory was its recognition of an inseparable connection between rational cognition and rational purpose; and that consideration it was which determined the preference for the name *Pragmatism*. (5.412)

It is not, therefore, the practical consequences of a conception that make it true and meaningful. They are, of course, criteria of its truth and meaningfulness (since one might expect a true and meaningful concept to have consequences), but do not in some crude sense constitute truth and meaning. This is but another way of repudiating the notion that action is man's end and the purpose of man's thinking. The key to meaning and to truth is the relation of a conception "to some definite human purpose," to some end which governs actions in the same way thirds govern seconds. Rational cognition is in the category of Thirdness and must be interpreted in terms of some other third. For Peirce, this is nothing other than rational purpose. The pragmatic maxim, then, is but a way of expressing this relation. Thus once again we see that Peirce intends meaning to be identical with rational purport and not with action alone. Of course, Peirce realizes that a *proof* that this is so would require a sustained exposition of his entire philosophy of logic, cosmology, and metaphysics, or, in his words, "the establishment of the truth of synechism" (5.415).

In the same article Peirce tries to answer certain objections to his position in the form of a little dialogue. The dialogue is particularly enlightening because it indicates as clearly as anyone could wish the connection he saw, or at least thought he saw, between pragmaticism and the normative sciences. It is objected, first, that according to the pragmatic position nothing enters into the meaning of a concept but an experiment; yet, an experiment in itself cannot reveal anything more than a constant conjunction of antecedent and consequent (5.424). This typically Humean objection, Peirce observes, betrays a misunderstanding of pragmaticism's fundamental point. In the first place, it misrepresents what is involved in an experiment. An experiment is not an isolated, "atomic" event; an experiment always forms a part of a connected series or system. An experiment essentially requires the following ingredients: (1) an experimenter, (2) a verifiable hypothesis concerning the experimenter's environment, and (3) a sincere doubt in the experimenter's mind about the truth of the hypothesis. The experimenter, by an act of choice, must single out certain identifiable objects on which to operate. Then, by an external (or quasi-external) act, he modifies those objects. Then comes a reaction of the world upon the experimenter through perception. Finally, he must recognize what the experiment teaches him. Now, while the chief elements in the *event* of the experiment are action and reaction, the *unity of essence of the experiment*, what makes the experiment an experiment, lies in its *purpose and plan* (5.424). In the second place, this sort of objection fails to catch the pragmaticist's attitude of mind. Rational meaning consists, not in an experiment, but in *experimental phenomena*. These phenomena, to which the pragmaticist refers, are not particular events that have already happened to someone or to something in the dead past, but are "what *surely will* happen to everybody in the living future who shall fulfill certain conditions" (5.425). Essential to experimental phenomena is that they have been predicted.

> The phenomenon consists in the fact that when an experimentalist shall come to act according to a certain scheme that he has in mind, then will something else happen, and shatter the doubts of sceptics, like the celestial fire upon the altar of Elijah. (5.425)

In the third place, this sort of objection overlooks in a very nominalistic way the fact that the experimenter is not interested in this single experiment or in that single experimental phenomenon. He is interested in *general kinds* of experimental phenomena, for what is conditionally true *in futuro* can only be general. In other words, experimental method, implicitly at least, affirms the reality of generals (5.426).

Notes

1. Cf. 5.494 (ca. 1906) where Peirce sketches the differences between his own position and those of James, Schiller, and Papini in a less polemical way.

2. "It [calculations of probabilities] goes to show that the practical consequences are *much*, but not that they are *all* the meaning of a concept. A new argument must supplement the above. All the more active functions of animals are adaptive characters calculated to insure the con-

tinuance of the stock. Can there be the slightest hesitation in saying, then, that the human intellect is implanted in man, either by a creator or by a quasi-intentional effect of the struggle for existence, virtually in order, and solely in order, to insure the continuance of mankind? But how can it have such effect except by regulating human conduct? Shall we not conclude then that the conduct of men is the sole purpose and sense of thinking, and that if it be asked *why* should the human stock be continued, the only answer is that that is among the inscrutable purposes of God or the virtual purposes of nature which for the present remain secrets to us?

"So it would seem. But this conclusion is too vastly far-reaching to be admitted without further examination. Man seems to himself to have some glimmer of co-understanding with God, or with Nature. The fact that he has been able in some degree to predict how Nature will act, to formulate general "laws" to which future events conform, seems to furnish inductive proof that man really penetrates in some measure the ideas that govern creation. Now man cannot believe that creation has not some ideal purpose. If so, it is not mere action, but the development of an idea which is the purpose of thought; and so a doubt is cast upon the ultra pragmatic notion that action is the *sole* end and purpose of thought" (8.211–212, letter to Mario Calderoni, ca. 1905).

3. As early as ca. 1875 Peirce distinguished action and conduct in terms of his categories: "Action is second, but conduct is third. Law as an active force is second, but order and legislation are third" (1.337).

4. Cf. 5.403 and the discussion below.

5. Cf. 1.322–323, where Peirce explicitly takes up the objection that law is essential to the very notion of one thing's acting upon another. To deny the distinction between action and action governed by law is to attack Peirce's categorical scheme. Tychism develops this distinction.

6. "In general, we may say that *meanings* are inexhaustible. We are too apt to think that what one *means* to do and the *meaning* of a word are quite unrelated meanings of the word "meaning" or that they are only connected by both referring to some actual operation of the mind. Professor Royce has done much to break up this mistake. In truth the only difference is that when a person *means* to do anything he is in some state in consequence of which the brute reactions between things will be moulded into conformity to the form to which the man's mind is itself moulded, while the meaning of a word really lies in the way in which it might, in a proper position in a proposition believed, tend to mould the conduct of a person into conformity to that to which it is itself moulded. Not only will meaning, more or less, in the long run, mould reactions to itself, but it is only in doing so that its own being consists. For this reason

I shall call this element of the phenomenon or object of thought the element of Thirdness. It is that which is what it is by virtue of imparting a quality to reactions in the future" (1.343).

7. In a letter to John Dewey, June 9, 1904, concerning a review of *Studies in Logic* about to appear in the September issue of *The Nation*, Peirce deplores the way in which his former pupil turns logic into a "natural history," instead of pursuing it as a normative science, "which in my judgment is the greatest need of our age" (8.239).

8. Peirce has in mind those who would make his maxim "stoical" (cf. 5.3). For his analysis of classical stoicism, cf. 6.36.

9. Under "Pragmatic and Pragmatism."

10. Cf. the letter to Calderoni cited in note 2 above (8.211–213).

11. Cf. 5.475–493 for Peirce's discussion of interpretants. He distinguished three: (1) the emotional, (2) the energetic, and (3) the logical. The final logical interpretant is habit. Action is the energetic, not the logical interpretant. But cf. 4.536 for a slightly different arrangement.

12. Elsewhere—for example, in a paper on the classification of the sciences (ca. 1902)—Peirce distinguishes "purpose" from "final cause." Purpose is one kind of final cause, the one "most familiar to our experience" (1.211). But he is not always careful to observe the distinction. The point he is making is that final cause does not always require consciousness (1.216).

13. "I also want to say that after all pragmatism solves no real problems. It only shows that supposed problems are not real problems. . . . The effect of pragmatism here is simply to open our minds to receiving any evidence, not to furnish evidence" (from a letter to James, March 7, 1904, 8.259; cf. also 5.13, note 1).

6

Peirce's Pragmatic Maxim: Realist or Nominalist?

MY PURPOSE HERE is to convince the reader that American pragmatism is not to be simply identified with positivism. By positivism I understand a rather extreme form of nominalism that developed along the lines of classical empiricism. By nominalism I understand any philosophical doctrine that denies the reality of general ideas as part of the ontological structure of things. A nominalistic view of reality makes of it nothing but a set of actual entities each of which is a discrete "absolute" and between which there are no real connections. Such a world is devoid of qualities and of causal relations. It is a world about which only statements of actual contingent fact can be made. To it no necessary statements apply since they are all nothing but logical truths.[1]

Admittedly, this is an incomplete characterization of positivism, but it is sufficient for my purpose since these essential notes of that form of nominalism are what I intend to deny of pragmaticism as developed by Charles S. Peirce. It should also be said at the outset that certain forms of classical rationalism are likewise nominalistic and have developed into a type of positivism all their own. The rationalism of Descartes, with its emphasis upon intuition of clear and distinct ideas, ultimately makes of the world a set of discrete, absolute, and actual entities. The only difference between the rationalism of Descartes and the empiricism of Locke or Hume is that for the former the ultimate building-blocks are abstract ideas while for the latter they are sense data. Both, however, assume the same model for philosophy and, consequently, are formally the same sort of thing. They assume that the world can be analyzed

---

An earlier version of this chapter appeared as "Peirce's Pragmatic Maxim," in *Tijdschrift voor Filosofie*, 35 (1973), 505–17.

adequately into ultimate and discrete entities out of which the real can be reconstructed—and that there is simply nothing more to it! We might call this the fallacy of "nothing but." It is the reductionist fallacy to which analysis is often prone. I do not mean, however, that we should do away with analysis in philosophy; nor do I mean that analysis cannot possibly avoid the "nothing but" mistake. I mean to indicate the historical fact that some philosophers have fallen into this trap and, because of it, have either simply given up the work of synthesis or made it exclusively the work of the human mind without an objective basis. Finally, some have been content to assert the fact of synthesis without being able to give it a satisfactory account.

Now, I intend to deny all this of Peirce's pragmatism. As developed by its founder, pragmatism was meant to be a method of clarifying our ideas and of proceeding in our investigations without falling into the fallacy of "nothing but." It does this by insisting on the reality of general ideas (Peirce calls it an extreme form of "scholastic realism") and by emphasizing the role of vagueness both as a necessary logical component of thought and as an ontological component of the real. An immediate corollary of these two claims is that there can be no such thing as the absolutely incognizable, and, therefore, that the real and the intelligible are co-extensive.

This is the general outline of what I will try to show with respect to Peirce's pragmatic maxim. But before I enter into the properly philosophical discussion, it will be useful to say something about the historical development of pragmatism during Peirce's own lifetime. The reason is that, then and there, a serious misunderstanding about the meaning of the maxim arose among Peirce's philosophical friends and colleagues, and this misunderstanding has led to the rather popular identification of pragmatism with some form of positivism.

Everyone who has tried to teach something or to give a lecture knows how difficult it is to popularize a technical idea without distorting it to some degree. Moreover, there is the constant danger of being misunderstood even about the simplified version. The risk is that the speaker communicates not the idea he had in mind but an entire family of ideas more or less like it. Such a situation is aggravated many times over if the lecturer himself has not clearly understood the technical idea he wishes to popularize. Now, this is just what happened with pragmatism. It was popularized by William James, and it was initially misunderstood by him. James thought that he was presenting Peirce's position and explicitly gave him the credit, but the fact is that James's doctrine was not exactly what Peirce had in mind. Thus, Professor R. B. Perry could write that the popular understanding of pragmatism is due largely to James's misunderstanding of Peirce.[2] As James's books and lectures were read by philosophers in America and Europe a whole family of "pragmatisms" grew up.[3] Lovejoy, for example, distinguishes some thirteen varieties.[4] Of these no doubt some are positivistic, and to the extent that they are, any similarity between them and Peirce's position is purely coincidental. Still the stage had been set for positivists to claim that their doctrine is substantially the same as American pragmatism. Thus, when the ideas of the Vienna Circle came to the United States along with several of its members, it was understandable that they should liken their views to those of the "pragmatic" school. Unfortunately, there is no one such thing as "American Pragmatism" except in popular imagination.

As early as 1897 Peirce began to feel uneasy about the version of his doctrine propounded by James. It was in that year that James's *Will to Believe*, dedicated to Peirce, appeared. In a letter of thanks for the dedication Peirce voiced his reservations (8.249–252). By 1900, with the rapid multiplication of "pragmatists," Peirce wrote to James asking for clarification as to who first used the term and what precisely James understood by it (8.253). From that time on, Peirce was seriously engaged in trying to dissociate his own view from those of James and the "ultra-pragmatists" (see 8.212). Besides his letters to James in this sense, he wrote to Calderoni (8.205–213) and published an article in *The Monist* (5.411–437) in which he suggests that his position no longer be called "pragmatism" but "pragmaticism"—a name "ugly enough to be safe from kidnappers."

Despite Peirce's protests and his attempts to save "his darling," the term "pragmatism" became popularly associated with James's view. The reason is simple enough—James had the audience and Pierce did not. James was the popular lecturer, the master of English prose, the distinguished Harvard professor, and the man of extraordinary personal charm. Peirce was the technical logician with little patience for popularization,[5] the writer of turgid and elliptical prose, the *ex*-professor from Johns Hopkins,[6] and a man of difficult personality. In short, for many reasons, at the time when pragmatism was becoming popular, Peirce found himself isolated in a small Pennsylvania community, without academic standing, without students, without readers, without money, and with failing health. Throughout these difficult years it was James who remained Peirce's most loyal and helpful friend, coming to his assistance again and again financially and through letters of recommendation,[7] and yet it was James's influence perhaps more than that of any other single man that turned pragmatism away from the intentions of its author.

Let me now turn to the philosophical issues and begin by stating the pragmatic maxim as Peirce first formulated it in 1878[8] and comparing it with one of James's versions. Once the difference has been made clear, I will follow Peirce's efforts to correct James's position or, failing that, to dissociate his opinion from James's. Last, I will point out some of the things implied in Peirce's understanding of pragmatism, namely, realism, the significance of the categories, and, finally, the significance of the theory of interpretants for an understanding of signs.

Peirce's maxim reads as follows:

> Consider what effects, that might conceivably have practical bearings, we conceive the object of our conception to have. Then, our conception of these effects is the whole of our conception of the object. (5.402)

Here is James's version of the maxim:

> To attain perfect clearness in our thoughts of an object . . . we need only consider . . . what sensations we are to expect from it, and what reactions we must prepare. The ultimate test for us of what a truth means is indeed the conduct it dictates or inspires. But it inspires that conduct because it first foretells some particular turn to our experience which shall call for just that conduct from us.[9]

The general similarity between the two versions is unmistakable. There is even a parallelism in expression. The differences, however, are crucial. In James's version the key words are "perfect clearness," "sensations," and "some particular turn to our experience." Not one of these terms appears in Peirce's text. There the key words are "that might conceivably have practical bearings," "object of our conception," and "our conception of the object." James seems to think that the maxim yields perfect clarity of thought. Peirce simply says that it yields the whole of our conception of the object. No doubt, the conscientious application of the maxim will yield a greater grade of clarity than the methods of Descartes or Leibnitz (criticized by Peirce in the same article), still it never yields "perfect" clarity because there is no such thing. All conceptions, because they are signs, are to some extent vague. James thinks sensations are the interpretants of our thought; Peirce holds that only other thoughts (conceptions) can be their interpretants. Hence, Peirce talks of the *conceivable* practical bearings the object of our thought might have.

In a word, James gives a nominalistic interpretation to thought as basically complexes of sense data; Peirce gives it a realistic interpretation as basically consisting in *general* ideas, not in singulars. James thinks of practical bearings in terms of *particular* experiences (this or that actual outcome); Peirce has in mind *kinds* of experience. James thinks of our relation to our environment as *nothing but* our action and reaction to it, and thus as consisting solely in what takes place in actual fact. Peirce, on the other hand, thinks of that relation as consisting in more than mere interaction and in more than what merely in fact takes place. He thinks of it as also consisting in what might conceivably happen and in what would happen if certain circumstances were realized. In a word, Peirce makes the possible and the destined constituent of the real along with, of course, the actual. But this means that generals, not merely particulars, have ontological status and must be the ultimate interpretants of thought (see, for example, 5.475–493, 4.536, 8.314–315).

Finally, it should be pointed out that James had the seed of a proper understanding in his statement of the maxim if he had only followed it through. He was on the right track in pointing out that meaning has a reference to our expectations and to our future conduct. If he had examined more carefully what expectation supposes, he would have seen that it requires the reality of generals since it involves habit and the tendency to take habits. If he had considered more carefully the requirements of conduct, he would have seen that it involves the notion of control, a reference to the future, and alternate *kinds* of experience. In a word, it requires the notion of *esse in futuro*, what *would* happen if certain circumstances *should be* realized. And this, of course, is Peirce's notion of real generals. The least that can be said is, the failure to bring this out leaves James's version open to the positivistic interpretation.

To be fair to James, however, it must be admitted that, although Peirce's 1878 formulation of the pragmatic maxim is accurate enough, and if read carefully, need not yield a nominalistic interpretation, still, some of Peirce's expressions and at least one of his examples are unfortunate and misleading. Take his analysis of "hardness" (5.403ff.). Peirce was to regret this passage and to make every effort in his subsequent writing to correct the mistaken impression it was to give. Let us examine it.

By something hard we evidently mean, says Peirce, that it will not be scratched by many other substances.

> The whole conception of this quality, as of every other, lies in its conceived effects. There is absolutely no difference between a hard thing and a soft thing so long as they are not brought to the test. (5.403)

This expression is surely unfortunate especially for one who would not be taken for a nominalist. But it is made even worse by what follows. Peirce asks us to imagine a diamond crystallized within soft cotton where it should remain until completely burned up. No other substance was ever rubbed against it so as to attempt to scratch it. The question is whether it would be correct to call the diamond hard or soft. Peirce answers that it would not be incorrect or even false to call it soft since nothing prevents us from saying that all hard bodies remain soft until they are touched when their hardness increases with the pressure until they are scratched. Such modes of speech "would involve a modification of our present usage of speech with respect to the words hard and soft, but not of their meanings. For they represent no fact to be different from what it is" (5.403).

It is not difficult to see that this analysis plays right into the hands of the positivist. Here practical consequences seem to mean actual sensible results, and facts are assumed to be nothing but actual states of affairs. Facts in this sense are identified with meaning. This, in effect, is what James says, but on Peirce's later reflection, this is not what should have been said. Perhaps at the time of this writing Peirce did not fully realize that his own presentation was still marked by the positivistic attitude even though at the time he would not have accepted positivism as a philosophical position. His later remarks seem to bear this out, because he first severely criticizes his example, then goes on to point out that it did not in fact fit the maxim as stated in the same article since that statement stressed that the effects to be considered are all those conceivable, not merely those actually realized. This implies, as Peirce pointed out later, that dispositional properties ("would-be's") are real. It is precisely this that nominalism does not understand or refuses to admit.

Writing to Calderoni in 1905, Peirce remarks that what most distinguishes his pragmaticism from other current forms of pragmatism is its complete break with nominalism.

> I myself went too far in the direction of nominalism when I said that it was a mere question of convenience of speech whether we say that a diamond is hard when it is not pressed upon, or whether we say that it is soft it is until pressed upon. I *now* say that experiment will prove that the diamond is hard, as a positive fact. That is, it is a real fact that it *would* resist pressure, which amounts to extreme scholastic realism. I deny that pragmatism as originally defined by me made the intellectual purport of symbols to consist in our conduct. On the contrary, I was most careful to say that it consists in our *concept* of what our conduct *would* be upon *conceivable* occasions. (8.208)

Peirce goes on to argue that an absolutely determinate individual would be incognizable and, therefore, unreal. The reason is that it could not function as a sign.[10]

One of the important conclusions from this understanding of the maxim is that although practical consequences in the sense of actual sensible effects are *much* they are *not all* in determining the meaning of our concepts. The other important factor is the notion of *purpose*—the purpose of human reasoning—namely, to regulate and direct human conduct. It has a normative role, and hence the intellectual *purport* of thought consists in what *would* happen in appropriate conceivable circumstances, not merely in what does in fact happen on actual occasions. This makes room for a judgment of what *ought to* happen, that is, of how we ought to act in order to achieve whatever might be the ideal purpose of God or Nature in putting us into the universe with the power to reason. Human reasoning is not mere action but the development of an idea. It must be doubted, then, that action can be the sole end and purpose of thought, as the ultra-pragmatists seem to claim (8.209–212).

Writing to James in 1902, Peirce avows that his conception of pragmatism in 1877 was "crude." He had not gotten to the bottom of it until he had established that logic is founded on ethics (of which logic is a higher development), and that ethics in turn is founded on aesthetics.

> These three normative sciences correspond to my three categories, which in their psychological aspect, appear as Feeling, Reaction, Thought. . . . The true nature of pragmatism cannot be understood without them. It does not . . . take Reaction as the be-all, but it takes the end-all as the be-all, and the End is something that gives its sanction to action. It is of the third category. Only one must not take a nominalistic view of Thought as if it were something that a man had in his consciousness. Consciousness may mean any one of the three categories. But if it is to mean Thought it is more without us than within. It is we that are in it, rather than it in any of us . . . .
> This then leads to synechism, which is the keystone of the arch. (8.256–57)[11]

From this point of view, the real cannot simply be a juxtaposition of fundamental building-blocks, no matter how carefully and intricately fitted together. It must be a highly complex set of relations which constitute it, and as such, the real must be of the nature of Thought. Furthermore, the relations that constitute the real cannot be only those that actually obtain but must also include those that might possibly obtain and those that would obtain under specified conditions. The real, in a word, includes a certain order and regularity which is normative of its development. It is the working out of Thought. This is what Peirce means by synechism—the real is a continuous set of relations and not a set of discrete, atomic, actual absolutes. Nor is the real something already absolutely determinate in every respect, for its order and regularity are always open to further development. Tychism, the doctrine that chance or spontaneity is real, is a corollary of synechism. "Value in a world of chance" (to borrow Wiener's expression) sums up well Peirce's position with respect to the real.[12] His categories give it technical expression.

The three fundamental categories for Peirce are: the possible, the actual, and the destined—may-be's, are's, and would-be's. Each category is really distinct from and irreducible to every other even though they cannot be separated in our experience. We can distinguish them in thought by precisive abstraction in a definite, non-reversible order. The possible is first—a monad. The actual is second—a dyad (action-reaction). The destined is third—a triad mediating between what may be and what is. The third category is properly that of thought, regularity, law-likeness, and so is most properly the category of the real. These three categories are both necessary and sufficient to account for the complexity of the real, since with these all higher polyadic relations can be constructed, while without any one of them some relation will be omitted. For example, without the triad as a distinct basic relation, not all three-termed relations can be expressed. X gives Y to Z cannot be accounted for by any combination of dyads and monads.

For Peirce, then, the pragmatic maxim implies realism. General ideas are real, not merely convenient mental constructs as nominalism would have it. This means that the real is more than what is actually the case but also that the real must also include what may be and what surely would be in specified circumstances. All scientific knowledge depends upon such realism and implies that it is so. If it were not, no scientific laws would be possible, and prediction would be nothing more than a sheer guess—it would not even be an "educated" guess. It is impossible here to trace Peirce's arguments for this conclusion, for that would demand a lengthy study of his vast logical works which show that human reasoning involves abduction, deduction, and induction. But I might hint at the line of argument by pointing out that abduction (forming an hypothesis) considers what may be the case and is the Firstness of reasoning; that deduction draws the consequences of the hypothesis—what would be the case in the actual world if the hypothesis were true—and is the Thirdness of reasoning; that induction tests the hypothesis through its consequences against what actually is the case and is the Secondness of reasoning.

Now, it is all this sort of thing that James did not completely understand. Perhaps after this too brief exposition the reader will sympathize with him. Be that as it may, James did fail to understand what Peirce meant. In the end James might have judged that Peirce simply was wrong, but that is quite different from not grasping his position in the first place. No doubt, a positivist would have something to say against Peirce's position and he would marshal arguments to refute it, but he could not in honesty any longer simply identify pragmatism with his own position.

As I have mentioned, Peirce made an effort to explain himself to James. Part of that effort included an explanation of his theory of signs as fundamental to the structure of thought. I would like to end by saying something about logical interpretants.

For Peirce, all human thought is a sign relation. Every sign relation is triadic: the relation of its ground to its correlate to its interpretant. Roughly speaking, the ground of a sign is that quality in it which renders it apt to stand for something else. Its correlate is what it so stands for, indicates, or otherwise represents. Its interpretant is what mediates these two and brings them into relation:[13]

> an Interpretant is that which the sign produces in the Quasi-mind that is the Interpreter by determining the latter to a feeling, to an exertion, or to a Sign, which determination is the Interpretant. (4.536)

In one place Peirce distinguishes interpretant into emotional, energetic, and logical: the emotional interpretant is the feeling produced by the sign; the energetic interpretant is the effort, physical or mental, elicited by the sign; the logical interpretant is the sign's rational purport. An analysis of the meaning of a concept must take all three into account. It is the logical interpretant that is important for us to consider since it refers to what would be on certain assumptions and therefore is of the nature of a general. Peirce gives an argument why the essence of the logical interpretant must be that of a habit, but that argument need not detain us. I need only remark that while Peirce admits that another concept, proposition, or argument can be *a* logical interpretant of a concept, he denies that any of these can be the *final* or ultimate logical interpretant, "for the reason that it is itself a sign of that very kind that has itself a logical interpretant." Only habit can fill the role of ultimate logical interpretant because, although itself of the nature of a sign, its interpretant is action. But action is an energetic, not a logical, interpretant because it lacks generality.[14]

Let me return to James's misunderstanding of pragmatism. It might now be stated as a failure to distinguish the energetic from the logical interpretant. While the actual effects determined by a sign are involved in understanding its meaning, they are *not* its meaning. While action is surely involved in habits, actions are *not* the habits.

> Intellectual concepts, however—the only sign-burdens that are properly denominated 'concepts'—essentially carry some implication concerning the general behavior either of some conscious being or of some inanimate object, and so convey more, not merely than any feeling, but more, too, than any existential fact, namely, the "would-acts," "would-dos" of habitual behavior; and no agglomeration of actual happenings can ever completely fill up the meaning of a "would-be." (5.467)

As I have said, for Peirce, actual effects are much but not all in determining what we *mean*.

It follows from all that has been said that the meaning of a proposition does not necessarily demand that the action denoted by it be carried out. And yet it is still true that "the sum of the experimental phenomena that a proposition implies makes up its entire bearing upon human conduct" (5.427) because pragmatism

> makes thought ultimately *apply* to action exclusively—to *conceived* action. But between admitting that and either saying that it makes thought, in the sense of the purport of symbols, to consist in acts, or saying that the true ultimate purpose of thinking is action, there is much the same difference as there is between saying that the artist-painter's living art is applied to dabbing paint upon canvas, and saying that the art-life consists in dabbing paint, or that its ultimate aim is dabbing paint. . . . (5.403, note 3)

This kind of pragmatism has nothing to do with positivism. Peirce advises us that "instead of merely jeering at metaphysics . . . the pragmatist extracts from it a precious essence, which will serve to give light and life to cosmology and physics" (5.423).

Notes

1. For a careful historical account of Peirce's move from an early nominalism to a mature realism see the following: Max H. Fisch, "A Chronicle of Pragmaticism, 1865–1879," *The Monist*, 48 (1964), 441–66, and "Peirce's Progress from Nominalism toward Realism," ibid., 51 (1967), 159–78; Jeffrey R. Di Leo, "Peirce's Haecceitism," *Transactions of the Charles S. Peirce Society*, 27 (1991), 79–109; John Peterson, "Can Peirce Be a Pragmaticist and an Idealist," ibid., 221–35; Susan Haack, "'Extreme Scholastic Realism': Its Relevance to Philosophy of Science Today," ibid., 28 (1992), 19–50; Claudine Engel-Tiercelin, "Vagueness and the Unity of C. S. Peirce's Realism," ibid., 51–82; Paul D. Forster, "Peirce and the Threat of Nominalism," ibid., 691–724; and Joseph Margolis, "The Passing of Peirce's Realism," ibid., 29 (1993), 293–330.

2. *The Thought and Character of William James*. II. *Philosophy and Psychology* (Boston: Little, Brown, 1935), p. 409.

3. For example, Papini, Calderoni, Schiller, Royce, Dewey.

4. "The Thirteen Pragmatisms," *Journal of Philosophy*, 5 (1908), 1–12, 29–39.

5. See, for example, his ironic remarks in "Detached Ideas on Vitally Important Topics" (1.616ff.).

6. Peirce taught at Johns Hopkins for only five years (1879–1884).

7. For example, to Harvard for the Chair of Logic. Peirce never got it.

8. See "How to Make our Ideas Clear" (5.388–410).

9. *Collected Essays and Reviews*, ed. R. B. Perry (New York: Longmans, Green, 1920), pp. 411–12.

10. See 3.93, where Peirce argues that there can be no such thing as a logical atom.

11. For an extended study of Peirce's synechism and tychism, see my *Charles S. Peirce: On Norms and Ideals* (Amherst: University of Massachusetts Press, 1967), Parts II and III.

12. The title of R. P. Wiener's edition of selected writings of Peirce (Garden City, N.Y.: Doubleday Anchor Books, 1958).

13. See "On a New List of Categories" (1.545ff., especially 1.553).

14. For a brief analysis of the points in this paragraph see my *On Norms and Ideals*, pp. 209–11.

7

Peirce on "Substance" and "Foundations"

CHARLES S. PEIRCE has a great deal to contribute both to understanding and to solving many of the philosophical problems that puzzle contemporary thinkers. In fact it is probably true that in some ways philosophers of our time are in a better position to understand Peirce's thought than those of his own day. Here I would like to consider but two puzzling notions: (1) the substantiality of things (including the "self") and (2) the foundations of human knowledge.

SUBSTANCE

The substantiality of things has been challenged at least since the time of the Enlightenment. The question was and is whether an existing thing (like the self) is, and can be known to be, something that lasts over time and keeps its identity through change. Both the British empiricists and the Continental rationalists undermined the very notion of substance. The rationalists, following Descartes's characterization of substance as a reality which is capable not only of existing in itself (*in se*) but also of existing completely independently of anything else (*a se*), so divinized the notion of substance that Spinoza's monism and Leibnitz's monadism were the results. Even some rationalists found these a strain on credulity.[1]

Hume all but eliminated the notion of substance by taking seriously Locke's characterization of it as an inert, unknowable substratum for sense qualities. Berkeley had already drawn the conclusion

---

An earlier version of this chapter appeared in *The Monist*, 75 (1992), 492–503.

that material substance is self-contradictory precisely because it is inert. Nothing completely inert can either be or be a cause. He admitted, however, spiritual substance since it actively perceived ideas. Hume made short work of Berkeley's spiritual substance (the self) by showing that it cannot be known since we have no impression of it whether of sensation or of reflection. But an idea having no corresponding impression is simply without any assignable meaning. For Hume, the notion of self as substance can at best be traced to a series of impressions of reflection and so really refers to a set of perceptions. Hence, the notion of self as unifying substratum of impressions is the product of either memory or imagination.[2] Hume might further have argued that whatever is completely inert is completely unknowable since there would be no interaction whatever between the knower and what is to be known. Such an entity would be completely unintelligible and therefore unreal.

Peirce's account of substance attempts to do justice to the empiricists' criticism of our knowledge of substance and to the rationalists' requirement of a principle of unity and continuity. Peirce's position on substance is connected with his discussion of the self, and that position he frequently states in negative terms. Peirce, I would contend, does have the elements of a positive position on both self and substance which, even if never put together in a systematic way, is worth a second look since it suggests a notion of substance different from that criticized by the Enlightenment and one that is perhaps much sounder.[3] I propose that we undertake a search for Peirce's view of substance by looking at his views about the self, since it is perhaps the most important example of substance.

As Vincent Colapietro has pointed out in *Peirce's Approach to the Self*, many passages from Peirce give the impression that his views about the self were purely negative. In the 1868 essays written for the *Journal of Speculative Philosophy*, for example, Peirce is emphasizing against the Cartesians that we have no intuition of the self or of anything else for that matter. Hence, he talks about our becoming aware of the self through our ignorance and proneness to error. Again, in the 1890s, emphasizing his synechism, Peirce denies in various ways that thoughts are confined to our own individual minds. In fact, our personal minds are not "individual" at all if by "individual" is meant isolated from other minds.[4]

The point of Peirce's negative presentation was to counter the assumption that the self in its existence is separated and isolated from all others. This is precisely Locke's assumption about substance—an isolated, inert, unchanging, absolute substratum for sensible qualities. In effect, such a substance would be a logical atom. Pierce holds that there can be no logical atoms. Hence, the notion of self as individual, if this is understood to mean without relation to, or connection with, anything else, is just an illusion. Peirce's positive understanding of the self emphasizes its connectedness with other selves and with the environment. The self is real insofar as it is in continuity with everything else and yet at the same time keeps its identity as this self and not that. This understanding required Peirce to rethink both the notion of "individual" and the notion of "substance" to overcome the misconceptions of the Enlightenment.

As one might expect, the key to Peirce's ability to rethink these notions successfully is his theory of categories. It would take us too far afield to review the entire theory, but it is probably enough simply to recall that for Peirce, while the categories—Firstness (mere possibility), Secondness (brute fact), Thirdness (law-likeness)—are real (not merely logical) and really distinct (one is not the other), they are *not* separable in the real order. We can distinguish them but we can neither find them in reality nor experience them in isolation from one another.[5]

> These universal categories, according to Peirce, are three in number, no more and no less, absolutely irreducible to one another yet interdependent, and directly observable in elements of whatever is at any time before the mind in any way. Firstness, Secondness, and Thirdness roughly correspond to the modes of being: possibility, actuality, and law. (1.23)[6]

Consider, first, Peirce's rethinking of individuality. He distinguishes individuality in a strict sense and in a wider sense. He characterizes strict individuality as reaction, and reaction, of course, is in the category of Secondness. On this account, strictly speaking, the individual is such only at the moment of an actual reaction. But for Peirce such an actual reaction can neither exist nor be understood in isolation from everything else (otherwise Secondness would be separable from the other categories). Furthermore, such an account of the individual does not square very well with our experience of physical objects and of other people as individuals lasting as individual over time. Peirce's category of Thirdness comes to the rescue, since, as the category of continuity, it allows him to characterize individuality in a wider sense as a "continuity of reactions" which constitutes a single logical subject:

> an individual is something which reacts. That is to say, it does react against some things, and is of such a nature that it might react, or have reacted, against my will. . . . It may be objected that it [the definition of individual in the strict sense] is unintelligible; but in the sense in which it is true, it is a merit, since an individual is unintelligible in that sense. . . . That is to say, a reaction may be experienced, but it cannot be conceived in its character of a reaction; for that element evaporates from every general idea. According to this definition, that which alone immediately presents itself as an individual is a reaction against my will. But everything whose identity consists in a continuity of reactions will be a single logical individual. (3.613)

The notion of the self as an individual in the sense of a continuity of reactions brings us to the notion of substance, since, as Colapietro points out, Peirce's substance is one and the same as continuity of reactions.[7]

By insisting upon continuity, regularity of behavior, the law-likeness of reality, Peirce in effect retains a notion of substance but one very much different from Locke's. In his well-known piece "A Guess at the Riddle" (ca. 1890), Peirce, speculating about the origin of things, writes:

> Pairs of states will also begin to take habits, and thus each state having different habits with reference to the different other states will give rise to bundles of habits, which will be substances. Some of these states will chance to take habits of persistency. . . . Thus, substances will get to be permanent. (1.414)[8]

The permanence of reactions is substance. Hence, the notion of substance is relational. It means regularity of behavior, continuity. This is a far different notion from the Lockean hidden substratum, absolute and inert. Peirce is right in suggesting that his use of the term is in an "old sense" (1.414, note). After all, in the past when various schemes of act and potency were common philosophical categories, at least some thinkers understood substance to be a co-principle of being inseparably related to accident, its corresponding co-principle. On such an account, then, substance is relational; in fact, it *is* a relation. The real, existing thing (Aristotle's "first substance") is a *composite* of substance and accident related in such a way that they are distinguishable but not separable.[9] Some called this kind of relation (between co-principles of being rather than between beings) a transcendental relation (to distinguish it from the more familiar predicamental relation). This older view would maintain that substance is known in and through its accidents (that is, its sensible manifestations and regular behavior). It would maintain that only some such scheme renders a changing thing intelligible. Finally, it would maintain that nothing unintelligible (even though perhaps as yet not understood by us here and now) is, or can be, real. These views I take to be Peirce's too.

Let me conclude my remarks on Peirce's general conception of substance by pointing out in Colapietro's words Peirce's distinction between existence and persistence:

> [For Peirce] existence is the mode of being of an individual substance considered as a continuity of *reactions*; insofar as it is *actually* reacting against other things, it exists. Persistence is the mode of being of such a substance seen as a *continuity* of reactions; insofar as it endures throughout a series of reactions, it persists. In other words, existence . . . designates the aspect of secondness exhibited by any individual substance, while persistence . . . designates one of the ways in which it manifests thirdness (1.487).

Both these aspects of substance are relevant to the cognitive enterprise of human agents. Substances are both designatable and knowable: designatable, by virtue of their brutally oppositional presence; knowable, by virtue of their inexhaustibly intelligible character.[10]

Foundations

Peirce steadfastly maintained that human knowledge is discursive, not intuitive. This also meant that there is no immediate knowledge of anything. Hence, for Peirce, if *all* human knowledge is discursive and mediated, both the question of "first principles" and the question of the "foundations" of human knowledge need to be rethought in a radical way.[11]

In 1868 Peirce (just turning thirty years of age) published a series of three articles in the *Journal of Speculative Philosophy*. The views set out there remained central to his thought throughout his long career. In those articles he makes a sustained attack on what he took to be the spirit of Cartesianism, which, according to him, consisted in a preoccupation with removing skeptical doubt by establishing human knowledge as immediate, intuitive, and certain. Peirce attributed this penchant to the empiricists as well, although what they claimed to intuit were sensible rather than "clear and distinct" ideas. In place of this Cartesianism Peirce strove to put a theory according to which human knowledge is thoroughly mediated and discursive. In a preliminary draft he makes the point that what we think is to be understood only in terms of the proper method for ascertaining *how* we think.[12] He begins, therefore, with an account of cognition, then of truth and reality, and finally of the grounding of inference.[13]

The first paper, "Questions Concerning Certain Faculties Claimed for Man," centers on whether we have any immediate or intuitive knowledge of ourselves, of our mental states, or of the external world. By intuition Peirce means cognition not determined by previous cognition. In the case of judgment this would be a proposition which can be a premise but is not itself a conclusion—a first principle in the traditional sense. His conclusion on this point is negative. All knowledge is inferential and mediated through signs. By introspection Peirce understands internal cognition of our internal states not determined by external cognition. He concludes that we have no such power. All knowledge of our mental states is by inference from overt behavior, not by an inward looking.

The second paper, "Some Consequences of Four Incapacities," focuses on a theory of cognition in terms of inference and sign-mediation. The argument proceeds on the assumption that language as the external manifestation of mental activity is to be taken as a model of that activity's structure. Language is a system of signs. Pierce works out an analysis of signs and the way they function. Mental activity, then, is viewed as "inner speech." What is more, the thought process manifested in language is inferential. Inferences are expressed in (and so can be analyzed into) a series of propositions (asserted in judgments). Judgments in turn are expressed through (and so can be analyzed into) concepts. But the thought process which is expressed in propositions and general terms and is analyzed into judgments and concepts is continuous and inferential. It is not the case that judgments are constructed out of concepts and inferences out of judgments. So to think would be to make a mistake comparable to thinking that because a line segment can be analyzed into points it can also be constructed out of points. The linguistic representation of inference (say, in the syllogism) is static and discrete. The process itself is dynamic and continuous. Such representation is no doubt useful, but it is inadequate. It would be an error to attribute to the process what is an attribute of its representation. It is this error that generates Zeno's paradoxes. Later in his career Peirce made this point very clear when he distinguished between an argument and an argumentation.[14] The former is the living inferential process; the latter, its representation in premises and conclusion.

If the human thought process is inferential, still that process is differentiated. Just as the color spectrum is continuous but differentiated, so the inferential process is continuous but differentiated. It can be analyzed into three sorts of inference: abduction, deduction, and induction. Abduction forms hypotheses (perceptual judgment is a limiting case), deduction draws their implications, and induction tests their truth. This process is continuous; hence, there is no first premise which is not itself a conclusion. What, then, according to Peirce, grounds this inferential process?

At the close of the second article Peirce introduces three notions necessary to handle this foundational question: the notion of truth, the notion of reality, the notion of community. From one point of view, truth is what is the case independently of what anyone happens to think. From another point of view, truth is what is *destined* in the long run to be agreed upon by investigators. It is not the agreement which constitutes the truth but the truth which in the long run brings about the agreement. To put it another way: it is the *opinion* of the community which converges; that opinion is *about* reality. But reality neither is an opinion nor is constituted by an opinion. The persevering application of the inferential thought process will correct error and bring about a convergence on the truth. Reality is that which is represented in the long-run agreement. Here and now it is the knowable. In the limit case of the long run it is what will be known. Here and now reality is what is intended in knowing. In the limit case it is knowledge of everything about everything. For Peirce there is no reality that is absolutely incognizable. Such a supposition is self-defeating. Truth and Reality, then, are convertible terms. These notions as merely intended by human cognition at any given time suppose the notion of a community without definite limits and capable of an indefinite increase in knowledge. In the last two paragraphs of this article, Peirce says:

> Finally, as what anything really is, is what it may finally come to be known to be in the ideal state of complete information, so that reality depends on the ultimate decision of the community; so thought is what it is, only by virtue of addressing a future thought which is in its value as thought identical with it, though more developed. In this way, the existence of thought now, depends on what is to be hereafter; so that it has only a potential existence, dependent on the future thought of the community.
>
> The individual man, since his separate existence is manifested only by ignorance and error, so far as he is anything apart from his fellow, and from what he and they are to be, is only a negation. This is man,
>
> ". . . proud man,
> Most ignorant of what he's most assured,
> His glassy essence." (5.316–317)

The third article, "Grounds of Validity of the Laws of Logic," sets out to justify inference in all its forms. Peirce begins with a consideration of deductive or necessary inference. He shows that each type of categorical syllogism is governed by the *dictum de omni* and refutes various classical objections to syllogistic reasoning. With respect to abductive and inductive (probable) inference, Peirce disposes of any attempt to justify them by turning them into a form of deduction or by appealing to the uniformity of nature. Since both abduction and induction are inferences from part to whole, they are essentially forms of statistical inference the validity of which depends upon the fact that in the long run any item selected is as likely as any other to be included in the sample.

Peirce maintains that this in turn follows from the very notion of reality which he previously developed. Suppose that men could not learn from induction. The reason would be that as a general rule when they had made an induction the order of things would change. But then the real would depend on how much men should know of it. But this general rule could be discovered by induction, and so it must be a law of a universe such that when the rule was discovered it would cease to operate. But this rule too could be discovered by induction, and so there would be nothing in such a universe which could not be known by a sufficiently long process of inference. But this contradicts the hypothesis that men cannot learn from induction. Finally, Peirce stresses:

> that logic rigidly requires, before all else, that no determinate fact, nothing which can happen to a man's self, should be of more consequence to him than everything else. He would not sacrifice his own soul to save the whole world, is illogical in all his inferences, collectively. So the social principle is rooted intrinsically in logic. (5.354)

To illustrate how a continuous process can begin in time and yet have no "first" members of the series, Peirce asks those readers to suppose an inverted triangle gradually dipped into water (5.263). Clearly there is a beginning in time of its being submerged, but there is no assignable first place on the triangle where it first contacts the water. Once the triangle is immersed, the surface of the water traces a line on it at some distance, say length a, from the apex. Such a line can be marked wherever one pleases and there will still be an infinite number of other places between it and the apex where it could be marked: at $1/2a$ or at $1/4a$ or at $1/8a$ . . . *Because* the series is continuous, there is no "first place" which must enter the water first. The apex itself is not that "first place" since it is the triangle's boundary and marks where the triangle is not yet in the water.

Peirce suggests that we think of the triangle as representing cognition and of the water as representing what is distinct from cognition. Thus, when the apex itself is at the water's surface, there is as yet no cognition. Now, let each line traced by the water on the immersed triangle represent a cognition, and let those lines nearer the apex represent cognitions which determine cognitions represented by lines further up the triangle. It is clear, then, that although every cognition is determined by one prior to it, there is no first cognition, that is, one which itself is not so determined.

Peirce contends, therefore, that one can conceive, without contradiction, of *every* cognition's being determined by another, although the whole process had a beginning in time. The term "first cognition" or "first principle" cannot mean "a cognition not determined by another" or "a premise which is not itself a conclusion." Whatever is to ground, or be the foundation of, cognition must be other than the "first principles" as abstractly conceived by at least some of the tradition.

It is here, I think, that the late Canadian philosopher Bernard Lonergan has something to offer Peirce. Lonergan holds substantially the same position as Peirce does with regard to the inferential and mediated character of all human knowing.[15] His helpful proposal is that what grounds the process of cognition (continuous as it is) is intelligence *in act*. The "foundation" of knowing is not itself an *abstract* knowing, but rather a concrete seizing of intelligence in action by the intelligent knowing agent. "First principles" (Identity, Contradiction, etc.) as abstract formulas are mere tautologies which, for all we know, have no truth value for anything outside the world of lexigraphical meaning. They are what Lonergan calls "analytic propositions." They are *principles* only insofar as they are grasped as existentially instantiated, and this is possible only in the concrete act of knowing. It is in the concrete act of knowing that their evidence is grasped as sufficient, that is, they are recognized as operating here and now because whatever be the conditions of their operation, they are fulfilled here and now. If the evidence is challenged, the response is to point out a *performatory* (not merely a logical) contradiction if such evidence is rejected. To challenge and reject the first principles as existentially instantiated in any concrete act of knowing itself requires a concrete act of knowing which instantiates the principles. For if the challenge were truly telling, it would bring intelligent acts to a stop and reduce everyone to silence. To put it another way: the very act of challenging the evidence produces the same evidence again. Notice that this response itself is an inference and is determined by another act of cognition. These concrete principles grasped in the act of knowing are the conditions of possibility of the act, not abstractly and tautologically enumerated, but grasped as fulfilled in the act of knowing itself. Hence, they are *a priori* but not outside the conscious appropriation of the act of knowing. They are *transcendental*, not in the Kantian sense of an object ever beyond the knowing experience, but in the sense of the immanent structure of every act of knowing.

I would like to conclude by returning to the three ideas central to Peirce's theory of knowing as continuous inference. The three central ideas are: the notion of truth, the notion of reality, and the notion of community.

Peirce adds to the traditional notion of truth (what is the case independently of what any finite knower may think) a heuristic notion of truth as that upon which the community of inquirers will agree in the long run. This emphasizes the search for truth rather than its possession (although it does not deny the latter). It introduces an historical and existential dimension which characterizes what actually goes on within the scientific community. Lonergan recognizes this implicitly when he points out that the canons of scientific method leave open the question of further relevant issues and thus make scientific inquiry a fallible and therefore indefinite quest.

Peirce's account of reality explicitly endorses the scholastic insight into truth and reality as co-extensive. There is nothing that cannot be known, for if there were, it would be inexplicable and so would block the road to inquiry. This is operative in Lonergan's notion of metaphysics as heuristic and of being as whatever is or can be known.[16] This insight is at the heart of both Lonergan's and Peirce's argument for God.

Finally, Peirce's account of truth and of reality requires the explicit recognition of the role of the community. This refers not just to any group of people but to the community of inquirers. Nor is this community merely a *de facto* requirement for arriving at the truth about reality. It is a necessary condition for the enterprise even to begin. This need for a community of inquirers, by the way, does not mean that there must be actually an endless community of researchers. All that is required is that the possibility of an endless community of researchers be real. As long as the possibility is real, the condition is fulfilled even if as a matter of fact the community destroys itself or is destroyed.

I would suggest that the essential role of the community in

Peirce's understanding of human inquiry rejoins Lonergan's insistence on the need for a series of personal conversions in order that there be any members of such a community dedicated to searching for the truth.[17] This includes what for Lonergan is the final and perhaps most important conversion, "falling in love." Peirce indeed could have written the following: "When he pronounces a project worthwhile, a man moves beyond consideration of all merely personal satisfactions and interests, tastes and preferences. He is acknowledging objective values and taking the first step towards authentic human existence."[18]

Much of what Peirce proposed may be of real help in overcoming the seeming bankruptcy of contemporary thought by shifting it away from the paralyzing self-doubt of skepticism. I would like this essay to be a small contribution to that project.

NOTES

1. René Descartes, *The Principles of Philosophy*, para. 51, in *Philosophical Works of Descartes* I, ed. W. D. Ross and E. T. Haldane (New York: Dover, 1955).

2. John Locke, *An Essay Concerning Human Understanding*, ed. Alexander Campbell Fraser (Oxford: Clarendon, 1894) Book II, chap. xxiii, 2; George Berkeley, *Principles of Human Knowledge* (New York: Bobbs-Merrill, 1970), pp. 85–96 (critique of material substance), pp. 135–42 (notion of spirit); David Hume, *A Treatise of Human Nature* (Garden City, N.Y.: Doubleday Dolphin Books, 1961), Part IV, sects. 5 and 6.

3. Several commentators have criticized Peirce for having no adequate account of the self. Among them are: Manley Thompson, *The Pragmatic Philosophy of C. S. Peirce* (Chicago: The University of Chicago Press, 1953); and Richard Bernstein, *Praxis and Action* (Philadelphia: University of Pennsylvania Press, 1971). Among those who have defended Peirce's account of the self are: Gresham Riley, "The Self, Self-Knowledge, and Pragmaticism," Ph.D. diss., Yale University, 1965; "Peirce's Theory of Individual," *Transactions of the Charles S. Peirce Society*, 10 (1974), 135–63; Stanley Harrison, "Man's Glassy Essence: An Attempt to Construct A Theory of Person Based on the Writings of Charles Sanders Peirce," Ph.D. diss., Fordham University, 1971; "Charles S. Peirce: Reflections on Being a Man-Sign," *Proceedings of the American Catholic Philosophical Association*, 53 (1979), 98–106; "Peirce on Per-

sons," *Proceedings of the C. S. Peirce Bicentennial International Congress*, Graduate Studies No. 3 (Lubbock, Tex.: Texas Tech Press, 1981), pp. 217–21; Vincent M. Colapietro, *Peirce's Approach to the Self: A Semiotic Perspective on Human Subjectivity* (Albany: State University of New York Press, 1989), pp. 61–65.

4. Colapietro, *Pierce's Approach to the Self*, pp. 61–65. See also Peirce's: "Some Consequences of Four Incapacities," 1868 (5.264–314); Responses to James, ca. 1891 (8.81–82); MS. from ca. 1892 (7.565ff.); "Detached Ideas on Topics of Vital Importance," 1898 (1.616–676).

5. I have treated Peirce's categories at some length in *Charles S. Peirce: On Norms and Ideals* (Amherst: University of Massachusetts Press, 1967), pp. 8–24.

6. Ibid., p. 11.

7. *Peirce's Approach to the Self*, p. 81.

8. In 1.409–416 Peirce sums up his "guess at the riddle" and shows that his system of categories is the key to his answer.

9. One such act/potency scheme looks like this:

	ACT (principle of perfection)	POTENCY (principle of limitation)
	ORDER OF	
Existence	esse	essence
Essence	substantial form	prime matter
Activity	accident	substance

10. *Peirce's Approach to the Self*, p. 83.

11. See, for example, Peirce's articles of 1868 published in the *Journal of Speculative Philosophy* (1.213–357).

12. See C. F. Delaney, "The Journal of Speculative Philosophy Papers" in *Writings of Charles S. Peirce: A Chronological Edition. II. 1867–1871* (Bloomington: Indiana University Press, 1984), pp. xxxvi–xlii.

13. Ibid.

14. Peirce, "A Neglected Argument for the Reality of God," 6.456ff.

15. See, "Insight Revisited," *A Second Collection: Papers by Bernard J. F. Lonergan, S.J.*, ed. W. Ryan, s.j., and B. Tyrrell, s.j. (Philadelphia: Westminster Press, 1974), pp. 265–69. He remarks that rather early in his career he came to think of human knowledge "as not intuitive, but discursive with the decisive component in Judgment." For Lonergan's account of judgment, see *Insight: A Study of Human Understanding* (New York: Philosophical Library, 1958), passim, esp. chaps. 9 and 10.

16. See, *Insight*, chaps. 12 and 19.

17. See, for example, Lonergan, "Theology in Its New Context," *Sec-*

ond Collection, pp. 65–67. To show that Peirce in effect requires the same sort of thing of his searchers after truth would require a study of Peirce's understanding of the Normative Sciences and how they are interdependent and hierarchically ordered.

18. "The Future of Christianity," in ibid., p. 152.

8

Peirce on Continuity

IN A LETTER TO William James on November 25, 1902, Peirce spoke of "the completely developed system, which all hangs together and cannot receive any proper presentation in fragments," and he went on to describe synechism as "the keystone of the arch" (8.255–257). Now, synechism, according to Peirce, is just "that tendency of philosophical thought which insists upon the idea of continuity" (6.169). Thus, it would appear essential to understand what Peirce meant by "continuity"—the master key which, he claimed, would unlock the arcana of philosophy (1.163). Here, I will show how Peirce's technical definitions changed as his thinking of continuity developed.[1]

Peirce did not have a single completed definition of continuity. On the contrary, from 1880 to 1911 his attempts to give continuity a precise mathematical expression show a clear development marked by several significant changes. Four main periods may be identified: (1) pre-Cantorian: until 1884; (2) Cantorian: 1884–1894; (3) Kantistic: 1895–1908; and (4) post-Cantorian: 1908–1911. Although exact dating of these transitions is difficult, the periods are approximately correct and the general characteristics of each stage are clear.

PRE-CANTORIAN PERIOD

In an article written for *The American Journal of Mathematics* in 1881, Peirce showed that he was still subject to the not uncommon confusion between the notions of continuity and infinite divisibility or compactness. He said, for example, that "a continuous system is one in which every quantity greater than another is also greater

---

An earlier version of this chapter, co-authored with Paul Shields, first appeared in the *Transactions of the Charles S. Peirce Society*, 13 (1977), 20–34.

than some intermediate quantity greater than that other" (3.256).[2] It is likely that this confusion persisted until around 1884, when Peirce first read Cantor's *Grundlagen einer allgemeinen Mannigfaltigkeitslehre* in volume two of *Acta Mathematica*.[3]

CANTORIAN PERIOD

The first published definition of continuity in Peirce's Cantorian period is that written for the *Century Dictionary* in 1889. Peirce stayed rather close to Cantor's *Grundlagen* in this article. He followed Cantor both in claiming that the notion of continuity must be defined independently of our conceptions of time and space, and in dismissing old definitions of continuity ascribed to Aristotle and Kant. He then said that Cantor's definition by perfect concatenation is "the less unsatisfactory definition" (6.164).

Over the next four years, Peirce proposed what are essentially modifications of the definition by perfect concatenation. It would be nice to report that he improved upon Cantor's definition. And, actually, there does appear to be some truth in Peirce's criticism that Cantor's definition "ingeniously wraps up its properties in two separate parcels but does not display them to our intelligence" (6.121, 1892). A series is perfect, for Cantor, when it is both closed (*abgeschlossen*) and condensed in itself (*insichidicht*). But every concatenated system can be shown to be condensed in itself.[4] This is why Peirce later wrote, in the margin of his personal copy of the *Century Dictionary*, that

> [Cantor] defines [a perfect system] such that it contains every point in the neighborhood of an infinity of points and no other. But the latter is a character of a concatenated system; hence I omit it as a character of a perfect system. (6.167)

Yet the alternative definition of continuity, by Kanticity and Aristotelicity, which Peirce proposed in 1892 (6.121–124), 1893 (4.121), and again in 1903 (6.166), did not improve the situation. Aristotelicity, in these formulations, is a rough analogue to Cantor's property of closure, that is, the requirement that every limiting point of the system be contained within the system. But Kanticity is just compactness or indefinite divisibility. It is, Peirce said, "having a point between any two points" (6.166). Except under special assumptions of completeness, this property is still not strong enough to provide concatenation (Cantor's *zusammenhangend*). Concatenation, in brief, ensures that there are finite gaps in the system. Infinite divisibility by itself cannot ensure this.[5]

In his 1895 memoir, "Beiträge zur Begründung der transfiniten Mengenlehre," Cantor replaced concatenation with an even stronger property, the postulate of linearity, which is required in order to keep all continua similar. But Peirce did not read this memoir until much later,[6] and by 1895 his criticisms of Cantor's definition had taken on a new dimension. There was no longer the basic agreement in spirit that seemed to have prevailed until 1893–1894.

Kantistic Period

I have called the new position that Peirce began to formulate around 1895 "Kantistic" because Peirce discovered one of its important ingredients in Kant's definition of a continuum as "that all of whose parts have parts of the same kind" (6.168, 1903). This should not be confused with the early property of Kanticity, which is merely infinite divisibility or compactness. Rather, it implies that a continuum cannot have point-like parts at all. To come to a full understanding of this new position, though, we must look at Peirce's doctrine of "postnumeral multitudes."

By the term "multitude" Peirce meant essentially what Cantor had called the "power" (*Mächtigkeit*) of a collection. Today these are called "cardinal numbers."[7] Peirce's theory of multitudes preceded, by many years, his earliest attempts to clarify the notion of ordinality. Hence, the series of transfinite or "postnumeral" multitudes that Peirce developed are those obtained solely by repeated application of Cantor's theory, that $2^m > m$. (Peirce, incidentally, seems to have discovered the general application of diagonalization independently of Cantor; see 4.204). Thus, Peirce's entire series of multitudes, using contemporary notation,[8] would look like this:

$$0, 1, 2, \ldots \quad \aleph_0, 2^{\aleph}, 2^{2^{\aleph_0}} \ldots$$

Peirce confused the "postnumeral" portion of this series, at times, with Cantor's series of cardinals, $\aleph_0$, $\aleph_1$, $\aleph_2$, ..., corresponding to the original number classes. This is why he sometimes called the "primipostnumeral" multitude, $2^{\aleph}$, the "smallest multitude which exceeds the denumerable multitude" (4.200-213, also 4.674). More often, Peirce was simply puzzled by the continuum hypothesis. He lacked the ordinal machinery necessary to understand the difficulty. Typical is a manuscript from about 1897 in which he first claims to prove the continuum hypothesis, and then has second thoughts, the word "prove" being crossed out and replaced with the word "argue" (MS 28).

By 1896 Peirce's theory of multitudes was sophisticated enough that he could begin to describe true continuity as coming at the end of the series of postnumeral multitudes. This was what he meant when he called a continuous collection "supermultitudinous" (MS 28) and when he said that "the possibility of determining more than any given multitude of points, or in other words, the fact that there is room for any multitude at every part of the line, makes it *continuous*" (3.568, 1900).

There were several philosophical motivations behind this "Kantistic" approach to defining continuity. On an intuitive level, it must have been extremely disquieting for Peirce, the synechist, to discover that the putative power of the continuum was only $2^{\aleph}$. If continuity can be distinguished from compactness by greatness of multitude, Peirce must have reasoned, why should not true continuity refer to the very upper limit toward which greatness of multitude can tend? But also, as early as 1892 (6.12), Peirce was concerned with the non-metrical properties of continua. One of his passing criticisms of Cantor was that Cantor's definition "turns upon metrical considerations; while the distinction between a continuous and a discontinuous series is manifestly non-metrical" (6.121). In 1893 Peirce asked himself the question: How can continua be colored if their proper parts, points, are not colored (4.126ff.)? By placing true continuity beyond the series of postnumeral multitudes, Peirce thought that he had solved this problem (because, in that case, points cannot be regarded as the actual constituents of a continuum at all [3.568]), while retaining the relation "greater than" to allow for the possibility of determining any multitude of points whatsoever on a continuum. In one sense, continuity is totally different from any collection of discrete elements;

but in another sense, the larger such a collection becomes the more it resembles a continuum. Peirce wanted both. This is the central theme of his "Kantistic" period.

Post-Cantorian Period

Peirce's "Kantistic" period extended to about 1908. The post-Cantorian period developed out of several instabilities in the "Kantistic" approach. First, there was the problem of how to interpret the relation "greater than" when it is applied to multiplicities. For a time Peirce tried to maintain that Bolzano's technique of defining order relations among multitudes is also applicable between multitudes and multiplicities (4.178). But a correspondence between a point and a possible point tends to turn into a possible correspondence that can establish only a possible order relation. And, in 1908, Peirce discarded the notion that a continuum is actually "greater than" every discrete multitude.

Second, Peirce began to question the sense in which a continuum can be thought of as a collection at all. This doubt was present as early as 1900 when Peirce suggested in a letter to the editor of *Science* that, because collections have multitude and obey Cantor's theorem, a continuum is not really a collection (3.568). But if a continuum is not a collection, Peirce must have developed some other way of explaining how the parts of a continuum come together as a whole—for a continuum clearly does have parts. His solution is anticipated in a passage from "The Bedrock Beneath Pragmatism," written in 1906. Peirce proposed the definition, "Whatever is continuous has *material parts*," emphasizing that a continuum should not be thought of as a collection of points (6.174). He then explained that the *mode of connection* between these parts contributes to the nature of the whole. In a collection, this mode of connection is just "co-being" (6.174), but in a continuum it may consist of something further.

But what this further connection is was not really made explicit until the addendum, dated May 26, 1908, to the note on continuity (4.639). Peirce wrote, "In going over the proofs of this paper, written nearly a year ago, I can announce that I have, in the interval, taken a considerable stride toward the solution of the question of continuity" (4.642). He then described a version of Kant's definition, according to which "all of the parts of a perfect continuum have the same dimensionality as the whole." This requires not only that all the parts have parts of the same kind, but that sufficiently small parts have a uniform mode of immediate connection. Such immediate connection has as its paradigm the notion of time. In a word, Peirce had come full circle since 1889, when he agreed with Cantor that the notion of continuity should be treated independently of the notion of time. His post-Cantorian definition of continuity can be stated completely in terms of the time-like mode of immediate connection that obtains between sufficiently small time-like parts. Peirce's continuum became indifferent to multitude and thoroughly non-metrical. Pierce still held this view in 1911 (3.631).

Peirce's final conception of continuity, then, comes to this: the accepted mathematical definition of "continuity" describes an "imperfect continuum" (4.642, and see 6.276, 6.168), but the "true continuum" (6.170) is something "other than" any metrical or even ordinal relation of elements. The true continuum has no actual element

Notes

1. One of the most important treatments to date is Murray G. Murphey, *The Development of Peirce's Philosophy* (Cambridge, Mass.: Harvard University Press, 1961), pp. 260ff.

2. Another example of this same confusion apparently occurs in "The Doctrine of Chances" (2.646). The original 1878 version says that continuity is "the passage from one form to another by insensible degrees." This was amended in 1893 to the effect that continuity only suggests the idea of limitless intermediation, that is, of compactness. And another 1893 note implies that there are other ideas besides this one involved in the notion of continuity. The presence of these corrections make this passage an interesting exhibit of the contrast between periods (1) and (2).

3. This was originally the fifth of a series of papers entitled "Über unendliche lineare Punktmanningfaltigkeiten," written in 1882, and published in 1883 in Volume 21 of *Mathematische Annalen*. It was reprinted, with an added preface and the full title, *Grundlagen einer allgemeinen Mannigfaltigkeitslehre: Ein mathematisch-philosophischer Versuch in der Lehre des Unendlichen*, in Leipzig in 1883. Portions of this latter were translated into French in *Acta Mathematica*, 2 (1884). See Georg Cantor,

Contributions to the Founding of the Theory of Transfinite Numbers, trans. Philip E. B. Jourdain (New York: Dover, 1955), p. 54, note. For references to Cantor's influence, see 3.563, 4.331, 6.223, 6.175, MS 316A–S.

4. The property of being condensed in itself is such that all the points of the system must be limiting points. Given the provision that it is specified whether these are to be upper or lower limiting points, this is equivalent to the property of compactness. And concatenation clearly implies compactness. Without this provision it is still true that compactness would imply being condensed in itself, even though the reverse implication would not necessarily hold, as in the case when a decimal ending in an infinite sequence of nines is distinguished from the decimal in which those nines are replaced with zeros and the preceding place increased by one unit. So, in any case, concatenation implies being condensed in itself. A good explanation of this is to be found in Bertrand Russell, *Introduction to Mathematical Philosophy* (New York: Macmillan, 1919), chap. 11; and *Principles of Mathematics* (New York: Norton, 1903), chap. 35 ("Cantor's First Definition of Continuity"), pp. 285–95.

5. Concatenation, according to Cantor, is the property of a collection such that if t and t' are any two of its points and epsilon is a given arbitrarily small positive number, a finite number of points, $t_1, t_2, \ldots, t_v,$ of P exist such that the distances $tt_1, t_1t_2, \ldots, t_v t'$ are all less than epsilon. While every concatenated collection is also compact, it is not the case that every compact collection is concatenated. For example, the series found by 0 and $2-m/n$, where m and n are integers such that m is less than n, is compact, that is, infinitely divisible, but not concatenated since the steps between 0 and any other point cannot all be made less than 1. The special conditions necessary to ensure that compact series are concatenated are spelled out in Russell, *Principles*, pp. 289, 290.

6. Cantor described the postulate of linearity as the property according to which an aggregate M "contains an aggregate S with the cardinal number $_0$, which bears such a relation to M that between any two elements m_0 and m_1 of M elements of S lie." Cantor, *Contributions*, p. 134. In 1900 Peirce said that he "never had an opportunity sufficiently to examine" these memoirs (3.563), but by 1911 he was quoting from the 1895 memoir (see 3.632).

7. Murphey, *Development*, pp. 251ff. Murphey is not sure that Peirce meant by "multitude" what Cantor meant by "cardinal number," but simply does not like Cantor's choice of words.

8. Unfortunately, the editors of the *Collected Papers* have substituted Cantor's aleph symbol, $\aleph$, for Peirce's original manuscript notation, which appears in MS 25. Peirce clearly meant to indicate the denumerable multitude (see 4.204), so I have used the more common symbol, $_0$.

9

Objective Chance: Lonergan and Peirce on Scientific Generalization

IN MANY RESPECTS the views of Bernard Lonergan and Charles Peirce concerning world process are strikingly similar. Thus, both outline an evolutionary cosmology[1] that pays attention to both the law-like and the chance elements required to think of the universe as developing. Both reject the notion that the universe is mechanistically determined even if it is ordered. Both look upon "chance" as an objective component of the universe, not merely as a cloak for our ignorance. The remarkable convergence of ideas of two thinkers separated by almost a century not only illuminates their place in intellectual history but, more important, adds an extrinsic confirmation of a cosmological view that takes motion and change seriously.

As might be expected, random differences play an important role in both Lonergan's and Peirce's account of physical laws. The insight into the significance of such differences amounts to this: the universe is in a process of growth and development from a state of lesser to greater complexity. Lonergan defines a situation as random "if it is 'any [situation] whatever, provided specific conditions of intelligibility are not filled.'"[2] The "specified conditions of intelligibility" are those provided by a systematic understanding of the process. To the extent to which a situation fails to fall under such a set of conditions, it is non-systematic or random.

An earlier version of this chapter appeared in *Method: Journal of Lonergan Studies*, 12 (1994), 91–107.

Lonergan

Let us consider first Lonergan's account of physical laws, and let us begin with his distinction between systematic and non-systematic processes. It is not so simple and clear-cut as it might at first seem. First of all, it is at least unusual to talk of a process that is non-systematic. It would seem that for a process to be a process at all it must be ordered in some way and thus be "systematic" in some commonsense meaning of the term. Of course, the point is that Lonergan uses the terms "systematic" and "non-systematic" in a technical, not a commonsense, meaning. In short, he uses them to indicate a definite type of order and its absence, as we shall see shortly. Even when we realize that Lonergan uses these terms technically, they remain difficult to grasp, because in experience processes always show both a systematic and a non-systematic aspect. They can be distinguished in understanding, but they cannot be separated in experience. They are, then, for Lonergan, complementary; but we must not allow their complementarity to obscure their real distinction lest we lose the significance of randomness for understanding our world.

A process is said to be systematic if it can be grasped in its entirety in a single insight or in a single set of unified insights.[3] Classical physics, for example, seeks to grasp such process precisely as systematic by looking for an answer to the question "What kind of process is this?" or, perhaps better, "What is the nature of this phenomenon?" It does so precisely by correlating measurable relevant variables (time, speed, temperature, pressure, or whatever) into differential equations. These equations are used to predict future events of the appropriate kind.

Systematic process then is commanded, as it were, by a single idea which allows us to know *a priori* and in principle (through differential equations expressing laws) all the events/situations that make up the process. Consequently, any event or situation in the process can be deduced from any other by virtue of the *idée maîtresse*. In a word, these physical processes are regarded as being subsumed under a *covering law* and so are ordered *deductively*.[4] Such a grasp of events/situations possesses a tremendous predictive power. It enables us to organize vast amounts of empirical data and to make predictions which are regularly fulfilled.[5] The insight into physical processes as systematic is that of so-called "classical" physics.

A process is said to be non-systematic if it has not been (and indeed ultimately cannot be) grasped in a single insight or set of unified insights. In such a case there is no one idea that governs the whole, and so one cannot *deduce* any event/situation from any other. (This does not mean that one cannot *infer* an event/situation from some other[s]; not all inference is deductive.) At best, predictions are based on probabilities calculated statistically. Indeed, Lonergan calls this model of science "statistical" physics, and he sees it as complementary to the classical model.

These models of science, classical and statistical, are *heuristics*. An heuristic is an intelligent anticipation of intelligibility of a certain kind. Thus, classical heuristic anticipates the *systematic and abstract* (the physical laws) on which the concrete observations converge. Statistical heuristic anticipates the *systematic and abstract* which sets a boundary (the ideal frequency) from which the concrete cannot systematically diverge (allows random divergence).

The statistical model deals with events as "coincidental aggregates." Events are assumed to have no relations to one another other than mere juxtaposition in space. Classical physics deals with events as intelligible wholes causally related. The laws that it formulates, however, always have added (explicitly or implicitly) to its generalizations the phrase "other things being equal." Hence, classical physics expects that there will be no differences between predicted and observed results. If such differences do appear, they are put down either to "observational error" or to arbitrary isolation of part of the physical universe, and so the observed results are expected to converge on the predicted as the observational errors or arbitrary isolation is overcome. To be sure, classical physics used statistical analysis when dealing with very, very large numbers (for example, the number of gas molecules in a container), but this was considered to be an unfortunate second-best and so to be a "cloak of our ignorance" of the actual behavior of such large populations. In principle, then, if one were to adopt the classical model as uniquely correct, statistical methods would be expected to be gradually eliminated.

Statistical physics, on the other hand, renders an account of discrepancies between predicted and observed results, thus giving them a kind of intelligibility by distinguishing deviations which are merely random from deviations which are themselves systematic. It sets limits (ideal frequencies) from which observed data cannot diverge systematically.[6] Non-systematic processes, then, manifest a certain intelligibility and thus a certain order, but an order and intelligibility different from that of systematic processes. Hence, statistical investigation, which deals with non-systematic process, anticipates a different intelligibility than does classical. The order studied by statistical investigation is that of actual relative frequencies of events as diverging from an ideal frequency only at random. In effect, it counts the number of times outcomes of a certain type actually occur. Thus, for example, the ratio of heads or of tails in tossing a fair coin turns out to be one half since the actual ratio of each for any series of tosses oscillates at random about the value 1/2.[7] Statistical techniques can then reveal a certain order in a run of events which from a classical point of view has no immanent intelligibility. The mind-set (heuristic anticipation) fostered by statistics is to expect that there will be differences which do not make a difference provided they are merely random. The classical mind-set, however, expects every difference to make a difference and puts down divergences from predicted values to observational error or to the arbitrary isolation of a physical system.

Perhaps an example will make the point clearer. According to classical kinetic theory, the interrelations of pressure, volume, and temperature of a gas (Boyle's and Charles's laws) are accounted for by supposing that the gas is composed of a very large number of molecules moving at random inside the container. Any molecule has as much chance as any other of hitting the container's wall. It was noted that the predicted values calculated for pressure or volume or temperature using statistical methods were only approximated by the actual values when observed. It was thought that, because every difference must make a difference, if the laws governing the relations between pressure, volume, and temperature were correct, the discrepancies must be due to faulty measurement and/or observational techniques. The expectation then was: improve the accuracy of measurement and observation and you will reduce the discrepancies between predicted and observed values. It turned out, however, that just the opposite resulted; the more accurate the observations the wider the divergence. Something, then, must have been wrong with the theory; it must be missing something. This realization led scientists completely to rethink Newtonian (classical) mechanics on which kinetic theory was built. The outcome, of course, was the elaboration of quantum mechanics.

It turns out, then, that statistical techniques do indeed give to runs of events a certain intelligibility indirectly and from the outside as it were—through the mathematics of probability, not through the unity of cause and of nature. In the case of deviations from the ideal frequency of any run of events, since they are all merely random they do not have even the intelligibility of non-systematic process. They are in fact the surd element of concreteness and finiteness.[8] In the real order, then, one finds no processes that are entirely systematic and no processes that are entirely non-systematic. Every real, observable world process exhibits aspects of each.

Both classical and statistical physics seek intelligibility in actual physical processes. Each, then, formulates "laws," and in each case observed values and predicted values differ; in the case of classical physics, those differences are unexpected and unwanted (merely "observational error"); in the case of statistical physics, they are expected and are permitted if and only if the differences are random. In both heuristics there is an inverse insight into the differences between observed and predicted results. In the case of classical heuristic, they are allowed as long as they are only the result of observational error that can be corrected by more careful and accurate measurement; in the case of statistical heuristic, they are allowed only when deviating from the ideal frequency at random.

Thus, the negative unintelligibility of random differences which make no difference to the generalization (the ideal frequency) is simply a recognition of the abstract character of our explanatory generalization. The positive unintelligibility of differences too large to be set down to mere observational error and too systematic to be ignored is recognition that our explanatory generalization has missed some relevant variable in the process and thus forces revision of the differential equation. Lonergan puts the matter like this: "when differences are not random (too large to be merely random) further inquiry is in order; but when differences are random, not only is no inquiry attempted but also the very attempt would be pronounced silly."[9]

Because of the complementarity of classical and statistical heuristics implied in the foregoing, they are not to be regarded as competing views. On the contrary, they are to be regarded as contributing positively to each other. Thus, to return to the example of kinetic theory cited above: the anticipation that the laws of gases as worked out in Newtonian mechanics would be perfectly confirmed by the coincidence of predicted and observed results was disappointed by further research, so that the very laws of mechanics had to be reformulated in such a way as to incorporate statistical method into the essence of the theory and not leave those statistical outcomes as simply a cover for ignorance.

Since these heuristics are truly complementary, it is plausible to assume *a priori* that they are irreducible in the sense that the greater development of one heuristic will not result in the elimination of the other. Suppose that classical physics succeeds in developing ever more inclusive frameworks in which to organize its data into more and more inclusive laws. Among other things this would mean that what was omitted by one framework was included in the next. Still, in the more inclusive framework there would be other items which escape the new laws. In every case these items which elude inclusion under classical law are considered in terms of statistical laws and are judged to be either random or systematic deviations. If the deviations are statistically significant, further investigation is in order. If they are merely random, no further research is required. In that case we are simply reflecting that the concrete, real situation reflects an *empirical residue* which can never be captured in laws whether classical or statistical. In a word, no matter how inclusive a framework is developed, in the concrete random differences will never be eliminated. Why is this so? What is the significance of differences which do not make a difference to any physical theory in question?

The classical heuristic if taken alone would have deduction as its model. Gödel proved that no non-trivial deductive system can be shown within the system to be both consistent and deductively complete. Deductive completeness means that every true statement appear as part of the system either as an axiom or as a theorem. Consistency, of course, means that the system is not self-contradictory. Clearly, all logicians want a deductive system to be at least consistent. But Gödel showed that no consistent, non-trivial deductive system can contain all true statements. There will always be at least one statement known to be true which is neither an axiom nor a theorem of the system. If one tries to fix up the axioms so that the truth previously not contained in the system is now so contained, another, different, statement will be found which, while known to be true, is neither an axiom nor a theorem. These "undecidables" are to the axiomatic system as the empirical residue is to classical physics. The strange, even disconcerting phenomenon is due, I think, to the abstract nature of our expressions of the world's intelligibility in general principles and laws. The reality of the concrete always involves more than the abstract can express.

The question whether world processes are systematic or not is an empirical question. It seems to have been settled that they in fact manifest aspects of each. Hence, insofar as there were a non-systematic aspect to actual world processes, the randomness they manifest would not be just "a cloak for our ignorance," but rather a property of what exists.

Lonergan points out that even if we accept that classical and statistical heuristics, correctly understood, are complementary, we still need an explanatory idea which accounts for the characteristics of each of those anticipatory schemes. As he remarks, the laws formulated under the classical heuristic (for example, Newtonian mechanics) not only do not give any insight into numbers, distribution, intervals of time, selectivity, and other elements that enter into statistical analyses, but rather abstract from all particulars and concrete conditions under which those classical laws actually function.[10] On the other hand, laws formulated under the statistical heuristic (for example, quantum mechanics) give no account of why there are "so many kinds of events or why each kind has the frequency attributed to it."[11] They merely provide in various cases an ideal frequency of the occurrence of the events. Lonergan concludes:

> To reach explanation on this level, it is necessary to effect the concrete synthesis of classical laws into a conditioned series of schemes of recurrence, to establish that such schemes, as combinations of

events, acquire first a probability of emergency and then a probability of survival through the realization of the conditioned series, and finally to grasp that, if such a series of schemes is being realized in accord with probabilities, then there is available a general principle that promises answers to questions about the reason for numbers and distributions, concentrations and time intervals, selectivity and uncertain stability, development and breakdowns. To work out the answers pertains to the natural sciences. To grasp that emergent probability is an explanatory idea, is to know what is meant when our objective was characterized as a generic, relatively invariant, and incomplete account of the immanent intelligibility, the order, the design of the universe of our experience.[12]

It is further evident that Lonergan is satisfied that the world process is, at least in some significant cases, non-systematic. In the section of *Insight* dealing with "emergent probability,"[13] he spells out in some detail what is to be expected from an empirical examination of the actual world if indeed *both* classical *and* statistical laws were supposed to be true of that world. We would then expect that world to exhibit both regularities and novelties, both lawful and chance events—in short, be a world of continuity and differentiation. We have only to go and look to judge whether such an heuristic anticipation is justified by empirical testing.

Peirce

Consider now what Charles Peirce has to say of the same subject. He is writing just before the turn of the century and so before Einstein, Heisenberg, and Planck. His notion of physics has been formed largely in the Newtonian, and so classical, model in which emphasis has been laid on events converging on predicted outcomes and in which divergence of actual observations from the norm were considered to be due to observational error of one kind or another. And yet in a paper published in 1893 in *The Monist*, he remarked:

> The *Origin of Species* was published toward the end of the year 1859. The preceding years since 1846 had been one of the most productive seasons—or if extended so as to cover the great book we are considering, *the* most productive period of equal length in the

entire history of science from its beginning until now. The idea that chance begets order, which is one of the cornerstones of modern physics . . . was at that time put into its clearest light. (6.297)

Peirce was convinced that Darwin's evolutionism and any mechanistic interpretation given to science and its laws were incompatible. In Peirce's opinion the use of statistical methods in science did not give any aid or comfort to "mechanical philosophy" as some, among them Peirce's friend Chauncey Wright (see, 5.64), supposed. To the contrary, Peirce regarded statistical methods as sounding the death knell for such views.

For Peirce the "mechanical philosopher" is "whoever holds that every act of the will as well as every idea of the mind is under the rigid governance of a necessity coordinated with that of the physical world" (6.38). Such a philosopher "will logically be carried to the proposition that minds are part of the physical world in such a sense that the laws of mechanics determine anything that happens according to immutable attractions and repulsions" (6.38). Peirce called this "the usual and most logical form of necessitarianism." We recognize in this "mechanical philosophy" the mind-set Lonergan spoke of as arising from the mistaken assumption that the classical model of physics is the uniquely correct one. It is against this view of things that Peirce, like Lonergan many years later, mustered all his considerable logical, scientific, and philosophical resources.

What, Peirce asks, are the reasons for holding such a view? Three sorts of arguments are usually proposed: (1) absolute determinism is a postulate of scientific reasoning; (2) absolute determinism is supported by observational evidence; and (3) various *a priori* arguments support it (6.39–65). The first class of arguments is based on a faulty understanding of scientific method; the second is simply gratuitously asserted; and the third does not exhaust all possible alternative hypotheses, in particular, the hypothesis that chance is in some sense real and not merely a function of our ignorance.

Let us consider Peirce's criticisms more closely. To think that absolute determinism is a postulate of scientific reasoning is to assume erroneously that induction is nothing but a special case of deduction. Peirce, of course, has in mind the sort of analysis of induction which grounds its effectiveness in the uniformity of nature. But he points out that in fact all inductive inference is based on the principle of sampling. He gives this example: from samples of a shipment of wheat we find that four-fifths of the samples contain quality A wheat; hence, we conclude "experientially and provisionally" (Peirce's words) that about four-fifths of all the grain in the shipment is of the same quality. Such an argument is based solely on what we have experienced of the wheat in the past and what we can experience of it in the future. Because that sort of reasoning is conditioned by experience (both actual and possible), its conclusion concerning the true proportion of quality A wheat in the shipment is only provisional. At any given moment, therefore, the inferred ratio is only an approximation of what would be found to be the case if more samples were to be taken. The inferred ratio, then, is really an hypothesis to be verified and/or modified by experience. If the outcomes of further sampling fluctuate irregularly so that no definite value can be assigned to this ratio, the limits within which it fluctuates can be discovered. If, however, further sampling yields definite ratios that change, that fact can be ascertained and the approximation modified accordingly. Thus Peirce remarks:

> in short, whatever may be the variations of this ratio in experience, experience indefinitely extended will enable us to detect them, so as to predict rightly, at least, what its ultimate value may be, if it has any ultimate value, or what the ultimate law of succession of values may be, if there be any such law, or that it fluctuates irregularly within certain limits, if it does so ultimately fluctuate. (6.40)

For Peirce, then, the process of sampling is self-corrective and because it is this process which grounds inductive inference, that type of inference needs no postulates whatever, not to mention a postulate of absolute determinism.

As for the claim that there is observational support for absolute determinism, Pierce cannot understand how anyone acquainted with scientific research from the inside could take it seriously. He points out that any scientist knows that no observation determines the value of a continuous quantity with a probable error of zero. But what about observations of continuous quantities which are discontinuous at one or two limits? For example, take a line segment drawn by someone on a sheet of paper. How to determine its length? Since it cannot have a length of less than zero, if no length at all is visible, the observed length is zero. All this means, however, is that the length of the line segment is less than the smallest length visible with the optical power employed. It does not immediately warrant the conclusion that no line segment had been drawn at all. To reach that conclusion legitimately one would have to have recourse to some indirect evidence, for example, that the person who supposedly drew the line in the first place was never anywhere near enough to the paper to do so (6.45–46). Peirce's general point is this: to conclude that some quantity or other is absent from a certain subject matter, there must be some experimental evidence, direct or indirect, to that effect. It is not enough simply to say that we are unable to detect it. Peirce points out further that when we try to verify a law of nature, the more precise our observations, the more certainly will they show irregular departures from the law (6.46).

Finally, consider Peirce's evaluation of the various *a priori* arguments advanced by the defenders of "mechanical philosophy." The most serious of these, in Peirce's view, is the claim that absolute chance cannot be an explanation of anything. The issue, then, is to determine in what an explanation consists and when one is required. Peirce maintains that regularity, not irregularity, is what *par excellence* requires an explanation. The reason is that an explanation is required only when questions arise, and questions arise only when there is some thwarted or disappointed expectation. Now, irregularity engenders no expectations whatever as to what is likely to turn up. Hence, it raises no questions and so needs no explanation. Again, purely formal regularities such as those found in mathematical laws (say, of probability) require no explanation either, since they are simply part of the *a priori* conditions of our knowing randomness at all. The situations that require explanation are: (1) those empirically observed in nature since they are the exception to the preponderance of our experience; (2) breaches in empirically observed regularities since they disappoint our expectations and so raise questions; and (3) failure to discover empirical confirmation of a postulated regularity. In this third case, what needs explanation is not precisely why there is no regularity, but rather why we were led to postulate it in the first place. In Peirce's view, then, in a universe such as ours regularity alone needs explanation. Consequently, law cannot be posited as the ultimate explanation of the cosmos. Such a position would lead to this rather curious reasoning: on the one hand, since law and regularity cannot explain irregularity and growing diversity, the latter would have to be set down as inexplicable; on the other hand, if laws cannot have evolved out of irregularity (precisely because of this account they are immutable and ultimate facts), then they have no explanation either. Hence, such a position would block the road to further inquiry and violate what Peirce took to be the most basic tenet of scientific method.

Peirce points out that all the laws of classical mechanics deal with conservative forces, that is, with forces which are reversible and which obey the laws of conservation of energy. He further remarks that in fact most physical phenomena here on earth are non-conservative and so seem to be inexplicable by the laws of classical mechanics: birth, growth, life, friction, heat conduction, combustion, capillarity, diffusion of liquids, etc.

Now, as a general rule, physicists explain those actions which seem to violate the law of conservation of energy through the action of chance. In some cases a uniform distribution can be understood to result from conservative forces acting upon a collection of things whose distribution is fortuitous. This process is known as sifting. The converse is not possible, however. By themselves conservative forces cannot bring about a fortuitous distribution; only another fortuitous distribution in the initial conditions can do that. Peirce gives this example. Suppose a jar to contain hot nitrogen. Add some cold oxygen. At first the nitrogen molecules will be moving with various degrees of force distributed fortuitously. The same will be true of the oxygen molecules. On the average, however, the oxygen molecules will be moving more slowly than the nitrogen. This is *not* a matter of chance. Furthermore, in the course of time there will be continual fortuitous encounters of the two sorts of molecules causing continual interchange of energy between them, with the result that gradually there will be an approximation to one fortuitous distribution of energy among all the molecules. Peirce observes:

> That which happens, happens entirely under the governance of conservative forces; but the character of fortuitous distribution to-

ward which there is a tendency is entirely due to the various fortuitous distributions existing in the different initial conditions of the motion, with which conservative forces never have anything to do. (6.81)

This is more remarkable, says Peirce, since, although the initial distribution of forces gradually tends to die out, the subsequent fortuitous distributions dependent upon the initial conditions not only hold their ground, but mark their effect wherever the conservative forces act. This is what Peirce means by the "action of chance" (6.81). The uniformity or regularity of a distribution, therefore, can be understood to have come about through the "action of chance" but not conversely. Conservative forces within a mechanical system cannot, by themselves, reverse the sifting process so that a completely fortuitous distribution results from a uniform distribution.

Not all uniform distributions are the result of the sifting of fortuitous distributions, however, and those that are also always involve some sort of regularity in their initial conditions. Peirce gives this example. The density of a gas varies directly with its pressure since more molecules confined to a smaller space will strike the walls of the container per unit time. This is not due to chance alone, however, since the initial conditions suppose that the parts of the molecules are all nearly rectilinear, for otherwise it might turn out that the molecules do not strike the container walls at all even though they are in motion. But such an initial condition is itself a regularity. Hence, regularity in a phenomenon requires some regularity in its initial conditions just as irregularity in a phenomenon requires some irregularity in its initial conditions. Thus regularity and irregularity are ultimate, irreducible, distinct yet inseparable, complementary aspects of all actual world processes. Peirce's hypothetical framework is called synechism (continuity), of which, he says, tychism (objective chance) is but a corollary. These rather exotic terms are perhaps best understood from the Greek roots. "Synechism" is coined from "syn" meaning "along with" or in general "accompanying," and from "echein" meaning "to have" or "to possess." Peirce meant it to stand for regularity of continuity. "Tychism" is coined from "tyche" meaning "chance" with the usual overtone of "good luck" ("dystyche" would mean bad luck). That continuity implies randomness as a corollary comes from the mathematics of continuous quantities, that is, their analysis requires the introduction of discreteness and so implies either the notion of limits to which continuous series converge or of infinitesimals of which continuous series are composed. I take it that Peirce looked on this as simply a generalized theory of evolution and that Lonergan would recognize it as the first cousin to his own heuristic hypothesis of emergency probability.[14]

For Peirce, then, the entire universe is in a process of development which can be thought of as hyperbolic:

> The state of things in the infinite past is chaos . . . the nothingness of which consists in the total absence of regularity. The state of things in the infinite future is death, the nothingness of which consists in the complete triumph of law and the absence of all spontaneity. (8.317)

These states (infinite past and infinite future) are, however, only theoretical limits which are approached asymptotically. Between them

> we have on our side a state of things in which there is some absolute spontaneity [chance] counter to all law, and some degree of conformity to law, which is constantly on the increase owing to the growth of *habit*. (8.317)

This is for Peirce *the* law of the universe, the law of habit-taking, the law of mind.

NOTES

1. To the best of my knowledge Lonergan's position as found in *Insight: A Study of Human Understanding* (New York: Philosophical Library, 1956) was developed quite independently of Peirce's views. Peirce wrote some fifty years before Lonergan and I find no evidence that Lonergan knew Peirce's work until several years after *Insight* was published.

2. Ibid., p. 51.

3. Ibid., p. 48.

4. Lonergan referred to his theory as "emergent probability" (ibid., pp. 121–28). He characterized it as both generic and explanatory. Peirce referred to his theory as "agapastic evolution," an explanatory account of

the growth and development of the cosmos which attempts to do justice to the role of the categories in world process by an appeal to the "action of love," that is, mediation between the necessity and the spontaneity of actual world process. I have treated this at some length in *Charles S. Peirce: On Norms and Ideals* (Amherst: University of Massachusetts Press, 1967), pp. 171–90.

Charles Peirce will also hold that classical (Newtonian) physics is deterministic in its view of the physical world because it took deduction as its model of explanation. Gerrit Smith, who was Professor of the Philosophy of Science, Fordham University, and who held his Ph.D. in Physics from Syracuse University, pointed out to me that while Peirce and Lonergan have in mind Newtonian mechanics as "classical physics," the real culprit behind this determinist mentality is more ancient and more profound. It is more ancient in that it goes back to the Pythagoreans and more profound in that it supposes a universe that is static and changeless, and so is capable of being completely expressed mathematically (geometrically, first, and then algebraically). (See the study of his student, Jamila Jauhari, "The Physics of Avicenna," Ph.D. diss., Fordham University, 1987.) Furthermore, the Pythagorean view would not allow anything like an "empirical residue" (Lonergan) or an irradicable "Secondness" (Peirce). Any discrepancy between predicted and observed outcomes would be put down not merely to "observational error" but also to the fact that, whenever an arbitrarily selected portion of the physical universe is treated as an isolated physical system, then, inevitably, some violation of the laws of conservation will appear and hence bring about discrepancies between predicted and observed results.

5. Lonergan, *Insight*, p. 48.

6. Some may find it helpful to think of "ideal frequency" in more precise, mathematical terms. Again I am in debt to Dr. Smith who brought this to my attention and who offered the following definitions: (a) *Cauchy Series*: a sequence of numbers is said to be "Cauchy" if and only if for any positive number ϵ ($\epsilon > 0$), there is a positive integer N such that for members x_n and x_m of the sequence with both n and m greater than N, $]x_n - x_m[< \epsilon$. Hence, the further one proceeds in such a sequence the more closely "bunched up" are the members. (b) *Limit "L" of Cauchy Series*: A Cauchy series is said to have a limit "L" if and only if for any positive number ϵ ($\epsilon > 0$), there is a positive number N such that for all $n > N$, $]"L" - x_n[> \epsilon$. (c) *Ideal Frequency*: a sequence ($x_1 \ldots x_n$) of statistical outcomes with average x is said to have an ideal frequency x_{id} if for any positive integer ϵ ($\epsilon > 0$), the *probability* that $]x[>]x_{id} \pm \epsilon[$ vanishes as N --- > infinity.

7. Dr. Smith points out that the difference between the expectations

for statistical studies in Newtonian mechanics and in quantum mechanics is just what Lonergan says is the difference between classical and statistical heuristic structures. Newtonian mechanics supposes that there are available to the observer other parameters which he simply neglects out of ignorance, laziness, or technological limitations. If these parameters were to be taken into account, the observed data would indeed converge on the predicted results. Quantum mechanics, on the other hand, supposes that there simply are not such other parameters. Lonergan's point is that, because classical and statistical heuristics are complementary, statistical techniques even when applied within classical physics are impossible to dispense with, since their reason for existence is the *empirical residue* that cannot be eliminated by any abstract laws whether classical or statistical. Statistics is *not* a mere cloak of our ignorance even in classical investigation. Peirce's agreement with the substance of this view may well have been what led him in fact to anticipate quantum theory. Lonergan's understanding of the physical universe is anti-Pythagorean and pro-hylemorphic, since "prime matter" is the analogue of the "empirical residue." Peirce is in the same camp by his insistence on "Secondness" as brute.

8. A convincing confirmation of a surd aspect, a brute and factitious element, in nature is the fact that physical constants, like K (specific gas constant), or R (universal gas constant), or C (speed of light), must be empirically measured and calculated. Indeed, a theory may posit that there is such and such a constant, but the theory cannot assign it a numerical value. That value simply is whatever it turns out to be.

9. *Insight*, pp. 54–55.
10. Ibid., p. 124.
11. Ibid.
12. Ibid.
13. Pp. 115–28.
14. Here are, according to Lonergan, some of the attributes the universe would in fact manifest if emergent probability were true: (1) there is a succession of world situations each one of which comes about, survives, and changes according to a schedule of probabilities; (2) world process is open, that is, not determined; (3) world process is increasingly systematic; (4) world process admits enormous differentiation; (5) world process admits of breakdowns; (6) world process includes blind alleys; (7) the later a scheme is in the conditioned series of schemes, the narrower its distribution in the cosmos; (8) the narrower the basis for the emergency of the later schemes of emergence, the longer the time interval; (9) the greater the probability of blind alleys and breakdowns, the greater must be the initial number if the whole series of schemes is to be assured. See ibid., pp. 125–28.

10

C. S. Peirce and Religious Experience

OVER THE YEARS two problems have engaged my attention as I have reflected on religion and religious experience. The first is classical empiricism's charge that religious language is meaningless, in the sense of bearing no cognitive content. The second is the tension felt by religious believers between the need for an authentic, or real, experience of God—a sense of awareness of God's nearness or presence—and the need for rational argument to ground and to legitimate (precisely as real or non-illusory) any such experience. Experience is required to make religion concrete and alive; argument is required to authenticate the experience.

The first kind of problem is well known and so requires no detailed elaboration here. The challenge to religious and metaphysical claims had its classical expression in Hume, but in more recent days the dismissal of such claims has been rethought even by contemporary empiricists. This re-evaluation has to do with a rethinking of classical empiricism's assumptions about experience and its role in human knowing. It is less fashionable nowadays to assume that only what is delivered in sensation and is expressible in perceptual language is cognitively significant—even though this assumption still has a haunting simplicity and a deceptive promise of scientific objectivity.

The second sort of problem can be found in Anselm's *Proslogion* where the so-called ontological argument is imbedded in a context of faith, prayer, and feeling. In more recent times within Christian circles the tension between faith and reason, between experience and argument, arose in the form of the fideist-rationalist controver-

---

This chapter is a slightly expanded version of "The Recovery of Religious Experience," which appeared in *Versus*, 49 (1988), 81–89.

sies. Among others, John E. Smith has written persuasively, in my opinion, on this matter. In an article entitled "The Tension between Direct Experience and Argument in Religion,"[1] he cites C. S. Peirce as one who successfully resolved this tension.

I will turn to Peirce, then, to answer both these problems in terms of his general theory of experience and cognition. I hope to show how he led the way in pragmatism's recovery of experience from the narrow empiricist view and showed us a way to resolve the tension between experience and argument in religion.

It is not easy to work out just how Peirce understood human experience. He, like so many others, used the term in a variety of different, if related, senses. Furthermore, his texts are notoriously difficult to interpret. It is hardly surprising that not all commentators agree on what his theory of experience is or on whether it (and his philosophical view in general) is internally coherent. I am convinced that his views are consistent and that a failure to understand this guarantees a misunderstanding of his theory of experience and cognition. This does not necessarily mean that Peirce's view is correct. One must determine that for oneself.

The Recovery of Experience

It is a well-established fact that the American pragmatic movement attacked British empiricism's notion of experience as too narrow.[2] These pragmatists pointed out that classical empiricism implied contrasts that were supposed to hold between sense perception, on the one hand, and reason or understanding, on the other. These contrasts were understood in terms of irreconcilable conflict. Hence, the British empiricists concluded that one had to choose between empiricism and rationalism. Furthermore, the pragmatic critics pointed out that empiricism insisted on the difference between the immediacy of *sensa* and the immediacy of physical objects. Empiricism believed that only sense data, not physical objects, could be the immediate object of experience. But such data are with the subject as modifications of his brain (or sense faculty or whatever). Hence, empiricism was forced to admit a gulf between what is immediately sensed and the world of physical objects. Hence, too, it was forced to face the insoluble problem of the bridge.

Pragmatism countered this drift into subjectivism in various ways. One move was to show a close connection between sense perception and reason or understanding. According to Peirce, for example, the basic unit of cognitive experience is the perceptual judgment, and every perceptual judgment involves inference. Hence, sense and reason work closely together rather than contend as rivals. Again, Peirce reacted against the Cartesian model according to which ideas "in" consciousness are what is immediately known. He argued that what we know directly, if not immediately, are physical objects. Furthermore, all pragmatists take human experience to be transactional and interactive. The subject is not just passive but an agent reacting to and transforming the environment. This dynamic model of human (cognitive) experience implies a view of the real as continuous rather than discrete. Interaction supposes change, and change supposes continuity amid diversity. In a thoroughly atomized world, change would be impossible, as Zeno so dramatically showed.

Let us consider more particularly Peirce's theory of experience. As we shall see, that theory is intimately connected with his categorial scheme.[3] Peirce frequently characterizes experience as what is forced upon us. It has the quality of insistence, compulsion, constraint (1.321, 2.139, 4.172, 4.318, 5.539, 5.581). Peirce agrees with the empiricists in admitting that experience is the source of *all* our knowledge (5.611). It is our sole teacher (5.50–52, 1.358). Yet he also admits that some aspects of *cognitive* experience come "from the depths of the mind as seen from within" (2.444, 5.50). Hence, experience manifests the category of Secondness—the category of fact, actuality, brute force. Yet experience, he insists, is what is forced on us over "the course of life" (1.426, 2.138–139, 5.539) and not merely in this or that isolated incident. Thus, while the insistent, forceful, brutish aspect of actuality given in experience is always a this-here-and-now, it is never just that; it is, rather, always a this-here-and-now-of-a-certain-kind. What we experience is always continuous over space and time. In short, it has a certain stability and law-like quality about it. But this aspect of experience is what Peirce called Thirdness—the category of the real, the intelligible, the continuous, the law-like (2.148–149, 3.435, 7.39, 1.426).

Finally, the stability of the law-like supposes another stability, namely, that of quality or kind of thing an actual entity might be. Peirce calls this Firstness—the category of possibility—which is usually expressed by the predicate of an attributive judgment. For Peirce, we cannot experience either pure Firstness or pure Secondness. Our experience is always of Thirdness mediating the other two categories. We may, however, upon reflection separate out mentally, by prescission, each of the categories. Hence, they are distinguishable although not separable.

It follows that experience for Peirce is wider than mere sensuous presentation (1.335). It has conceptualization and judgment as constitutive elements. Hence, any sensuous perception is experienced, even though not all experience is sensuous perception. Peirce would admit that all experience is rooted in perceptual presentation to begin with, but that, properly speaking, experience consists in changes in these presentations and thus in actual encounter. We do not encounter, and so do not experience, forms of experience; we encounter, rather, objects themselves directly in their insistence, brutishness, and resistance (6.95) precisely as objects of a certain general kind following definite law-like regularities.

As I said above, not all commentators would agree with this account. Goudge, for example, argues that Peirce's thought is riven into naturalism, on the one hand, and transcendentalism, on the other. According to him, this explains Peirce's double account of experience. Goudge gathers under naturalism all those texts that speak of experience as the forced, compulsive, brutish, unreasonable element in our lives. All those that "idealize" experience, turning it into a functioning of mind or a mental construct, he assigns to Peirce's transcendentalism. Thus, Peirce is "naturalistic" when he insists that we experience directly things-in-themselves, not our ideas of things; he is "transcendentalist" when he insists that experience is a mental construct. In the naturalistic account, experience is the non-cognitive source of all cognition and the ultimate test of all knowledge claims; experience as our sole teacher is brutal and unreasonable. In the transcendentalist account, experience is cognitive; it is the cognitive whole made up of Peirce's three categories.

Surely, Peirce spoke of experience in these ways. The question is whether we must choose between them. I think the answer to that is no, and a more careful reading of Peirce will show this was his opinion as well. He was convinced that his 1868 rejection of "intuition" and of all immediate knowledge, together with his theory of categories (begun with the "New List" in 1867), shows how to interpret him in this matter. In the New List Peirce had already proposed that all thought is in signs, that those signs are triadic in structure, and that any thought is determined only by another thought. These ideas were further developed in the 1868 *Journal of Speculative Philosophy* articles. There the "Cartesian" assumption that knowing is an intellectual "taking a look" in an unmediated grasp of the thing itself was rejected as making any cognition impossible. (It makes cognition causal rather than representational and has thought determined by something other than thought—remember, for Peirce there is no first cognition, that is, a cognition not itself determined by another cognition.)

Furthermore, Peirce's account of how the categories are related to one another precludes the possibility of our ever experiencing them one in isolation from the other—the only supposition that gives the incoherence thesis plausibility. Without belaboring the point, Peirce distinguishes three grades of separability of ideas: (1) dissociation, (2) prescission, and (3) distinction. The categories can be separated only by prescissive abstraction. They cannot be imagined apart from one another; we can suppose one without the other only in a definite order: we can suppose Firstness (possibility) without Secondness (actuality) and Secondness without Thirdness (necessity) just as we can suppose space without color. In none of these cases, however, can we either experience or imagine them as separated. We can merely discern a logical priority and recognize them as distinct from one another. Hence, Peirce can speak of experience in different ways without contradicting himself. Experience is understood in terms of the categories. Experience as experienced, if I may put it that way, is for Peirce the synthesis of Firstness and Secondness and so is properly a Thirdness—hence, representational and cognitive. It involves the grasp of a this-such which has both the insistence and the compulsion of a this-here-now and the generality and intelligibility of a this-kind-of-thing. Secondness surely characterizes that aspect of lived experience which is opposition—which resists our wills—which presents the world whether we like it or not. But this is understood by abstractive analysis; it is neither encountered nor experienced in isolation from Firstness and Thirdness. Two accounts of experience emphasizing one or the other are neither inconsistent nor mutually exclusive.

One place where the elements of Peirce's understanding of experience come together in a striking way is in his "A Neglected Argument for the Reality of God" (6.452–493). There Peirce refers to the three universes of experience which correspond precisely to his three categories. Beyond any doubt, then, Peirce includes Thirdness in experience. But Thirdness, as generality, is beyond all particulars and hence beyond all sense content. Peirce can then hold that we have direct, if mediate, experience of God. God is not a spatio-temporal object but is real nonetheless—just as Thirdness is not Secondness but no less real.

The Recovery of Cognitive Experience

In what follows I will confine my remarks to cognitive experience. This does not mean that I think experience is only cognitive, but only that the empiricist challenge to religious language is insofar as that language claims to express cognitive experience of something beyond or more than the sensory content of consciousness. I do suppose that experience in the formal sense is conscious. This does not mean to deny that we are influenced by unconscious or subconscious factors.

First, it might be well to transpose Peirce's categorial analysis of experience into the more familiar terms of cognitive theory. I suggest we use the terms presentation, understanding, and judgment to replace Peirce's Secondness, Firstness, and Thirdness, respectively. Sensuous presentation is the Secondness of cognitive experience inasmuch as it involves actual encounter with a physical object. Understanding is its Firstness in that it proposes what kind of reality the physical object encountered might be. Finally, judgment is its Thirdness inasmuch as it links the "might-be" (the predicate) to the "is" (the logical subject) in virtue of sufficient evidence grasped as such. This declares that understanding has indeed "gotten it right"—that the proposition is true.

Cognitive experience has levels which are distinct yet interrelated cumulatively and incrementally. Thus, cognitive experience involves presentation, understanding, and judgment. The first is nearly what the empiricists mean by experiencing; the second is thinking about what is presented; the third is knowing that one's thinking is correct. Only when this last stage is reached is intelligence satisfied that it has grasped what truly is the case.[4]

Now, "narrow" empiricism assumes that knowing is "taking a look," that is, nothing but having sensory impression vividly and forcefully present to consciousness. It follows that the objectivity of knowing consists simply in that encounter with the sensory given. And, finally, the real is simply that which is grasped in such an encounter. It is these assumptions concerning knowledge, objectivity, and the real which must be examined more closely. What one holds on these cardinal issues determines what one can hold consistently on a host of other issues including the possibility of meaningful religious language.

It is not true that the fundamental assumptions of classical empiricism are its assumptions alone. Similar positions are taken by classical rationalism. The only difference between them is what each takes the given to be and hence what each considers "taking a look" to be. For rationalism, what is given as the basic element in cognitive experience is the idea (usually clearly and distinctly conceived), and taking a look consists in an intuition of the idea rather than a physical seeing. It is an inward or spiritual look, but a look nonetheless. The real, then, is what is thus intuited—an essence, a form.

In both classical empiricism and classical rationalism it was also frequently assumed that cognitive experience is a mental product (since it consists in looking at sense data or at abstract ideas as the case may be).[5] What is cognitively experienced is itself an idea, perception, or impression which is thought to be "in" consciousness. The problem that arose was, in what sense, if any, is cognitive experience objective. Such experience risks becoming subjective, not merely in that it involves a subject, but also in that the extramental status of what is known becomes problematic. The objective status of the content of cognitive experiences, then, requires some special characteristic that guarantees that the object represented in the idea, perception, or impression is both independent of the subject and veridically "copied" in the idea, perception, or impression. Thus, Descartes required that ideas be clearly and distinctly perceived. Locke required a distinction between primary and secondary sense qualities. Berkeley simply identified the being of sensible things with their being perceived. And Hume merely distinguished impressions from ideas in terms of liveliness and vividness without inquiring whether the original impressions were impressions *of* anything.

More recent empiricists have tried to circumvent this problem, not by questioning the assumption that generated it, but by claiming that the content of cognitive experience can be ascertained by an analysis of the language used to express it. This amounts to limiting objective cognitive experience to what so far has been successfully described in language.[6] This seems to me implausible enough (experience consists in linguistic expression) but it becomes even more arbitrary when linked to the restriction that only perceptual or observational language counts as meaningful.

Let us consider briefly each of these assumptions. It is at best doubtful that knowing is merely taking a look (with the eye or with the mind), even if taking a look is involved in knowing.[7] Granted: it is easy to think of knowing as taking a look (self-awareness as taking an inward look at ourselves) since knowing is knowing something. Knowing, surely, involves being aware of something confronting us and to which we are mysteriously "present" much in the way that we are present to what we see. Hence, it is understandable to suppose that knowing is essentially a gazing, an intuiting, a contemplation. Attractive as this account is because of its simplicity, it is its simplicity that renders it inadequate. Knowing indeed begins with some sort of sensuous presentation, but in that presentation the subject seeks to discover an immanent intelligibility or pattern which would answer the spontaneous question, "What is this presentation?" Moreover, a little reflection will confirm that not even an answer to that question satisfies the cognitive drive since the issue remains whether or not such an understanding of the presentation is correct. Not all possible ways of understanding sensuous presentations turn out to be tenable. Otherwise there would be no distinction between merely entertaining an hypothesis and affirming that an hypothesis is in fact the case. Intelligence is not satisfied that it has experienced what and how things are until it can assert that its understanding of what is given to it is correct. It pushes its inquiry until it can decide what conditions must obtain if its understanding is correct and whether or not those conditions are fulfilled. Then and only then is the drive to know satisfied, and then and only then can one be said to have had cognitive experience. This is precisely the dynamic intentionality of knowing toward being.

But if knowing is not merely taking a look, then objectivity cannot be simply a matter of extroversion.[8] It cannot be merely a matter of determining the already-out-there-now-real. If it were, human cognitive experience would not be any different from that of other animals. The kitten "knows" the difference between milk and a picture of milk in that the former satisfies its biological needs while the latter does not. But the kitten gives no evidence of understanding what milk is, what its nutritional value is and why, what the principles of perspective and color are which make the picture so lifelike. Humans do so understand (or try to), and their cognitive experience is considered incomplete until they can answer such questions correctly. There is no doubt that "givenness" (empirical objectivity) is involved in all true judgments (even those that concern self-awareness). Yet rather than this being the end-all and be-all of cognitive experience, it is only the occasion for questions concerning the nature and status of what is so given. If the human subject did not experience a drive to ask questions about the given, it would remain just present but not understood. Objectivity in human cognitive experience involves not just the presentation of data but also the attempt to understand it. But this supposes questions and questions suppose inquiry and inquiry supposes that the drive to know is allowed unrestricted play untrammeled by bias or prejudice which would cut it off from the truth. In a word, human cognitive experience requires normative objectivity. This is opposed to subjectivity where preconceived ideas, hopes, desires, or wishes become father to the thought. Finally, the objectivity intended in human cognitive experience is the grasp of what is actually the case independently of what anyone might think, wish, or desire. In a word, it intends to reach being, and in this sense objectivity implies the possession of absolute and unconditioned (albeit only virtually so) fact. It is in the grasp of this virtually unconditioned that the intentionality of knowing is fulfilled.[9] This absolute objectivity is proper to each and every true judgment precisely insofar as it is true. Finally, reality is not coincidental with the already-out-there-now-real. It is, rather, what is intended in knowing—the objective of the pure desire to know.[10] That intention is to understand the given intelligently and to affirm it rationally. That is what reality *is*.

In terms of this alternative theory of cognitive experience, it is evident that such experience cannot be satisfactorily characterized merely in terms of some specific content of consciousness. It must be understood as the product of an ongoing process of interaction between what there is and the subject encountering it, understanding it, and affirming it.[11] The subject reacts and interacts with what it thus affirms through deliberation and decision, shaping his behavior as rational. If experience is an interaction between a given and an intelligent subject, it cannot be supposed to be merely mental. Our experience is not merely of ideas or perceptions or impressions. It is of things presented, understood, and affirmed. The contribution of the subject is not such that it removes the demand of intelligence "to get it right." Yet "getting it right" is not merely passively reflecting the transmissions of our sensory apparatus. Human experience does not merely reflect nature. It refracts it, in the sense that it abstracts the intelligibility immanent in the given and, if certain conditions are fulfilled, affirms it to be real. Furthermore, if human experience is an interaction between subject and object, the subject transcends its own psychic states and so is open to the other—other things and other subjects from whom it learns and with whom it communicates. Hence, human experience cannot reasonably be confined to the individual. It is also social. Hence, the assumption that human cognitive experience is a "mental" record or that it is essentially dependent upon linguistic expression of a canonical sort has no claim upon one's assent as having been established as the truth of the matter.

The Recovery of Religious Experience

Once the notion of human cognitive experience has been expanded in terms of a theoretical explanation of knowing, objectivity, and being, it then follows that religious language can have meaning even though it goes beyond perceptual predicates. Hence, the question of whether there is religious experience and how it is to be understood is again open.

William James in *Varieties of Religious Experience* had a powerful influence in making the phrase "religious experience" popular.[12] His book also contributed to the rather common opinion that religious experience is identical to some kind of feeling which was variously identified as the sense of presence, of peace, of joy, of the holy, and so on. Not only is this understanding of religious experience unsatisfactory; it is also a challenge to religion as threatening as the challenge of narrow empiricism. It is unsatisfactory because it does not succeed in specifying what the religious element in experience is; it is threatening to religion because it supports the claim that God is nothing but the name we give to a certain kind of human experience. God is a projection and reification of feelings of a certain kind.

The model for this understanding of religious experience might be characterized as the adjectival model. It takes the term "religious" to be an adjective signifying a specific difference within the genus "experience." If one uses this model, it makes sense to search amid human experiences for some special set that are religious. Religious experience would be a species of human experience and thus differ from other species *in kind.* Not only does such an interpretation easily lead to the assumption that God is but the name given to a certain kind of experience (perhaps a feeling), as I have said, but it also fosters the idea that to be religious one must have some kinds of experiences (feelings). Since they are *essential* to being religious, they must be actively sought out if one is to be religious. The consequences of such a conclusion have sometimes been disastrous to the individuals and communities involved. I have in mind various cultic practices designed to induce whatever feelings or experiences the particular group takes to be specifically religious. I have in mind various groups of "illuminati" or "enthusiasts" down through history who considered themselves beyond ordinary moral law and whose behavior became destructive of themselves and others.

It might be argued in defense of this adjectival theory that it is the natural interpretation of the phrase's grammatical form; that it does not necessarily make God a projection of human feeling but only that such feelings are a sign of God's presence; that it does not necessarily entail dangerous emotional arousal. Perhaps there is a way in which these errors and dangers can be avoided without abandoning the notion of religious experience as a species of a genus. But I think that the avoidance of these undesirable consequences would require explanation so radical as to have implicitly changed the adjectival model altogether. Surely, to argue from the grammatical form of the phrase is inconclusive because, frequently, popular yet grammatical phrases are inaccurate or they are elliptical expressions of something more complex. To say that certain kinds of experiences are signs of God's presence is on the face of it satisfactory, but it could not mean that only *certain* kinds of experiences are such signs, for that would arbitrarily restrict the ways in which God could make Himself known. Furthermore, it would have to be shown what it is about the particular experience that makes it the uniquely possible and infallible indication of God's presence. Would this mean that God is present only in those experiences and not in others? This would be rejected as simply false by Christianity at any rate. Would not the recognition that a certain kind of experience is a sign of God's presence require that the experience be interpreted and understood and thus entail something more than simply some quality of the experience itself? Finally, it is difficult to imagine that one would think oneself religious (perhaps "saved") without ever having had the appropriate experience, and so anyone who wanted to be saved would at least welcome and foster such experience.

Is there, then, some other model in terms of which one could interpret "religious experience"? I suggest that there is. I would call it the adverbial model. On this understanding, the phrase "religious experience" is an ellipsis for "experiencing the world religiously." What makes experience religious is not some special content but rather the realization that it has another aspect or dimension, as a sign or representation, directly but mediately disclosing or revealing God.[13] In a word, it is a question of understanding the significance of what humans experience, that is, of experience as interpreted. This is not a special feeling, although as a consequence of realizing the religious dimension any of a number of emotions may follow or become intensified. In principle, any and all human experiences may disclose this other dimension, that is, they may be the occasion for one's finding God, or, better, for God's disclosing Himself. Religious experience, on this view, is not some species of experience but an understanding of the significance of experience as God-bearing. The deeply religious or holy have this understanding habitually so that they can recall it explicitly at will. In these terms it is easier to make sense of the spiritual advice to find God in all things and of praying always. Formal acts of worship, public or private, have the role of making explicit this habitual orientation toward God. When one is religious in this sense, all one's experience is transformed so as to have new significance. It is like the difference between binocular and monocular vision. In both cases the same items or content is seen. But for the one, these objects have depth; for the other, they are flat.

Finally, such an understanding of religious experience permits one to maintain that although our knowledge of God is mediated, it is nonetheless a real experience and an experience of something real and objective. We can (and I hold that we do) have genuine cognitive experience of God (Peirce's position) mediated through the structure of experience as presentation, understanding, and judgment. This is beyond what is delivered by the senses alone and beyond what is understood by concepts alone. A cognitive experience of God is not the result of inference alone. There must be a moment of "disclosure" in which "transcendence" of mere sense is a constituent part of human knowing, and in which the "transcendent" is recognized as a possibility (that is, is recognized as implicitly affirmed in every cognitive act). The so-called arguments for the existence of God play an important role in the maturing of religious experience by rendering the implicit explicit—"God" as mere possibility (hypothesis) is grasped and affirmed as actual and necessary. It seems to me that, among other things, these arguments play the role of removing obstacles that prevent us from grasping what is directly, if mediately, in all our experiences—the presence of God.

So far I have said very little directly concerning how Peirce's recovery of experience might help resolve the tension between the demand for direct experience and that of argument in religious conviction. A brief look at Peirce's "Neglected Argument for the Reality of God" may help to see how it does.[14] The argument has three stages. The first consists in a free play of thought which Peirce called "musement." He once likened it to "building castles in Spain"—a free romp of the imagination without any particular pre-conceived purpose. Peirce suggests that such playful meditation be brought to bear on the universes of our experience—the possible, the actual, and the necessary—and their interconnections. Musement is direct experiencing, as Peirce says, of "what is about or within you" (6.461). When this free mediation is directed at the universes and their relations, the hypothesis of God is suggested. The second stage is a reflection on the first which yields the Humble Argument, namely, that the tendency of human nature to believe in God is rooted in *wonder* at the universes, their relations, and their origin. What this second stage adds to the direct experience of the first is a grasp of how the hypothesis of God arises from such musement—from wonder—and, of course, a realization that the human mind has the capacity to form such an hypothesis. The third stage recounts the three stages of scientific inquiry, reproduction, deduction, and induction, and authenticates the Humble Argument by showing that the forming of the God-hypothesis has its counterpart in scientific inquiry. This, in Peirce's mind, gives no deductive proof of God's reality but does give reasonable support for the God-hypothesis. That hypothesis must be put to the further test of having influence upon our conduct.

Notes

1. In *Religious Studies*, 17 (1981), 487–97.
2. See, for example, John E. Smith, "The Reconception of Experience in Peirce, James and Dewey," *The Monist*, 68 (1985), 538–54.
3. See, for example, my *Charles S. Peirce: On Norms and Ideals* (Amherst: University of Massachusetts Press, 1967), passim, esp. pp. 8–24 for a brief treatment of the categories.
4. This terminology is developed by Bernard J. Lonergan in *Insight: A Study of Human Understanding* (New York: Philosophical Library, 1958), esp. in chaps. 1–10.
5. See John E. Smith, "The Reconception of Experience," in *Experience and God* (New York: Oxford University Press, 1968; rev. ed. New York: Fordham University Press, 1995), pp. 21–45.
6. See ibid., p. 23.

7. See Lonergan, *Insight*, pp. 320ff.
8. See ibid., pp. 375–84.
9. See ibid., chaps. 9 and 10.
10. See ibid., chap. 13.
11. See Smith, *Experience and God*, pp. 21–45.
12. (New York: Longmans, Green, 1912).

13. See Smith, *Experience and God*, pp. 46–67, for a fine treatment of the religious dimension of experience. To my knowledge this way of putting it is Professor Smith's.

14. For a full discussion of this argument, see chap. 12 of the present collection of essays.

11

"Vaguely Like a Man": The Theism of Charles S. Peirce

PEIRCE'S THEISM is not calculated to please many philosophers—at least not at first sight. His theism, he says, is "sound pragmatism," and this is not likely to attract positivists who have adopted its maxim as an expression of their own views concerning verification. His theism, he says, is a consequence of anthropomorphism—a claim not likely to enthuse either traditional theists or hardheaded scientists. Finally, his theism is intrinsically infected with vagueness, a disease which surely will be diagnosed as fatal by many analysts and logicians. I have failed to remark perhaps the most disturbing claim of all: Peirce's theism is supported by a form of the ontological argument! This will perhaps please no one at all.

Yet there it is in all its outrageous boldness: a theism supported by an "exact logician" trained in natural science; a theism that is the consequence of pragmatism; a theism vague and anthropomorphic, and, *therefore*, indubitable in the strictest sense. These are hard words, and who among philosophers will hear them? The point of this essay is to help the philosopher, if he is still willing to read on, to understand the precise import of these shocking claims and perhaps suggest at least that they are not so shocking—that, in the end, they are not so bad even if unusual and/or distasteful.

In a letter to William James (July 23, 1905), Peirce remarked that his own belief in theism was "good sound solid strong pragmatism" (8.262). Three years later he published his well-known "Neglected Argument for the Reality of God" (6.452–493) in the *Hibbert Jour-*

An earlier version of this chapter appeared in *God Knowable and Unknowable*, ed. Robert J. Roth, s.j. (New York: Fordham University Press, 1973), pp. 241–54.

nal where he gave a "poor sketch" of that argument and a mere "table of contents" of what would be required to show its validity. This poor sketch is in reality a rapid and terse outline of that philosophical view called "pragmaticism" which he had elaborated over the preceding half-century. The "table of contents" is nothing but a marshaling of the conclusions he had reached concerning the nature of reasoning worked out with so much labor over that same period.

In a short essay I cannot hope to do justice to Peirce's thought on this matter. I will simply try here to expound some of his reflections which may serve as a propaedeutic to his well-known article in the hope that it will aid the reader, first, to understand the unusual kind of argument it is, and, second, to help focus properly critical evaluation. I will not attempt an analysis of the argument itself; that alone would require an essay or two. I restrict myself, then, to preliminaries: what Peirce had to say about God-talk in general and why in general he held what he did. While this essay does not seek critical evaluation *in recto*, it does so *in obliquo*, since it pretends not only to expound but also to explain and interpret. That explanation and interpretation intend to be a presentation of the truth of the matter as this writer sees it, while at the same time remaining faithful to Peirce. The presentation will consist of three parts: (1) traditional theism, (2) anthropomorphic theism, (3) vagueness.

Traditional Theism

In a letter to William James (June 12, 1902), Peirce says that he has been reading Royce's *The World and the Individual* and finds it not in very good taste "to stuff it so full of the name of God" (8.277). The reason is that "the Absolute is strictly speaking only God, in a Pickwickian sense, that is, in a sense that has no effect" (8.277). The point of this remark seems to be that, although it may be true that God is absolute, such a characterization is altogether too abstract and formal to make of God an object of belief. An object of belief in the strict sense according to Peirce must be such that it is capable of influencing human conduct. Peirce seems to think that Royce's absolute if not allowed other attributes would be precisely incapable of such influence because it is too abstract and empty. It is God in a Pickwickian sense, in a sense that has no effect, and so literally is incapable of belief. The reality (or unreality) of God as merely "the Absolute" would make no difference to human conduct. Whatever attributes over and above "absoluteness" we decide "God" must have, they must be such as to show God to be intimately related to and "concerned with" what men do. To be an object of belief, the reality of God must make a difference to human conduct. The meaning of "God," then, must be rooted in human experience and at the same time must indicate in some way that that reality is not confined to space and time. Let us consider how Peirce describes the absolute reality called "God."

In the opening lines of his article on the Neglected Argument, Peirce defines the term "God" as *the* definable proper name signifying *Ens necessarium* (6.452). This reality is not only necessary but also one, personal, not immanent in creation but creating the universe (5.496, 6.505–506), omniscient (6.508), omnipotent (6.509), infallible (6.510), not subject to time (4.67), and not finite (8.262). These attributes are recognizable as the traditional ones of theistic natural theology. But what is different in Peirce's description is that he will not allow that God exists, in the strict sense of that term, but rather that he is real (cf. 8.262). The reason is that existence strictly belongs to the category of Secondness, of brute force or interaction. Whatever belongs to Secondness must be capable of action and reaction and must, therefore, be spatiotemporal. Consequently, such a reality would be limited and finite. But this will not do for God, since he is the Creator of the three universes of which the actual—the realm of existents—is but one. God, then, must be said to be real (as opposed to unreal, fictitious, non-being) but not to exist.

The term of Peirce's argument, therefore, is a non-finite, necessary reality that can best be described in traditional theistic terms, because such a description makes of that reality more than an abstract and empty Absolute. It makes of that reality something that would make a difference to human conduct if acknowledged as real. It is a conception that would arise from meditation upon human experience and which in turn would affect that experience insofar as it is subject to self-control. It was such considerations as these which led Pierce to try to write down a description of his argument:

> If God really be, and be benign, then, in view of the generally conceded truth that religion, were it but proved, would be a good outweighing all others, we should naturally expect that there would be some Argument for His Reality that should be obvious to all minds, high and low alike, that should earnestly strive to find the truth of the matter; and that this Argument should present its conclusion, not as a proposition of metaphysical theology, but in a form directly applicable to the conduct of life, and full of nutrition for men's highest growth. (6.457)

In a word, Peirce believed that there is no more adequate way for us to conceive of the adequate cause of the universe than as vaguely like a man (5.536). The theistic notion of God, then, is both anthropomorphic and vague. According to Peirce, it is precisely because that notion is anthropomorphic that it is believable and because it is vague that it is a notion of God.

Anthropomorphic Theism

Peirce's claim that theism must be anthropomorphic to be believable is, to say the least, unusual. One might have expected that a theist would try to avoid the charge of anthropomorphism as an objection to any theory of God. The medieval theologians were at pains to avoid precisely this sort of objection by developing at length a negative theology and a doctrine of analogous predication. Whether these attempts by some of the leading proponents of theism were successful or not is not the point here; what is important is the lengths to which defenders of theism have gone in order to avoid this sort of criticism. And yet not only does Peirce not reject the allegation, he seems to revel in it.

What, then, does he understand by anthropomorphism? Peirce contrasts his use of this term with Schiller's "humanism." While humanism is allied with anthropomorphism and is in perfect harmony with pragmatism, it does not deal precisely with the same question, because Schiller, in Peirce's view, identifies it with the "old humanism" which was not so much a scientific opinion as an aim. Pragmatism as a scientific opinion is best expressed by the term "anthropomorphism." The scientific opinion to which Peirce refers is, of course, the correct analysis of scientific method at which all his logical researches were directed. It is this analysis which implies theism:

> if by metaphysics we mean the broadest positive truths of the psycho-physical universe . . . then the very fact that these problems can be solved by a logical maxim is proof enough that they do not belong to metaphysics but to "epistemology," an atrocious translation of *Erkenntnislehre*. (5.496)

Among other things, *Erkenntnislehre* shows that man has powerful and accurate instincts besides reasoning. In fact, reasoning is nothing but a development of instinct and so is continuous with it. Instinct is more basic than reasoning, and no adequate account of reasoning and scientific research can be given without recognizing its role. This, of course, is not to say that reasoning is identical with instinct. It is not. But a correct analysis of scientific reasoning will show, according to Peirce, its roots in human instinct. Thus Peirce can say:

> For those metaphysical questions which have such interest [human interest], the question of a future life and especially that of One Incomprehensible but Personal God, not immanent in but creating the universe, I, for one, heartily admit that a Humanism, *that does not pretend to be a science but only an instinct*, like a bird's power of flight, but purified by meditation, *is the most precious contribution that has been made to philosophy for ages*. (5.496; emphasis added)

Peirce argues that almost all human conceptions are at bottom anthropomorphic. This is true even of scientific hypotheses, and to say that an hypothesis is unscientific simply because it is anthropomorphic is an objection "of a very shallow kind, that arises from prejudices based upon much too narrow considerations" (5.47). According to Peirce, this is the objection for the nominalist. In opposition to these "much too narrow considerations," Peirce maintains that all man's knowledge, including all scientific and philosophical theories and hypotheses which can have any meaning, is based upon experience.

> I hold . . . that man is so completely hemmed in by the bounds of his possible practical experience, his mind is so restricted to being the instruments of his needs, that he cannot, in the least, *mean* anything which transcends those limits. (5.536)

All man's conceptions, then, are anthropomorphic, in the sense that they depend upon the limits of his possible experience. But to say this is like passing a law forbidding man to jump over the moon; such a law would not prevent him from jumping as high as he could. Man will continue to try to conceive of a supreme and indeed transcendent cause or agency of the entire universe, but there will be no more adequate way of conceiving than "as vaguely like a man." Furthermore, Peirce repeatedly recalls that the only satisfactory explanation of man's ability to form any hypothesis applicable to the universe is his affinity to the universe.

> And in regard to any preference for one kind of theory over another, it is well to remember that every single truth of science is due to the affinity of the human soul to the soul of the universe, imperfect as that affinity no doubt is. To say, therefore, that a conception is one natural to man, which comes just about to the same thing as to say that it is anthropomorphic, is as high a recommendation as one could give to it in the eyes of an Exact Logician. (5.47)

Peirce's anthropomorphism, therefore, is nothing other than his metaphysical realism.

> They [the great realists] showed that the general is not capable of full actualization in the world of action and reaction but is of the nature of what is thought, but that our thinking only apprehends and does not create thought, and that that thought may and does as much govern outward things as it does our thinking. (1.27)

The basic mistake of nominalism is that it violates the fundamental rule of exact logic: do not block the road to inquiry. By denying that anything is real except the actual, it at once renders all knowledge of the world inexplicable and posits an unknowable "thing-in-itself." It renders knowledge of the world inexplicable because all knowledge of the world involves generals. If generals are not real but only figments of the mind, then knowledge is not of the world. Rather, it posits a mere "out-there-here-and-now," about which nothing can be said, conceived, or judged. It would be positing the utterly unintelligible and inexplicable as the ultimate explanation, thus cutting off all further questions and inquiry. For Peirce such a position turns out to be in the strictest sense meaningless in view of the pragmatic maxim.

> The elements of every concept enter into logical thought at the gate of perception and make their exit at the gate of purposive action and whatever cannot show its passports at both of those gates is to be arrested as unauthorized by reason. (5.212)

Peirce's "anthropomorphism," it must be concluded, is but another name for his realistic pragmatism (pragmaticism).

Vagueness

Theism, it has been remarked, is only implied by anthropomorphism. The middle term, as it were, for this inference is to be found in Peirce's critical common-sensism, itself a consequence of pragmaticism (5.439). It is so, in my view, because it takes seriously the role of "instinctive mind" by which man has an affinity to nature (5.47) and to God (8.262; see 6.516).

> Our logically controlled thoughts compose a small part of the mind, the mere blossom of a vast complexus, which we may call instinctive mind, in which this man will not say he has *faith*, because that implies the conceivability of distrust, but upon which he builds as the very fact to which it is the whole business of his logic to be true. (5.212)

This "instinctive mind" through which every concept enters into logical thought Peirce elsewhere calls "Insight . . . into Thirdnesses, the general elements, of Nature." Again he refers to it as a "faculty" that man must have, because otherwise there would be no accounting for his undeniable ability to guess right among the millions of possible hypotheses often enough to allow him to make genuine discoveries (5.171ff.). This is man's *il lume naturale*, the natural disposition with which man comes into the world (see 1.80, 2.750, 5.47, 5.603–604, 6.10, 5.504). Ultimately, then, instinctive mind must consist of "*in posse* innate cognitive habits, which is all that anybody but John Locke ever meant by innate ideas" (5.504).

Instinctive mind, then, is "pre-scientific"; it is the ground of reasoning both as an activity and as a developed habit; it is the affinity of the mind to reality which makes any scientific inquiry possible. Insofar as science strives for greater and greater precision in its terms and concepts, instinctive mind will escape scientific analysis. It will always remain vague and indeterminate because it is the innate source and origin of reasoning itself whose function to a large extent is to analyze and make precise what it apprehends. No attempt to inquire scientifically into instinctive mind (no matter how useful and informative such investigation may prove to be) can be adequate to the reality so investigated. Something will always be "left over" which is vague and indeterminate. This is true not only of instinctive mind but also of any reality investigated by science. The real is continuous and so intrinsically affected by vagueness and generality, both forms of indeterminateness. This is why the real is intelligible, why it must be said to be "mind-like," and why, finally, there is any affinity between human minds and the universe.

The point that I am trying to make is that for Peirce it is a serious mistake not to take vagueness seriously. It would be an even greater mistake to think that whatever remains vague after investigation can be disregarded as unreal. And perhaps the greatest mistake of all would be to think that in principle all vagueness can be eliminated even from science in the strictest sense. These errors in understanding human knowing are found in varying forms and degrees in the several nominalistic interpretations of inquiry. Peirce's pragmaticism was meant to avoid them. Critical common-sensism and "scholastic" realism, both consequences of pragmaticism, argue for vagueness and generality as essential ontological as well as logical categories.

In an attempt to show that there is nothing contradictory in holding a common-sensism that is at the same time critical, Peirce lists six characteristics that distinguish his position from the Scotch school. The fourth and most important of these he states as follows:

> By all odds, the most distinctive character of the Critical-Common-sensist, in contrast to the old Scotch philosopher [Reid], lies in his insistence that the acritically indubitable is invariably vague.
>
> Logicians have been at fault in giving Vagueness the go-by, so far as even to analyze it. (5.446; see 5.505)

The recognition of vagueness as an important logical category is essential to Peirce's discussion of theism. Our ideas of the infinite are extremely vague, he writes to James, and become contradictory the moment we attempt to make them precise (8.262). It is true to say of God that He is omniscient and omnipotent providing that we leave these concepts vague (6.508–509). And yet these predicates "are not utterly unmeaning" for, as a matter of fact, they can be interpreted "in our religious adoration and the consequent effects upon conduct" (8.262). The vagueness of our notions of God, therefore, ought not for that reason rule them out from rational belief. Indeed, this vagueness acts as a corrective to anthropomorphism by negating the limitation of human experience and classification in the infinite reality. In a word, it is vagueness that allows our notions to be about God.

Vagueness is a form of indeterminateness. Generality is another. A subject is said to be determinate with respect to a character when that character is predicated of it universally and affirmatively. Such a subject, of course, would also be determinate with respect to the negative of such a character. In all other respects the subject is *indeterminate*. A sign is objectively *general* if it leaves it to the *interpreter* to supply further determinations. Thus, in the sentence "Man is mortal" the term "man" is objectively general because the answer to the question "Which man?" is "Any one you choose." A sign is objectively *vague* if it reserves *for some other possible sign* (and not for the interpreter) the function of completing the determination. Thus, in the sentence "This month a great event will happen," the term "great event" is objectively vague because the answer to the question "Which event?" is not "Any one you like" but rather "Let us wait and see" (5.447, 5.505). Now, every utterance leaves the right of further exposition to the utterer, and so every utterance is to that extent vague. Its vagueness is removed to the extent that the signs it uses are rendered general. According to Peirce, it is usually the case that an affirmative predication covers generally every essential character of the predicate, while a negative predication vaguely denies some essential character (5.447). It turns out, therefore, that in every communication situation *absolute* determinateness and precision are not and cannot be attained:

honest people, when not joking, intend to make the meaning of their words determinate, so that there shall be no latitude of interpretation at all. That is to say, the character of their meaning consists in the implications and the non-implications of their words; and they intend to fix what is implied and what is not implied. They believe that they succeed in doing so, and if their chat is about the theory of numbers, perhaps they may. But the further their topics are from such precise, or "abstract," subjects, the less possibility is there of such precision of speech. (5.447; see also 2.357)

Another way of distinguishing vagueness and generality as two forms of indeterminateness is as follows: "anything is general insofar as the principle of excluded middle does not apply to it and is vague insofar as the principle of contradiction does not apply to it" (5.448; cf. 5.505). Thus, Peirce observes, a triangle in general is not isosceles, not equilateral, not scalene. It is false neither that an animal (in a vague sense) is male nor that an animal is female (5.505). While no sign can be both vague and general in the same respect, still every sign is to some extent indeterminate and to that degree is both vague and general. The only way in which it could escape being either vague or general would be for it to be completely and absolutely determinate. According to Peirce, this is simply not possible. While every proposition actually asserted must refer to some non-general subject, still no communication between persons can be entirely non-vague. The reason for this, without going into detail, is that there is no such thing as a logical atom in the strict sense, that is, a term incapable of logical division (see 3.93). It follows, then, that none of our conceptions, even the most intellectual and scientific, are absolutely precise, that is, without some vagueness.

Peirce holds that our acritically indubitable beliefs are invariably vague. To submit such beliefs to criticism involves an attempt to render them more precise. To the extent that they are rendered more precise, Peirce admits that they are open to doubt. His point is this: "Yet there are beliefs of which such a critical sifting invariably leaves a certain vague residue unaffected" (5.507). The question, then, is simply whether that vague residue itself would disappear under persevering attempts at precision.

> But the answer . . . is that it is not because insufficient pains have been taken to precise the residuum, that it is vague: it is that it is vague intrinsically. (5.508)

The example of such an indubitable belief offered by Peirce is that of order in nature. A host of critics have submitted to criticism every precise statement of that order which has been proposed. Each of these precise statements is open to doubt. "As precisely defined it can hardly be said to be absolutely indubitable considering how many thinkers there are who do not believe it" (5.508). All this shows, however, is that any precise statement of nature's order is open to doubt. In fact, it is the very precision that allows room for doubt and therefore for criticism. And yet for all that, "who can think that there is *no* order in nature" (5.508)? For Peirce, such a claim is literally unthinkable. Pure chaos cannot be thought; the notion of chaos itself is parasitical upon the notion of order; it is *relative* disorder, that is relative to an order we expected to find or hoped to find. Any number of doubts can be cast upon this or that or the other characterization of nature's order, but there always remains a vague residue to that original belief which cannot be done away with. This residue is indubitable and indeed acritical, but it is not indubitable precisely because it is acritical in the sense of simply not having been criticized. Rather, it remains indubitable because it cannot be criticized since it remains essentially vague.

Peirce is convinced that there is a relatively fixed list of such original beliefs which is the same for all men. He tells us that he was not always so convinced but that experience and reflection led him to this view. He admits to always having been strongly attracted by a form of common-sensism which holds that there is "no definite and fixed collection of opinions that are indubitable, but that criticism gradually pushed back each individual's indubitables, modifying the list, yet still leaving him beliefs indubitable at the time being" (5.509). A better understanding of vagueness, however, changed his mind. From very early on (at least from the paper "Some Consequences of Four Incapacities" in 1868), Peirce held that there is no first, indubitable proposition that occupies a privileged epistemic position. This basic criticism of what he took to be the "spirit of Cartesianism" is compatible with the position outlined in the preceding paragraph. Every proposition is indeed open to criticism, revision, and doubt to the extent that it is precise, that is, non-vague. On the other hand, every proposition remains to some extent and in some respect vague; otherwise it simply would not function as a symbol (see 2.357). Every proposition, therefore, is to be interpreted in terms of another proposition and thus *ad infinitum*.

To the extent that the vagueness of a proposition is intrinsic to it, that proposition remains an element of the indubitable. Hence, every proposition is open to revision both in the sense that it can always give way to a more adequate expression and in the sense that an erroneous proposition (that is, a false proposition) can give way to a true one. Indubitables in the sense of primitive, original beliefs are indubitable because they remain intrinsically vague not only with respect to the individual logical subjects to which they refer but also with respect to the character or characters predicated of them. No amount of analysis will render those predicates absolutely precise and determinate since they will always carry the rider "vaguely like." This rider, of course, warns the hearer or reader that some unspecified character of that predicate does not apply to the subject, and so that the subject is also vaguely *unlike* the character applied to it. Some predicates, for example, infinite, omnipotent, etc., carry this warning in themselves since they contain in their own comprehension the negation of some general predicate (non-vague in that respect).

Perhaps all this is not well put and an example might be worth a thousand vague and general explanations. Let us consider Peirce's own example: there is order in nature. The logical subject of this indubitable is a non-vague, non-general reality vaguely and generally characterized in the first place by the predicate "nature" and further specified by the vague and general predicate "order." What is intended in this proposition is not at all indefinite, and consequently the subject term partakes of the nature of an index in that it functions so as to force attention on its object. Still, the logical subject of a symbol is not strictly an index because it indicates its object only as a result of being intended to do so (a true index is a sign independently of anyone's intending it to be). Since only a true index can be absolutely determinate and since the subject of a proposition is only *like* an index, the logical subject of our proposition is not absolutely non-vague. This sort of vagueness attaches to the logical subject of any proposition whatsoever.

This is what Peirce means by saying that there is no logical atom. Both predicates in our example are also vague and intrinsically so. "Nature" is vague because it is understood to be the denial of "artifact" and, further, is a collective term for all such non-artifacts. More precision can be accomplished only by further indicating what "nature" is not or by pointing to objects that go to make up "nature" without being nature—natural objects. The positive content of that term remains imprecise although not empty on that account. "Order" is vague because it is a relational term and can be made precise only with respect to some standards of comparison antecedently specified. What this comes to is that this or that particular order might be rendered non-vaguely indicated, but not order as such. Similarly, non-order is a relative term. It indicates the absence of some anticipated kind of order. But absolute non-order is literally unthinkable and cannot be even vaguely indicated. Since non-order is not real in any absolute sense at all, it has no positive content at all. It is pure negativity—the limit notion of "no thought at all." The proposition under consideration, then, is at least doubly vague, with respect to its subject and with respect to its predicates.[1] Its predicates are vague not because of any lack of diligence on the part of analysts but because of their very nature. Order is unity amid multiplicity—one and many—and, of course, this is *the* paradox!

Belief in the God of theism is for Peirce an original belief. It is one of the indubitables in that relatively fixed list that is the same for all men. Doubts about God's reality or about the attributes that most aptly describe Him arise from attempts at precision. Every formula about God which claims to be non-vague is to that extent open to real doubt. The ultimate ground for such doubt is the fact that insofar as such formulas succeed in being precise they are false. An infinite being is not the sort of thing that can be precisely classified. If it were, then it would fall under a genus and so would entail the possibility of many Gods (8.262). Doubts about God's reality, therefore, are in fact doubts about various formulas meant to express that reality in relatively non-vague terms. Such doubts, however, are not about God's *reality*; indeed for Peirce such a doubt is impossible because belief in it is instinctive; it is an acritical indubitable in the sense already discussed. Doubt about it, according to Peirce, vanishes once it is recognized that all appropriate formulations of that reality are intrinsically vague. Thus Peirce claims that any argument for God's reality is really a form of the ontological argument.

Note

1. Peirce remarks that "indefiniteness and generality might primarily affect either the logical breadth or the logical depth of the sign to which it belongs" (5.448, note). In the case of a proposition, logical breadth is the subject denoted and logical depth is the predicate asserted (5.471; see 2.394ff.).

12

C. S. Peirce's Argument for God's Reality: A Pragmatist's View

CHARLES SANDERS PEIRCE, one of America's greatest logicians and perhaps her most original philosopher, founder of the movement called pragmatism, was also a theist. According to his own account he is a theist because he is a pragmatist. Thus, he could write to William James that theism is nothing but "good sound solid strong pragmatism" (8.262).

Nevertheless, religion for Peirce is a topic of "vital importance" and so is a matter more of the heart than of the head. He writes that all sensible talk about religion, morals, and aesthetics "must be common-place, all reasoning about them unsound, and all study of them narrow and sordid" (1.677). When it is a question of great decisions affecting our lives, it is the wise man who knows that sentiment and instinct are sure guides, while reasoning about such matters is out of place since that faculty is a notoriously fallible instrument (1.650–653).

Again, Pierce never seems to tire of telling us that when it is a question of belief, theoretical argumentation has little or no place. Conversely, when it is a question of theoretical or scientific inquiry, there is little or no room for belief. How is it, then, that Peirce presents us with an argument for God's reality? He calls it sometimes the Humble Argument, sometimes the Neglected Argument, and humble though it might be and neglected though it surely has been, it is nonetheless an argument.[1] The answer to this question

---

An earlier version of this chapter appeared in *The Pappin Festschrft*. II. *Wisdom and Knowledge: Essays in Honour of Joseph Papin*, ed. Joseph Armenti (Villanova: Villanova University Press, 1976), 224–44.

can only come from a study of the kind of argument it is, and this, of course, is the aim of this essay.

This much can be said now. Peirce's point in those remarks about the relation of a belief to scientific inquiry is that the conviction required to make a theoretical proposition (or at least a proposition capable of theoretical investigation) into an operative principle influencing our conduct is rooted in instinct rather than in scientific inquiry itself. Scientific inquiry, as a form of human conduct, is ultimately rooted in instinct too. Of course, it is possible, even necessary, for a reasonable man to submit beliefs to critical evaluation once he has begun to doubt those beliefs. But this does not take away from the fact that the scientific inquiry which evaluates doubted beliefs itself depends upon other beliefs which are in fact undoubted.

According to Peirce, some beliefs remain undoubted because of the instinctive basis of reason itself. Scientific inquiry itself is a function of a natural disposition or instinct in man—his rationality. In effect, Pierce tries to give a theoretical argument based on the nature of scientific inquiry why instinct is to be trusted as a guide to human conduct and why in the end this trust is reasonable. Truly instinctive beliefs are essentially vague, and insofar as they are vague, they are strictly indubitable. Any attempt to render such beliefs non-vague will fail, in that a residue of the old vague belief not touched by the non-vague formulation will remain. To the extent that some particular formulation of an instinctive belief is definite (non-vague), that formulation is open to doubt and demands critical review. Thus, in Peirce's view, belief in God is instinctive. The formulation of that hypothesis comes naturally and spontaneously to anyone who seriously engages in the activity he calls "musement." Furthermore, critical reflection upon the hypothesis, Pierce contends, shows that although any non-vague formulation of that hypothesis may be doubted as true and accurate, still some residue of the belief remains and some formulations can be shown to be less false than their opposites. In the end the God-hypothesis is supposed by a correct analysis of scientific inquiry. Insofar as the hypothesis remains vague, it is indubitable, and insofar as it is made definite, it is truer (less false) than its opposite.

Of course, we are well ahead of ourselves already. What has been sketched in the preceding paragraph is what we must consider in some detail in the rest of this essay. From the list of items involved in Pierce's thought in the matter it is not surprising that in the *Hibbert Journal* article where he presented his "argument," Peirce could give only a "poor sketch" and a "sort of table of contents" of a complete inquiry into God's reality. I can do little more than follow his example. I will try to pass in review the elements of his outline and comment upon them in the light of his other work and in terms of certain problems that they raise. It is hoped that by throwing some light upon the "Cimmerian darkness" which James found surrounding Pierce's "flashes of brilliance,"[2] this will tempt the reader no longer to "neglect" Peirce's "humble" argument. Perhaps, however, this effort will succeed only in confirming the reader in the opinion that such an argument has only received its just deserts in being neglected. Either way it is hoped that it will be of some use.

Definitions

Peirce begins with a glossary of terms (6.452–456). A defense of his usage would require a presentation of his entire categorial scheme and theory of knowledge (according to Peirce a bad translation of *Erkenntnislehre*). Let us examine these terms which he thinks necessary to an understanding of his argument.

(1) "God": *the* definable proper name of *Ens necessarium*, Creator of the three Universes of Experience. In another place (6.494), in answer to the question "Do you believe in the existence of a Supreme Being?" Pierce explains that he prefers the term "God" and that the latter term is the common English word. As the common word it is in one sense understood by everyone and in another sense remains extremely vague. Its vagueness is not reduced by saying that "God" imports "infinity" or "necessity" or any other traditional attribute, because these are equally vague. Now, it is the very vagueness of the term "God" which recommends it as the more appropriate term. We shall see why presently.

(2) "Real": to be real is to have properties sufficient to identify their subject whether or not anyone actually attributes them to it. "Real" is not a synonym for "actual" or "existent." It is a broader term which includes these. Whatever is actual or existent is real,

but not the converse. The "actual or existent is what is encountered in space and time. It interacts with the spatio-temporal environment" (6.454, 6.495). Strictly speaking, therefore, God cannot be said to be actual or to exist, because this would make God simply another spatio-temporal object. God can properly be said only to be real.

In answer to the question cited in paragraph (1) above, Peirce also makes these remarks:

> I will also take the liberty of substituting "reality" for "existence." This is perhaps overscrupulosity; but I myself always use *exist* in its strictest philosophical sense of "react with the other like things in the environment." Of course, in that sense, it would be fetishism to say that God "exists." (6.495)

Perhaps the reader already familiar with Peirce's thought recognizes the peculiar brand of "scholastic realism" which prompts this distinction.

(3) "Experience": a conscious effect produced upon a subject by brute interaction with the environment such that it contributes to the formation of a habit, self-controlled yet so satisfying upon deliberation that it cannot be destroyed by any mere exercise of internal vigor. Such habits are broken or modified only by further brute interactions which come as a shock. All knowledge, Pierce holds, is based on direct experience. This includes knowledge of God. Furthermore, the real and the knowable are co-extensive. There is, then, no such thing as the absolutely incognizable. Consequently, if God is real, He is knowable, and whatever knowledge of Him we can achieve, vague as it must be, comes through direct experience. It follows, then, that although God cannot be just another object in space and time, His reality is manifested there or not at all (6.492–493):

> as to God, open your eyes—and your heart, which is also a perceptive organ—and you see him. But you may ask, 'Don't you admit there are any delusions?' Yes: I may think a thing is black, and on close examination it may turn out to be bottle-green. But I cannot think a thing is black if there is no such thing to be seen as black. Neither can I think that a certain action is self-sacrificing, if no such thing as self-sacrifice exists, although it may be very rare. It is the nominalists and the nominalists alone, who indulge in such scepticism, which the scientific method utterly condemns. (6.493)

Peirce once remarked in a letter to James that he held a form of the "ontological argument" (8.262). Presumably the Neglected Argument is supposed to help us open our eyes—and our hearts.

(4) "Universes of Experience": the three constitutive elements of any experience. They are Possibility, Actuality, and Mediation ("connectedness"). These, of course, are an application of the categories of Firstness, Secondness, and Thirdness. The Universe of Possibles comprises all mere Ideas, "those airy nothings" dear to poets and mathematicians, whose reality consists, not in their actually being thought or in their instantiation, but in their capability of either. The Universe of Actuals is that of brute fact and of things whose reality consists in their reaction against brute force. The third universe is made up of "everything whose being consists in active power to establish connection between different objects, especially between objects in different universes" (6.455). Peirce includes here all regularity of nature, mediation, continuity, and representation. This third category is the category of the real and the intelligible *par excellence* because it is the synthesis of the other two.

(5) "Argument": "any process of thought reasonably tending to produce a definite belief" (6.456). It is to be distinguished from argumentation. Argumentation is an argument proceeding from definitely formulated premises. Argument is a living process of thought; argumentation is the representation of that process in judgments expressed in non-vague terms. No judgment can be non-vague in every respect. If it were, it would be absolutely determinate and so would lose its character as a representation. Arguments are of three types: retroductive, deductive, and inductive (see, for example, 2.266–270). Any of these arguments becomes argumentation when and to the extent that its premises are definitely formulated. Argumentations, then, are to arguments what still shots are to motion pictures—or what position is to motion. There is always more to argument than can be caught in an argumentation. Since, for the purposes of analysis, arguments must be formulated, it would be easy to assume that the only form of argument is argumentation. Peirce thinks that this sort of mistake is one reason why his argument has been neglected:

> of all those theologians . . . who, with commendable assiduity, scrape together all the sound reasons they can find or concoct to

prove the first proposition of theology, few mention this one, and they most briefly. They probably share those current notions of logic which recognize no other Arguments than Argumentations. (6.457)

In particular, Peirce considered the first step in the complete inquiry into God's reality, the retroductive step, to be a form of argument rather than argumentation (6.469). Failure to distinguish argument from argumentation springs from two oversights. The first is failure to take vagueness seriously. Adherents of "those current notions of logic" assumed that vagueness had no place in logic and must be eliminated. This mistake might have been avoided if they had analyzed vagueness (see, for example, 5.446 and 5.505ff.). The second is failure to distinguish lived experience from its representation (see 6.435–439).

General Characteristics of Peirce's Theism

Before we proceed to a presentation of the argument, it will be helpful to review Peirce's idea of what sound theism must be like. It must be pragmatic, anthropomorphic, and vague.[3]

(1) "Pragmatic": to be a belief at all, belief in God must make a difference to human conduct. Furthermore, if belief in God is a true belief (and not merely truly believed), God must be a reality that makes a difference to human conduct. Not only must belief or non-belief make a difference, but so also must the reality or non-reality of God. The way in which God is described, the attributes by which we characterize Him, must show Him to be intimately involved in human life. Still, this characterization must be such that it does not make God any less God. According to Peirce, the traditional predicates of natural theology fulfill these requirements.

In a letter to James, Peirce complains that Royce's Absolute "is strictly speaking only God in a Pickwickian sense, that is, in a sense that has no effect" (8.277). God may well be absolute, but if nothing more is said, God is left too abstract and formal to be an object of belief. While such a characterization has the merit of indicating that God is not merely another spatio-temporal object, it does not connect Him with human experience and does not show that knowledge of Him arises from experience. Peirce gives God the abstract predicate *Ens necessarium* but adds that He is one, personal, transcendent, Creator of the universes of experience, omniscient, omnipotent, infallible, not subject to time, not finite, provident.

(2) "Anthropomorphic": this follows from what has just been said. Peirce refers to anthropomorphism as but another term for pragmatism considered as the analysis of scientific method (8.262). Human reasoning as a development of instinct depends upon conceptions taken from experience. Hence, at bottom, all human conceptions, scientific hypotheses included, are anthropomorphic (5.47, 5.536).

> I hold . . . that man is so completely hemmed in by the bounds of his possible experience, his mind is so restricted to being the instrument of his needs, that he cannot, in the least, *mean* anything which transcends those limits. (5.536)

Thus, God must be known in and through experience (God must be immanent), and yet He must be known as other than any object of experience (God must be transcendent). To say that man cannot go beyond the limits of his possible experience does not and need not prevent him from trying to conceive of "a supreme and indeed transcendent cause or agency of the entire universe." Peirce remarks that it would be like passing a law prohibiting man from jumping over the moon; this would not prevent him from jumping as high as he could. When all is said and done, Peirce opines, man will find no more adequate way of conceiving this "supreme agency" than as "vaguely like a man" (5.536).

> To say, therefore, that a conception is one natural to man, which comes to just about the same thing as to say that it is anthropomorphic, is as high a recommendation as one could give to it in the eyes of an Exact Logician. (5.47)

(3) "Vague": vagueness is a form of indeterminateness. Generality is another. A subject is said to be determinate with respect to a character when that character is predicated of it universally and affirmatively (this holds also for the character's complement). In all other respects the subject is indeterminate. A sign is objectively general if it leaves to the interpreter to supply further determina-

tions. Thus, in the sentence "Man is mortal" the term "man" is objectively general because the answer to the question "Which man?" is "Any one you choose." A sign is vague if it reserves for some other possible sign, and not for the interpreter, the function of completing the determination. Thus, in the sentence "This month a great event will happen," the term "great event" is objectively vague because the answer to the question "Which event?" is not "Any one you like," but rather "Wait and see" (5.447, 5.505). Since there is no term absolutely incapable of logical division (no logical atom), every term is to some degree indeterminate (3.93–94). Furthermore, every sign leaves to the utterer some further degree of determination. Its vagueness is removed only by rendering it general. Thus, an affirmative predication covers generally every essential character of the predicate, while a negative predication vaguely denies some essential character (5.447). Since, then, every sign is both vague and general (though not in the same respect), absolute determination and precision *cannot* be attained (5.477; see also 2.357).

Vagueness and generality may also be distinguished as follows: "Anything is general in so far as the principle of excluded middle does not apply to it" (5.448; see also 5.505). Thus, Peirce observes that a triangle in general is not isosceles, nor equilateral, nor scalene. Anything "is vague in so far as the principle of contradiction does not apply to it" (5.448). Thus, it is false neither that an animal is male nor that an animal is female (5.505).

On Peirce's account, instinctive beliefs are acritically indubitable, and acritically indubitable beliefs are invariably vague. To the extent that an instinctive belief is rendered precise, it is open to doubt. "Yet there are beliefs of which such a critical sifting invariably leaves a certain vague residue unaffected" (5.507). Would this vague residue disappear under persevering efforts at precision? It would not" . . . it is not because insufficient pains have been taken to precise the residuum, that it is vague: it is that it is vague intrinsically" (5.508). Peirce gives us an example: the notion of "order in nature." Every formulation of that order in a precise way is open to doubt, and yet for all that, "who can think that there is *no* order in nature" (5.508)? Such a claim is literally unthinkable since pure chaos cannot be real or be even thought. This residue, then, is indubitable and acritical: indubitable because it is acritical and acritical because it is essentially vague. The notion of God is *essentially* vague; God's reality must be such that it cannot be subsumed under a genus.

According to Peirce, therefore, our notion of God must be anthropomorphic if it is to be capable of belief, and it must be vague if it is to be a notion of God.

The Argument

The obvious is usually the most difficult thing to grasp and, when grasped, even more difficult to express. For Peirce, God's reality is (and *must* be) obvious (6.450):

> If God really be, and be benign, then, in view of the generally conceded truth that religion, were it but proved, would be a good outweighing all others, we should naturally expect that there would be some Argument for His Reality that should be obvious to all minds, high and low alike, that should earnestly strive to find the truth of the matter; and that this Argument should present its conclusion, not as the production of metaphysical theology, but in a form directly applicable to the conduct of life, and full of nutrition for men's highest growth. (6.457)

Such an argument merits to be called the "Humble Argument." Still, its very simplicity raises problems insofar as reason seeks to analyze and to express the reality in formulas. Augustine of course *knew* very well what time was until he sought to define it. Peirce's argument presents something of the same impression. But perhaps to be forewarned is to be forearmed. To expect or require an argument couched in the language of "metaphysical theology" is to be disappointed. For one thing, this would be to assume that every argument is an argumentation. For another, Peirce's argument requires a certain kind of activity which leads to a certain kind of experience without which the point of the argument is lost (this does not imply that this activity and this experience are out of the reach of most or even some men). Again, the theoretical justification of the argument, in the sense of showing its reasonableness, depends upon a correct understanding of logic and methodology (6.468). For a certain type of man at least (see 6.486), the force and validity of the argument is tied to the correctness of the pragmatic analysis.

The "Humble Argument" is the first step in a complete inquiry concerning God. The other steps are deductive and inductive. This first step results from an "agreeable occupation of the mind" called *musement* or free meditation (6.458). It is nothing but *Pure Play* whose only rule is the law of liberty. It is an exercise which has no ulterior purpose, no preconceived notion as to its outcome—in short, no prejudices of any kind. In effect, it is the ideal frame of mind for the scientific inquirer because it supposes an openness to entertain and explore every suggestion inspired by the wonders of nature. Musement may take the form of esthetic contemplation, or of free imagining (castle-building), or of considering some wonder in one of the three Universes of Experience, or of wondering at "some connection between two of the three with speculation concerning its cause" (6.458). It is musement in this last form especially from which the Neglected Argument "will in time flower" (6.458).

Peirce was always very hard on "theologians" and "seminary men." He opposed to their mentality that of the "laboratory man" or experimentalist. The latter was the man imbued with the spirit of scientific investigation—an openness to learn the lessons of nature. Such a man does not have his heart set on proving some hypothesis, but rather welcomes disconfirmation of "pet ideas" with as much as or more enthusiasm than he does confirmation. For the laboratory man hypotheses are just that; they are not principles of conduct and they are not objects of belief. In this sense science does not deal with "topics of vital importance."

> One who sits down with the purpose of becoming convinced of the truth of religion is plainly not inquiring in scientific singleness of heart, and must always suspect himself of reasoning unfairly. So he can never attain the entirety even of a physicist's belief in electrons, although this is avowedly but provisional. (6.458)

The same remark, of course, applies to one who sits down with the avowed purpose of becoming convinced of the falsity of religion. Peirce's recommendation to practice musement is meant to avoid this sort of false beginning.

But let religious meditation be allowed to grow up spontaneously out of Pure Play without any breach of continuity, and the Muser will retain the perfect candour proper to Musement. (6.458)

From the nature of the case each one must practice musement for himself. Peirce begins with some advice gathered from personal experience which might help the beginner: the time, the place, the subject matter, and so on (6.459). The one essential, however, whether these particular suggestions prove helpful or not, is to adhere to the law of liberty. He warns that the road to inquiry should not be blocked by prejudice masked as maxims of wisdom (6.460). The course which musement might take, therefore, cannot be prescribed beforehand. Certain kinds of consideration, no doubt, are likely to arise, such as "psychological and semi-psychological questions" which in turn will lead to metaphysical and logical ones (6.463–464).

Such meditation might go something like this: (1) consider the "unspeakable variety" of each Universe; (2) consider the "homogeneities of connectedness" within each Universe; and (3) consider the "homogeneities and connections" between two or more Universes (6.464–465). Peirce uses but two brief paragraphs to sketch this threefold consideration. He barely develops each point, for two reasons: first, each must make the meditation for himself in liberty in order to grasp the force of the argument; and, second, justice could not be done to such considerations except by a thorough presentation of synechism and tychism—an impossible task within the scope of the article.[4] Let us, however, take each of the three points in turn and comment briefly on it.

Point (1): "Variety in the Universes." Peirce maintains that variety, change, and growth are the most immediate, the most striking, and the most pervasive characteristics of our experience. The world of our experience is in constant flux. Now, such a situation in itself does not create any particular expectation concerning the course phenomena are likely to follow or the order that is likely to appear. It can engender only the expectation of further, endless, variety. Where there is no particular expectation concerning the order of events, there can be no surprises, since in such a world anything would be as likely as anything else. Where there are no surprises, there are no questions, and where there are no questions, no explanations are required. What *is* surprising in our endlessly varied experience, however, is the fact that there is some order and regularity. It is the law-like character of experience, then, which *par excellence* needs explaining. Peirce elsewhere developed this line of thought in his polemic against mechanistic determinism. It is not the law-like character of events which "explains" our experience; rather, it is that regularity which must be explained.

Point (2): "Regularity in the Universes." The surprising fact is that amid the flux of experience there are uniformities, not absolute, not exact, but regularities nonetheless. These "laws of nature" are not rigid; they themselves admit of variations ("sporting") and so themselves can change and develop. It is the regularity in experience which renders it intelligible and, Peirce argues, it is regularity which makes the real to be real (since there cannot be an absolutely incognizable). This sort of regularity (less than absolute and exact) is what constitutes reality. This sort of regularity engenders expectation concerning our future experience, allows for surprises, and so is the source of questions.

Point (3): "Regularities between Universes." In the phenomenon of growth all three universes conspire, for "a universal feature of it is provision for later stages in earlier ones" (6.465). Peirce asks whether this might not be accounted for by chance. Can regularity be explained by random interaction? In one sense the answer is yes—in some cases order does in fact arise from random distribution (for example, the action of "conservative forces" in physics). Furthermore, the action of chance is required as at least part of any explanation, since it is order which must be explained. Still, pure chance or absolute randomness cannot be real, since it would be unintelligible. In a word, the action of chance itself has its own law, the "Law of Mind" as Peirce calls it, which is such that, without being absolute and rigid, tends to make it more likely that future activity of an agent will be of a certain sort than some other because the agent has so behaved in the past.[5] In a word, this peculiar law is the tendency to take habits. Chance or randomness, then, is relative to some expected order. But expected order is based on habit, and habits are not rigidly necessary. In the end, therefore, all processes manifest some degree of regularity, although it may not be the regularity expected. They involve the action of real or objective change (tychism), but also have some, perhaps only "the smallest conceivable dose," of the higher element, the Law of Mind (synechism). Absolutely rigid laws of nature as conceived by the mechanistic determinists cannot explain growth and development. In such a world nothing new could ever happen. In fact, law in such a world would be strictly unknowable, since *ex hypothesi* it would be absolutely determinate, that is, incapable of generalization and therefore incapable of representation by a sign. The law of laws, then, is the Law of Mind, the tendency to take habits (6.102–103, 6.238–268, 6.287–306).

It is this sort of consideration, according to Peirce, which will make the hypothesis of God very attractive. The hypothesis of God as *Ens necessarium* will itself require that the laws of nature be as synechism describes them, and so if synechism is even approximately correct, the hypothesis has confirmation:

> in the Pure Play of Musement the idea of God's reality will be sooner or later to be found an attractive fancy, which the Muser will develop in various ways. The more he ponders it, the more it will find response in every part of his mind, for its beauty, for its supplying an ideal of life, and for its thoroughly satisfactory explanation of his whole threefold environment. (6.465)

So far we have traced how the hypothesis of God might arise through meditation on the order and variety of the real. We have tried to fill in some consideration of Peirce's ontology and cosmology developed over a number of years which are operative in his presentation and which he himself admits the Muser could not critically explore in odd half-hours. Once meditation has suggested the hypothesis, the task of developing its consequences and of investigating its validity and truth remains (6.464).

> At this point a trained mind will demand that an examination be made of the truth of the interpretation; and the first step in such an examination must be a logical analysis of the theory. But strict examination would be a task a little too serious for the Musement of hour fractions, and if it is postponed there will be ample remuneration even in the suggestions that there is no time to examine; especially since a few of them will appeal to reason as all but certain. (6.464)

Peirce now explores some of the peculiarities of the God-hypothesis and some of its consequences. After that there is a consideration of its logicality. Let us follow his order.

THE HYPOTHESIS

According to the pragmatic maxim, the entire meaning of any conception is constituted by the conceivable practical effects it would have upon our future conduct (5.402). Peirce appeals to this principle in analyzing the God-hypothesis. Its meaning is its conceivable effects upon our conduct, and its truth is confirmed insofar as it has power to make men strive to regulate their conduct according to those consequences. Yet the hypothesis is a "peculiar one" (6.466) not only because of its extreme vagueness, but also because "it supposes an infinitely incomprehensible object, although every hypothesis, as such, supposes its object to be truly conceived in the hypothesis" (6.466). As we have seen, every proposition (hence, every hypothesis) is to some degree vague. Hypotheses can be judged true or false only to the extent that they are made definite. Black, for example, maintains that all terms which require for their application the recognition of the presence of sense qualities are vague.[6] There are no rules for "drawing the line" between cases that fit the description and those that do not. Still, in order to reason with "loose concepts," some decision procedure must be adopted. Black suggests one for empirical concepts. But what about concepts like "order of nature" or "God"? If we are truly to conceive of an infinitely incomprehensible object, then according to Peirce our conception must be "vague yet . . . true so far as it is definite, and as continually tending to define itself more and more and without limit" (6.466).

To approach this logical problem we must return to the notion of vagueness. Concepts can be vague with respect to logical breadth or logical depth. Vagueness in logical breadth means that there are individuals about which there would be disagreement as to whether they belong to the class or not. Thus, the class "chair" (to use Black's example) is vague in logical breadth because, although we can define the concept well enough not to confuse it with another (say that of "table"), and there are individuals that indisputably belong to the class, there are others that are "borderline" cases. Vagueness in logical depth means vagueness with respect to the notes that define the class. It is not so much that there are borderline cases as that we cannot say just what the defining characteristics are—not because of ignorance, but because what we are trying to define resists classification.[7] In such a case we can better say what the concept does not mean, and still what is intended is not something merely negative. Such vagueness in logical depth may not necessarily mean that there is any doubt as to which individuals are meant. The transcendentals—being, unity, truth, goodness—have this sort of vagueness. It would be begging the question to say that therefore these notions are meaningless. The notion of God has vagueness in logical depth.

How can such a notion be rendered definite enough to be capable of a true or false judgment? Since no sign is absolutely determinate, the sign "God" can be made definite only by rendering it general. But all such attempts fail in one way or another since what is intended by "God" is not the sort of thing that can be in a class. It would seem, then, that all claims about God must be neither true nor false because of their irremediable vagueness. Yet this will not do either, because we do in fact discriminate between predicates applicable to God and those that are not. This is independent of whether we admit God's reality or not. It might be claimed that all predicates applied to God are inappropriate precisely because the notion has no meaning. The same would apply to all "metaphysical" claims. The inconvenience, of course, as has been pointed out numberless times, is that this claim itself is "metaphysical." Again, one might wish to exclude the notion of God on metaphysical grounds. In that case, either one is claiming that the statement "God is real" is false (and so admitting it has meaning) or one is claiming meaninglessness for the concept on grounds other than its vagueness.

It is impossible here to enter into all the problems raised by "God-talk." Perhaps in the end one will be forced to some version of the ancient *via negativa, via affirmativa*, and *via eminentiae*. In such a case, the reality intended would be said to show itself in the very failure of every attempt adequately to express it. Such a disclosure[8] would be different from the disclosure that something is without meaning at all, since in that case one would see either that the expression is syntactically incorrect or that it contains a contradiction, logical or performatory. But is this the case with "God" and the "transcendentals"? Perhaps we simply have to face the paradox of admitting a type which cannot be a type at all. Peirce struggles with this sort of puzzle but does not come to any clear resolution. He says, for example, that to think of God as having a purpose is *less false* than the opposite (6.466). It seems that he is getting at the paradox we just mentioned, although he does not state it in so many words. Peirce seems to mean that from the supposition that God has purpose we can draw true conclusions about the Universes of Experience (for example, that they are in continual process of development), while from the opposite we can draw no conclusion at all. This would make the former supposition preferable, and so while not exactly true of God (since God's having a purpose does not entail change in God, while ours does), still it is "less false" in its consequences.

Conceiving God as purposeful poses another puzzle for Peirce. He argues that if the hypothesis of God is subject to growth in that it tends to define itself without limit, it must represent God as subject to growth too. But the representation of God as "growing" is "contradicted in the hypothesis from its very first phrase," and yet since this cannot be eradicated from the hypothesis it "cannot . . . be flatly false" (6.466). There must be something like growth in God's reality although we have no precise idea what it is like. This follows from Peirce's understandings of Thirdness as *the* category of the real—and Thirdness involves mediation and continuity. The real and the intelligible are identical, and both are thirds. God, then, must be conceived after the analogy of Mind (6.502).

It may be that what leads Peirce into this sort of difficulty is the extreme version of realism which he espoused. He seems to think that whatever characterizes the representation of some reality must also characterize what is represented. This thesis is open to doubt, and many philosophers would flatly deny it. One might want to distinguish the proper and proportional object of finite intelligence from a transcendent and disproportionate object which must be represented to finite intelligence in a discursive way even if the object itself is not subject to such limitation. There is something of this idea in the attempt to understand continuity (a subject dear to Peirce), in that continuity must be represented conceptually through the use of discreteness—a series is continuous if between any two members of the series there is always another. Such a representation always carries a clause (explicit or implicit) negating what in the representation is subject to limitation. This supposes of course some theory of limitation such as the Scholastic development of act and potency. Peirce does have a theory of limitation of a sort. The category of Secondness is meant to account for it, and, as we have seen, this is the category of existence. This was the reason why God could not properly be said to exist. Still, we cannot have an experience of anything not related to existents in some way, since our experience is constituted by all three categories. The categories cannot be experienced in isolation but can only be distinguished within experience through "precission" or abstraction (1.353, 1.549).[9] This would require Peirce to say that we have no experience of God *immediately* but only in and through the world of intelligible actuals. This would be direct but mediated knowledge. Again, we have seen that Peirce contends that we know God by direct experience.

According to Peirce, therefore, it is "less false" to speak of God as having a purpose than as being purposeless. It cannot be simply true because "a *purpose essentially involves growth* and so cannot be attributed to God" (6.466; emphasis added). Whether it does *essentially* involve growth is the question.[10] It may be the case that for us to have a purpose in fact always has concomitant with it growth of some sort. But might not this be only accidental? Could it be, for example, that having a purpose might look only to the development of something else? It might be that to accomplish the purpose with respect to the other, the purposer might have to act and in acting himself develop by reducing his potentialities to act. But is this essential to having a purpose? To put the same thing in another way: is it essential to the notion of actively accomplishing something that the agent undergo change? Is it conceivable that only the patient change? Is not this just what we would expect of an infinite agent? Insofar as we have a purpose we undergo change, but this may be due not to our having a purpose but to the fact that we do not have actually infinite power. Then it would follow that God cannot be said to have a purpose in just the same way as we do, but that He has something like a purpose in that what He intends in His creative act is accomplished in the creatures—that is, they come to be and develop according to His will. Peirce seems in fact to be getting at this notion since he tells us that the implications of thinking of God as "growing" (having a purpose) will be maintained insofar as it concerns the Universes, "while its implications concerning God will be partly disavowed" (6.466). Still, with respect to God these implications will be "held to be less false than their denial would be" since that denial would lead us to think of God as purposeless.

Justification And Validity

The logical justification of the God-hypothesis would require: (1) an examination of the elements of any complete inquiry; (2) a discussion of the logical validity of each element; and (3) an appraisal of the place of the Neglected Argument in this process. Peirce merely summarizes items (1) and (2). They are treated copiously in his other logical writings. Item (3), however, receives special attention.

The validity of deduction and induction need not detain us. What is important is the justification of retroduction since the first stage of the Neglected Argument is of that form. Every real advance in knowledge comes through retroduction. "Neither deduction nor induction contributes the smallest positive items to the final conclusion of the inquiry" (6.475). Deduction merely draws out explicitly what the hypothesis contains. Induction seeks to evaluate its truth in terms of experience. It is retroduction which supplies the major premise for the deduction and tells the inquirer what to look for in applying inductive techniques. Retroduction is the light of intelligence itself, "*il lume naturale*," and, according to Peirce, it testifies to the affinity of mind and nature. The conjectures it produces are the spontaneous offshoots of instinctive reason.

It is the notion of instinctive reason that Peirce finds to be at the base of retroduction as an argument form. The spontaneous and overpowering impulse to form hypotheses is a "symptom of its being instinctive" (6.476). This is, in general, the natural disposition of intelligence.

To give the lie to his own consciousness of divining the reasons of phenomena would be as silly in a man as it would be in a fledgling bird to refuse to thrust its wings and leave the nest, because the poor little thing has read Babinet, and judged aerostation to be impossible on hydrodynamical grounds. (6.476)

The real question is whether men in fact have this ability to discern in particular cases which among alternative hypotheses is "instinctive." Peirce gives an affirmative answer:

> Not, I reply to the extent of guessing right the first time, nor perhaps the second; but that the well-prepared mind has wonderfully soon guessed each secret of nature is historical truth. (6.476)

Following scientific procedure, man has "wonderfully soon" guessed correctly among the infinitely many possible hypotheses which might explain perplexing phenomena. The implication is that the correct method itself is a matter of instinct. This does not mean that every analysis of method is correct, but only that the actual use of the method is instinctive and that if the method be persevered in, it is self-corrective even with respect to formulating it properly.

But perhaps this "guessing right" in a relatively few tries is mere coincidence and not due to the instinct of reason? Peirce's answer is twofold: (1) the probability of this being *mere* chance is so small "that it would be ridiculous to suppose our science so to have come to pass" (6.476); and (2) even granting the element of chance as an "explanation" of any purposed human action, this still leaves unaccounted the role played by reason in that action, or else it must suppose that reason has nothing to do with it at all (6.476). Peirce concludes:

> There is a reason, an interpretation, a logic, in the course of scientific advance, and this indisputably proves to him who has perceptions of rational or significant relations, that man's mind must have been attuned to the truth of things in order to discover what he has discovered. It is the bedrock of logical truth. (6.476)

This "bedrock of truth" was called by Galileo "*il lume naturale*," and the heuristic principle that it dictates is to prefer the *simpler* of two hypotheses. But simpler does not necessarily mean *logically* simpler. It is to be understood as referring to the "more facile and natural" hypothesis—the one instinct suggests. As we have seen, a symptom of the instinctive nature of an hypothesis is its initial compulsive force, but this has to be put to the test and controlled by the techniques of scientific method.

> It was not until long experience forced me to realize that subsequent discoveries were every time showing I had been wrong (i.e., in supposing that "simpler" meant "logically simpler"), while those who understood the maxim as Galileo had done, early unlocked the secret . . . that it is the simpler Hypothesis in the sense of the more facile and natural, the one that instinct suggests, that must be preferred; for the reason that, unless man have a natural bent in accordance with nature's, he has no chance of understanding nature at all. . . . I do not mean that logical simplicity is a consideration of no value at all, but only that its value is badly secondary to that of simplicity in the other sense. (6.477)

Application to the Neglected Argument

Peirce imagines three sorts of men and their reactions to his argument:

> the first, of small instruction with corresponding natural breadth, intimately acquainted with the N.S., but to whom logic is all Greek; the second, inflated with current notions of logic, but prodigiously informed about the N.S.; the third, a trained man of science who, in the modern spirit, has added to his specialty an exact theoretical and practical study of reasoning and the elements of thought, so that psychologists account him a sort of psychologist, and mathematicians a sort of mathematician. (6.478)

No space is given to the reaction of the second type of man, because "the current notions of logic" are full of errors. Even though such a man were well-informed about the argument, he would not be able to understand it, much less criticize it. The first type, however, is naturally well-disposed to grasp the argument and to accept it, because he follows his instincts in the matter without the complications suggested by critical reflection. Such a man would have learned that "nothing has any kind of value in itself . . . but only in its place in the whole production to which it appertains" (6.479). Thus, he is disposed to think of God as having a purpose. He will perceive evil as leading ultimately to good in that the fight against it is required by the cosmic law of growth. Thus

> he may hope that it (evil) be best *for them* (his dear ones who suffer evil), and will tell himself that in any case the secret design of God will be perfect through their agony; and even while still hot from the battle, will submit with adoration to His Holy Will. He will not worry because the Universes were not constructed to suit the scheme of some silly scold. (6.479)

Thus, this man will "shape the whole conduct of his life and all the springs of action into conformity with that hypothesis" (6.466). This is Belief.

The third type of man, while well-disposed to entertain the hypothesis because he feels its initial attraction, still because of his training requires that it be put to the test:

> the third man, considering the complex process of self-control, will see that the hypothesis, irresistible though it be the first intention, yet needs Probation; and that though an infinite being is not tied down to any consistency, yet man, like any other animal, is gifted with power of understanding sufficient for the conduct of life. (6.480)

The test to which the hypothesis must be put, therefore, "must lie in its value in the self-controlled growth of man's conduct of life" (6.480). This man requires critical reflection upon the dictates of "common sense" and also "instinct" to see whether they are authentic. If they are, they will survive, since in the end what is real will out. Intelligence is nothing but the natural disposition to learn the lessons of experience. The third man, therefore, has come to know that the first and basic principle of "common sense" and of "instinct" is identical with correct scientific procedure. Pragmatism, according to Peirce, is the proper analysis of such procedure. It is, then, in accord with instinct and indeed is called "Critical Common-sensism."

> This brings him, for the testing of the hypothesis, to taking his stand upon Pragmaticism, which implies faith in common sense and in instinct, though only as they issue from the cupel furnace of measured criticism. (6.480)

The hypothesis of God is to be explored for its implications concerning human conduct. Those implications are to be considered according to the requirements of proper thinking, acting and feeling explored in the normative sciences: logic, ethics, and esthetics. As speculative sciences these three do not set down particular practical imperatives but only the general requirements for anything to be true, good, or beautiful.[11] The hypothesis of God is tested in its ability to render practical and operative what those sciences only generally and formally characterize.

A man of the third type, then, might reason as follows: since there is a strong, initial impulse to believe some proposition (say, that God is real, or that there is order in nature, or that incest is wrong), there is a strong presumption in its favor. This presumption is further strengthened if history shows that such belief has been held by most men over long periods of time. Consequently, it would be unreasonable not to take such beliefs seriously or to abandon them simply for theoretical reasons (recall the example of the fledgling bird). It would be unwise to begin to practice incest because one has theoretical difficulties in establishing its immorality. It would be irrational to abandon entirely the notion of order in nature simply because all such precise statements of that order are open to doubt. It would be unreasonable to reject belief in God simply because the hypothesis is essentially vague, and it would be unreasonable to suspend indefinitely such belief on the grounds that there is no *apodictic* argument in its favor. All these conclusions have a theoretical justification in terms of a proper understanding of human inquiry. If all knowledge comes through experience, then experience is the great teacher. If these beliefs are in fact false, experience will sooner or later find it out since induction is self-correcting. To take the God-hypothesis: if it arises spontaneously in musement as highly plausible, if it unifies otherwise fragmentary experiences, and if its consequences for human conduct are to impel men to conform their lives to the ideals it offers (described in a formal way in Normative Science), then reason requires that the hypothesis be approved not only theoretically but also practically—that it be *believed*. In such a case reflection confirms impulse. The desire to conform action to belief and to control belief through critical reflection is the drive of intelligence itself. The outcome is reasonable belief.

Summary: A Nest of Arguments

In an "Additament" at the end of his argument, Peirce sums up the results. The Neglected Argument is really a nest of three separate but related arguments. The first and innermost of the nest is the Humble Argument properly so called. It is humble because "it is just as good an argument, if not better, in the form it takes in the mind of the clodhopper" (6.483). It is the argument which has the most religious force since it is nothing but "the honest, sincere and unaffected, because unprepense, meditation upon the Idea of God" (6.486). The pure play of musement shows the Idea itself to be so admirable and wonderful as to be worthy of adoration. It is this movement of the spirit which tends to produce a truly religious belief in God's reality and nearness. This argument is reasonable because it arises naturally and results in the Muser's determining to shape his conduct in accord with the Idea.

The second argument of the nest is the Neglected Argument properly so called. It consists in showing that the Humble Argument is indeed the natural fruit of free meditation and that the Idea is so beautiful and awesome as to be adorable. In a word, it tries to show that the Idea of God, far from being vicious or superstitious, is instinctive. This is done by showing that the Idea is the natural outcome of meditation upon the three Universes of Experience, especially from the point of view of their origin. Peirce sees this moment as an apology for the Humble Argument. The Humble Argument is a lived process which one has to experience for oneself in order to feel its force (6.435–439). It is, therefore, strictly speaking, an argument and not an argumentation. Its formulation and defense in the Neglected Argument involves argumentation.

The third argument of the nest is a further development of the Neglected Argument and completes the vindication of the Humble Argument for the man trained in science and familiar with logic. It is based upon careful study of scientific method. Once such an analysis has been made, one compares the process of thought of the Muser as he reflects upon the Universes of Experience with the process of thought employed in scientific discovery. One finds that the Humble Argument is nothing but the first stage of such discovery—the formulation of an hypothesis through observations and reflection. The hypothesis so formed, however, differs from ordinary scientific hypotheses in three ways: (1) it has an extraordinary degree of plausibility (so much so that those not used to critical reflection will be tempted to give up any further investigation in the belief that the hypothesis is fully justified); (2) the hypothesis is very vague, so that all attempts at precision render the hypothesis less satisfying, indeed open to doubt with respect to that precision, and yet an indubitable residue remains after each such attempt (recall the example of "order in the universe"); (3) the hypothesis has continuing influence on human conduct. It is in terms of this last characteristic that the scientific man must continue to investigate the hypothesis beyond its initial attractiveness. He must put it to the "pragmatist's" test. If the hypothesis is seen to have powerful consequences in shaping human conduct in the good, then according to Pierce it is a reasonable object of belief. In terms of its truth, it is seen to be "less false" than its opposite, to use his own unusual expression.

Intelligence is a natural capacity (an instinct) for discovering the "secrets of nature" (see 6.414–418, 6.499). Intelligence supposes the intelligible. The intelligible and the real must be co-extensive since otherwise there would be the unknowable thing-in-itself. If the real were only partially intelligible, something would be real which was not only not known but could not in principle be known. Such an hypothesis would be to give as an explanation not merely the inexplicable but also the unintelligible. Such a view of explanation cannot be formulated without giving the lie to itself. There is, then, an "affinity" between intelligence and the real. Peirce calls "God" that reality which is the source and origin of this integration—of the intelligibility of phenomena. The notion remains vague but true insofar as it can be made definite; it is strictly indubitable insofar as it remains vague. The difficulties in attempting to render the notion definite are many, and insofar as generalizations serve in the attempt, those are acceptable which are less false than their opposites. It is less false to say of God, therefore, that He has purpose than to say that He is purposeless, because the first allows us to deduce the world's intelligibility (already known as a fact from the nature of inquiry itself) and to conform our conduct to the highest ideal of love, while the other does not.

Knowledge of God, like all human knowledge, is based upon direct experience, even though God is not experienced as an object among other objects. God must remain vague and mysterious. God is encountered rather than deduced, and this encounter takes place along with and within experience of the world of space and time. As so encountered, He is recognized as not confined to the spatio-temporal conditions of our experience of objects. Though God is not grasped as a result of reasoning, reasoning can help us recognize God in the encounter (6.493). Thus, Peirce argues that those theologians who hold exclusively to negative theology to the exclusion of any positive content have made a mistake. We can have some positive idea of God through the world of experience which insofar as it is intelligible is nothing but His Thought.

> Of course, various great theologians explain that one cannot attribute "reason" to God, nor perception . . . and, in short, that his "mind" is necessarily so unlike ours, that some—though wrongly—high in the church say that it is only negatively, as being entirely different from everything else, that we can attach any meaning to the Name. This is not so; because the discoveries of science, their enabling us to *predict* what will be the course of nature, is proof conclusive that, though we cannot think any thought of God's, we can catch a fragment of his thought, as it were. (6.502)

Notes

1. Peirce's article "A Neglected Argument for the Reality of God" first appeared in the *Hibbert Journal*, 7 (1908), 90–112, and is included in the *Collected Papers*, 6.452–91. The discussion will concern this article.

2. James's remark (in *Pragmatism*, p. 5) was made concerning Peirce's lectures on Pragmatism given at Harvard in 1903. See editor's note, *Collected Papers* V, p. 11.

3. I have developed these ideas in another essay, "'Vaguely Like a Man': The Theism of Charles S. Peirce"; see chap. 11, above.

4. For a detailed exposition of Peirce's synechism and tychism see my *Charles S. Peirce: On Norms and Ideals* (Amherst: University of Massachusetts Press, 1967), parts 2 and 3.

5. See Peirce's essay, "The Law of Mind" (6.102–163).

6. "Vagueness: An Exercise in Logical Analysis," *Language and Philosophy* (Ithaca: Cornell University Press, 1949), pp. 25–58.

7. Vagueness in depth is not to be confused with ambiguity as defined, for example, by Black (ibid., p. 42n33). According to him, ambiguity "is constituted by inability to decide between a finite number of alternative meanings having the same phonetic form (homonyms)." Ambiguity can be removed; vagueness in depth cannot be in all cases.

8. See W. de Pater, *Linguistic Analysis and Theology* (Louvain: Acco, 1970); *Taagalanalytische perspektieven op godsdienst en kunst* (Antwerp: Nederlandsche Boekhandle, 1970); *Theologische Sprachlogik* (Munich: Lösel-Verlag, 1971).

9. For a further discussion of the categories and their interrelation see my *Norms and Ideals*, part 1, chap. 1.

10. In 6.502 Peirce explicitly says that "it is impossible to say that *any* human attribute is *literally* applicable" to God.

11. See 5.14–40, and my *Norms and Ideals*, for an exposition of normative science.

Appendix:
Response to Hartshorne's
"Peirce and Religion"

PROFESSOR HARTSHORNE'S ESSAY is a remarkable summary of his contribution to recent philosophical theology and an illuminating account of the way Peirce has influenced his thinking in the subject. Beyond that, Hartshorne's critical evaluation of Peirce's philosophical approach to God is a valuable contribution to the understanding of pragmaticism.

For my part here I would like to accomplish three goals: first, to react to some selected remarks of Hartshorne's in his evaluation of Peirce's reflections on God (his essay is much too rich for me to deal with all the points it makes); second, to select two aspects of Peirce's thought for further development; and, finally, to offer my own assessment of Peirce's accomplishment in reasoning about God. I hope to achieve these goals *per modum unius*, that is, without breaking them out separately.

In the first place, then, let me say immediately that I agree almost completely with Hartshorne's assessment of Peirce's strengths and weaknesses. I thoroughly agree that Peirce might indeed be characterized as between two worlds—the world of classical theism (from which he moved away) and the world of process theism (at which he had not arrived). Peirce's philosophical theology is neither Aquinas's nor Hartshorne's. This fact will probably endear him to neither of these schools. Whether Peirce's shortcomings in theological reflection are properly remedied in the ways Hartshorne suggests I leave to the reader to decide. That some of Peirce's reflections on God need clarification, if not correction, I think will become evident as we proceed, if it is not already so.

As is well-known, for pedagogical reasons Scholastics frequently

---

This essay under the title "Response to Hartshorne" and Professor Hartshorne's paper appear in *Peirce and Contemporary Thought: Philosophical Inquiries*, ed. Kenneth Laine Ketner, American Philosophy Series No. 1 (New York: Fordham University Press, 1995).

divided their treatises on God into two parts: namely, into the two questions *"An sit Deus?"* and *"Quid sit Deus?"* Ultimately, of course, the two questions cannot be kept apart, because the answer to the first depends upon the answer to the second. Still, I shall use that division as a convenient way of lining up some of Hartshorne's important remarks about Peirce. My impression is that Hartshorne would give Peirce rather higher marks for his treatment of the first question—that is, "Is there a God?"—than for his treatment of the second—"What is God?" I would like to consider Peirce's proof more closely to show how, in fact, his answer to the question of whether there is a God is connected to his answer to the question of what God is.

Now, to begin with Hartshorne's positive assessment of Peirce, I take it that he thinks that two of Peirce's most important contributions to philosophical theology are (a) his emphasis on the fact that human beings have access to God's reality in ways other than conceptualization and ratiocination; and (b) his recognition that all traditional proofs for God—ontological and cosmological—contribute something important to the issue (see, for example, 6.504); in the case of the ontological argument, that either God exists necessarily or else the very notion of God is self-contradictory and incoherent; in the case of the cosmological argument, that the experience of the world shows God's existence to be neither self-contradictory nor incoherent. I agree completely with this assessment.

Peirce constantly insisted that religious belief is instinctive (see, for example, 6.497–500). It is a matter of sentiment, of the heart rather than the head. He thought that mankind can perceive God directly and, in fact, if mankind cannot so perceive God, God cannot be known at all. It is this instinctive belief that is at the heart of the first of Peirce's "proofs"—from musement or free contemplation. Moreover, it is well-known that the pragmatic movement, following Peirce's lead, set out to recover experience from the narrow and arid thing it had been made to be by certain forms of empiricism. For Peirce, experience is so rich that it is the sole source of whatever man knows—including God (see, for example, 6.492–493). Hence, for Peirce, some form of religious experience is necessary (although not sufficient) for any *rational* belief in God.

Peirce frequently remarked that all reasoning about religious matters must be unsound and that all study of them must be sordid and narrow. Nonetheless, Peirce did reason about God, and he did undertake a serious study of religious issues. He did so because he considered Reason to be a development and extension of Instinct. One might say he considered Reason to be the specifically human instinct with which evolution equipped mankind to deal with the as-yet-unfamiliar. But instinctive belief in God is indubitable as long as that belief is left sufficiently vague; but once questions arise which call for attempts at precision which in turn open the instinctive belief to doubt, then only Reason can serve the need, albeit in a halting way. For a pragmatist, furthermore, no belief should be fixed merely by tenacity or authority; doubts and questions must be explored by Reason.

For Hartshorne's second major commendatory point—Peirce's proofs for God's reality. I suggest we rely on Peirce's 1908 *Hibbert Journal* article (6.452–491), since it represents his mature thought on this matter. There Peirce offered us three nested arguments for God's reality (not God's existence, since existence for Peirce is the category of contingent matter of fact, of physical objects interacting in space and time—and to apply this category to God would, in Peirce's eyes, be making God simply another object among objects). These arguments are nested, in that the third argument includes within it the second and the first; the second includes within it the first (in just that way in which the categories are related). The first argument is the so-called Humble Argument based on the exercise of musement or free contemplation of the three Universes of Experience (the Possible, the Actual, and the Necessary). The point of this exercise is that our instinctive belief in God will assert itself on the occasion of considering the beauty and coherence of each of the Universes and of their interconnections. Although the Humble Argument issues in the hypothesis of God, the second nested argument, the Neglected Argument, shows that this hypothesis is the *God*-hypothesis, that is, that the reality so postulated is not merely finite and contingent, but infinite and necessary. Writing to William James in 1905 Peirce remarked:

> The God of my theism is not finite. That won't do at all. For to begin with, existence is reaction, and therefore no existent can be *clear supreme* . . . . In the next place, anthropomorphism for me

implies above all that the true Ideal is a living power, which is a variation of the ontological proof. . . . That is, the esthetic ideal, that which we *all* love and adore, the altogether admirable, has, *as ideal*, necessarily a mode of being to be called living. Because our ideas of the infinite are necessarily extremely vague and become contradictory the moment we attempt to make them precise. But still they are not utterly unmeaning, though they can only be interpreted in our religious adoration and the consequent effects upon conduct. (8.262)

I would point out (1) that this formulation of the ontological argument in terms of a real infinite Ideal might also have been articulated in terms of the moral Ideal of Goodness or the logical Ideal of Truth; (2) that it is a step away from the classical formulation of the argument toward what I would call a pragmatist variation, since it is not merely in the conceptual order but in the conceptual order insofar as it is linked to human conduct. I think Peirce chose the esthetic formulation as more readily seen to be available in musement.

The third nested argument situates the God-hypothesis within the logic of rational inquiry and so puts it immediately in the context of human conduct. Again, I take this to be a move away from the classical formulation of the cosmological argument insofar as it does not move merely from contingency to necessity by effect to cause, but rather from human thinking, willing, and feeling to their adequate sufficient reason, which is in turn a living ideal of that sort of human behavior. Completely to appreciate what Peirce understood by this third argument from conduct (hence, from the world to God—the cosmological move with a pragmatist twist!) one would have to know his doctrine concerning the normative sciences, his understanding of scientific method, and the hierarchy of the sciences. In brief, unless God were a reality, a non-fictional ideal, with real living power, all human inquiry would be meaningless. Conversely, once that Ideal is acknowledged, how we behave is affected.

Perhaps now is the time to make our transition to the second question posed by the Scholastics in the philosophy of God: namely, *"Quid sit Deus?"* Far and away Peirce's favorite characterization of God is "creator." Peirce began the *Hibbert Journal* article by defining God as *Ens necessarium*, but as Donna Orange pointed out in *Peirce's Conception of God*,[1] this is the only place that Peirce explicitly used this attribute of God. She also shrewdly pointed out that the entire set of nested arguments can be read as an attempt to bring the conception of God to the third degree of pragmatic clarity as achieved through the use of the pragmatic maxim. That maxim would take God to be above all creator. Peirce wrote: "God is *the* definable proper name, signifying *Ens necessarium*; in my belief Really Creator of all three Universes of Experience" (6.452). Note that he immediately qualified *Ens necessarium* in terms of creator. No doubt, Peirce used the term *Ens necessarium* to elicit a connection with both the Anselmian and the Aquinate argument from contingency (the third way). I suspect, too, that he had in mind Royce's Absolute, which he conceded might be an appropriate abstract characterization of God but which was empty since it had no implications for human conduct. If the Absolute as *Ens necessarium* is given the pragmatic interpretation of super-order, of which order and uniformity of the created universes are but particular varieties, then Peirce thought he could argue from the predictability that general laws governing matters-of-fact bring, to the need for such a super-order. The growth of the universe from chaos to order is what Peirce meant by the growth of concrete reasonableness and is probably what he meant by the pragmatic import of *Ens necessarium*. In effect, if the universe is intelligible, as science assumes that it is, it must exhibit generality, and the source of that generality must be necessary reasonableness.

This brings us to a central unclarity or waffling in Peirce's philosophy of God. The issue comes down to this: Is "God" for Peirce God or Reason? Is the growth of concrete reasonableness in the universe (Peirce's *summum bonum*) what he means by "God," or is this the sign of God? In a word, is God immanent or transcendent? Is he both? If so, in what sense or senses? Donna Orange concluded, in her study of Peirce's conception of God, "these texts . . . confirm my suspicion that Peirce's theism amounted to a belief that certain inescapable beliefs we hold can be expressed in religious language when such expression is appropriate or necessary for worship and the conduct of life."[2]

Hartshorne has astutely pointed out that because of Peirce's insistence on the role of experience in our understanding of God, some form of anthropomorphism is to be expected and that the only real issue is to find which analogies are fitting and proper—that is, to find which predicates of God Peirce would characterize as "less false." In this regard Hartshorne is completely correct, in my opinion. Again, he is right in holding that the merely negative attributes alone will not do. They do serve a purpose, however, and cannot simply be dismissed as "abstractions," since they do set certain boundary limits beyond which predicates are unacceptable and perhaps even "vicious," to use Hartshorne's expression. Still, "negative theology," when coupled with "less false" positive attributes, is useful, even necessary, for theological discourse. Peirce seemed to think that the classical predicates—such as infinite, omniscient, omnipotent, creator—fit the bill better than some of those suggested by William James, for example.

Hartshorne approves of Peirce's attributing growth and change in some sense to God. But this is an area of Peirce's thought which needs clarification. It would perhaps be helpful to quote a passage where Peirce made such an assertion to see the extent to which he hesitated in this matter:

> The hypothesis of God is a peculiar one, in that it supposes an infinitely incomprehensible object, although every hypothesis, as such, supposes its object to be truly conceived in the hypothesis. This leaves the hypothesis but one way of understanding itself; namely, as vague yet as true so far as it is definite, and as continually tending to define itself more and more, and without limit. The hypothesis, being thus itself inevitably subject to the law of growth, appears in its vagueness to represent God as so, albeit this is directly contradicted in the hypothesis from its very first phase. But this apparent attribution of growth to God, since it is ineradicable from the hypothesis, cannot, according to the hypothesis, be flatly false. Its implications concerning the Universes will be maintained in the hypothesis, *while its implications concerning God will be partly disavowed*, and yet be held to be less false than their denial would be. Thus the hypothesis will lead to our thinking of features of each Universe as purposed; and this will stand or fall with the hypothesis. Yet a purpose essentially involves growth, *and so cannot be attributed to God*. Still it will, according to the hypothesis, be less false to speak so than to represent God as purposeless. (6.466; emphasis added)

This paragraph deserves careful study and requires some close analysis to determine just what is being maintained and whether it is defensible. In the first place, it is evident that Peirce hesitated about attributing growth to God. He was still enough under the influence of the classical notion of God as immutable because infinitely perfect—that is, as possessing every perfection in a supereminent way (the classical understanding of "pure act")—that he thought that the hypothesis of God as *Ens necessarium* "directly contradicts" the notion of change and growth in God. What I find curious is the argument that because the hypothesis of God is vague but true insofar as it is definite, and because that hypothesis tends to define itself more and more, "it" (the hypothesis? God?) is subject to growth. Certainly, it is true that the hypothesis in its expression and articulation grows. I fail to see, however, that it follows necessarily that what is true of the hypothesis as expressed is true also of what the hypothesis expresses. Such an error would be the same as attributing to what is measured the properties of the measure. It might be urged that Peirce really meant to attribute growth (and so purpose) to the created Universes, and that insofar as those Universes are a sign of God (as a great poem is a sign of the poet), in some sense something like growth can be attributed to God, but not literally—unless, of course, Peirce meant that in the case of God and the Universes, sign and signified are identified. Again, it seems unlikely to me that Peirce would hold *that*, because then the notion of sign becomes vacuous. It is more likely that Peirce held some partial identity of God and the Universes, a point to which I will return shortly.

In very abstract terms one can ask whether God for Peirce is transcendent or immanent. No doubt, Peirce thought that God is not *merely* immanent. God is immanent in the sense that, as creator, He is a living power present to (even if not identical with) the created Universes. But God is, after all, creator of the Universes (or at least of some of them!): He is their source, and so cannot be simply identical with them. The Universes as created depend upon God and so do not exhaust God's reality. Again, in Peirce's version of the ontological argument, God is characterized as the Ideal (esthetic, moral, logical) and so transcends any instance of beauty, goodness, or truth. The question is whether this transcendence means that God is outside and beyond the Universes of experience or whether God is at least partially identified with those Universes. Hartshorne put his finger on the problem when he asked whether or not, for Peirce, the categories apply to God. Hartshorne rightly points out that you will find indications that seem to support each of these views. It seems to me that Peirce should maintain that the categories apply to God (since they are strictly universal) in some way or other. The real question is: How?

The hesitation in this matter can be seen in the *Hibbert Journal* article when Peirce, laying out the Neglected Argument, described the activity of musement as "that course of meditation upon the three Universes which gives birth to the hypothesis and ultimately to the belief that they, *or at any rate two of the three*, have a Creator independent of them . . ." (6.483; emphasis added). It seems clear from the context that Peirce thought God to be creator of, and so other than, the Universes of Possibility and Actuality, since neither of these alone accounts for reality—possibilities are merely what may be, while actuals are a contingent matter of physical fact. But is God identical with the third Universe? Is God Reason, Mind, Concrete Reasonableness? Or is God perhaps the totality or wholeness of Reason as penetrating actuals and as source of possibilities? Peirce might argue that the pragmatic conception of "God" is the ideal wholeness of Reason which alone could be fully real and so in that sense could alone be transcendent creator.

Hartshorne also pointed out in his essay what he takes to be a "real blunder" on Peirce's part, in that he held that only our faults or defects distinguish us from one another. This might also account for his difficulty in relating God's transcendence and immanence. If Peirce had no positive account of individual distinctness, he could hardly think of God as a distinct positive individual reality transcending (and so standing outside of) the three Universes. Thus, for example, Peirce spoke of God as Absolute First (Alpha) and Absolute Second (Omega). Must he also have said that God is all the rest in-between—or at least the wholeness of the in-between? Or might he have said that God is also Absolute Third outside the world and continuously creating and conserving it. The analogy here is that of an hyperbola defined by its asymptotes and generated by an algebraic function. This, then, could be read as a distinct individual reality (distinct from the created arguments). I am not at all sure about what I have just suggested, but raise it more as a question. I would like to say, however, that attempts have been made to use Peirce's principles to construct a positive account of the self and of the subject.³ Hence, I am not sure that this was so much a blunder as simply an omission, although we still might call such an omission a blunder. At any rate, this raises the correlative question of whether Peirce exaggerated the role of continuity in *identifying* (or seeming to identify) it with reality. It is one thing to maintain that nothing can be real without partaking in continuity; it is another to claim that continuity exhausts reality. The latter claim would, of course, eliminate the category of Secondness from reality—a charge often brought against Peirce by his critics, but something which Peirce, at his best at least, would not hold.

The final issue I would like to raise is whether or not for Peirce creation is free. Hartshorne makes a distinction between creation's being free in specification and being necessary in exercise. Hence, this particular world is radically contingent and so it need not have been, but the creation of some world or other is necessary, since, if God is creator at all, he is creator necessarily. I tend to think that Peirce would be in substantial agreement with that, while I would not. I would prefer to say that any particular instantiation of the possible is contingent, but some actual entity must be necessary in order for anything else to be possible at all. Since there is no realm of entities called "possibles" which have ontological status independent of the actual and the necessary being, God creates *freely*, not necessarily, from all eternity. My question is whether such freedom, as Hartshorne allows God in creating, is sufficient to do justice to God's transcendence. Must there not also be, with respect to creation, freedom of exercise; that is, must not God be free not to create any world, where "any" has both the collective and the distributive sense? Isn't this required in order for God to be completely independent of the created world? Perhaps the difficulty here is a certain ambiguity in the term "necessary." The term is used in several ways: first, in the usual sense of "causal connection," according to which, when the necessary and sufficient conditions for an event are present, the event happens necessarily—more exactly, when those conditions for the event are fulfilled, the event itself is virtually unconditioned (necessary in that sense); second, in the statistical sense of "what is logically inevitable" given an unlimited long run. Each of these senses of "necessary" is *hypothetical*, not absolute. That is, each requires only that there be *in fact*, not that there must be, some actual world or other. There is yet another sense of "necessary"—a reality which simply *is* unconditionally. It simply has no conditions at all. This is the classical notion of God's necessity. Is this Peirce's sense? Again, I think there is hesitation and waffling here in the same way, and for the same reason, that there is hesitation and waffling about how to understand God's transcendence.

I hope that these reflections, prompted by Hartshorne's essay, will encourage interest in Peirce's religious philosophy in such a way as to clarify further what Peirce himself held, and more important, to show how his reflections might help us to a deeper understanding of that Ideal whose living power bears upon human conduct.

Notes

1. Donna M. Orange, *Peirce's Conception of God: A Developmental Study*, Peirce Studies 2 (Lubbock, Tex.: Institute for Studies in Pragmaticism, 1984).

2. Ibid., pp. 81–82.

3. See Stanley Harrison, "Man's Glassy Essence: An Attempt to Construct a Theory of Person Based on the writings of Charles Sanders Peirce," Ph.D. Diss., Fordham University, 1971; and Vincent M. Colapietro, *Peirce's Approach to the Self: A Semiotic Perspective on Human Subjectivity* (Albany: State University of New York, 1989).

Bibliography

Abbot, Francis E. *Scientific Theism.* Boston: Little, Brown, 1885.
Apel, Karl-Otto. *Charles S. Peirce: From Pragmatism to Pragmaticism.* Trans. M. Krois. Amherst: University of Massachusetts Press, 1981.
Berkeley, George. *Principles of Human Knowledge.* New York: Bobbs-Merrill, 1970.
Bernstein, Richard J. *Praxis and Action.* Philadelphia: University of Pennsylvania Press, 1971.
——. "Peirce's Theory of Perception." *Studies in the Philosophy of Charles Sanders Peirce, Second Series.* Amherst: University of Massachusetts Press, 1965).
Black, Max. "Vagueness: An Exercise in Logical Analysis." *Language and Philosophy.* Ithaca, N.Y.: Cornell University Press, 1949. Pp. 25–58.
Boler, John. *Charles Peirce and Scholastic Realism.* Seattle: University of Washington Press, 1963.
——. "Peirce, Ockham, and Scholastic Realism." *The Relevance of Charles Peirce.* Ed. Eugene Freeman. The Monist Library of Philosophy. La Salle, Ill.: The Hegeler Institute, 1983. Pp. 93–106.
Cantor, Georg. *Contributions to the Founding of the Theory of Transfinite Numbers.* Trans. Philip E. B. Jourdain. New York: Dover, 1955.
——. *Grundlangen einer allgemeinen Mannigfaltigkeitslehre: Ein mathematisch-philosophischer Versuch in der Lehre des Unendlichen.* Leipzig: Teubner, 1883.
Charles Sanders Peirce: Contributions to the Nation. Ed. Kenneth Laine Ketner. Graduate Studies No. 30. Lubbock: Texas Tech Press, 1987.
Charles Sanders Peirce: Schriften zum Pragmatismus und Pragmatizismus. Trans. Gerd Wartenberg. Ed. Karl-Otto Apel. 2nd ed. Frankfurt: Suhrkamp, 1976.
Charles S. Peirce: Über die Klarheit unserer Gedanken. Ed. and trans. Klaus Oehler. Frankfurt: Klostermann, 1968.
Colapietro, Vincent M. *Peirce's Approach to the Self: A Semiotic*

Perspective on Human Subjectivity. Albany: State University of New York Press, 1989.

Delaney, C. F. "The Journal of Speculative Philosophy Papers." *Writings of Charles S. Peirce: A Chronological Edition* II. Bloomington: Indiana University Press, 1984. Pp. xxxvi–xlii.

Descartes, René. *Philosophical Works of Descartes* I. Ed. W. D. Ross and E. T. Haldane. New York: Dover, 1955.

Di Leo, Jeffrey R. "Peirce's Haecceitism." *Transactions of the Charles S. Peirce Society,* 27 (1991), 79–109.

Ducasse, C. J. "Whewell's Philosophy of Scientific Discovery." *Philosophical Review,* 60 (1951), 56–69, 213–34.

Einstein, Albert. *Ideas and Opinions.* New York: Crown Publishers, 1954.

Eisele, Carolyn. *Studies in the Scientific and Mathematical Philosophy of Charles S. Peirce.* Ed. Richard M. Martin. The Hague: Mouton Publishers, 1979.

Engel-Tiercelin, Claudine. "Vagueness and the Unity of C. S. Peirce's Realism." *Transactions of the Charles S. Peirce Society,* 28 (1992), 51–82.

Experience, Reason, and God: John E. Smith in Dialogue. Ed. Vincent M. Colapietro. New York: Fordham University Press, 1996.

Faris, J. A. "C. S. Peirce's Existential Graphs." *Bulletin of the Institute of Mathematics and Its Application,* 17 (1981).

Fisch, Max H. "Alexander Bain and the Genealogy of Pragmatism." *Journal of the History of Ideas,* 13 (1954), 413–44.

———. "A Chronicle of Pragmaticism, 1865–1879." *The Monist,* 48 (1964), 441–66.

———. "Peirce as Scientist, Mathematician, Historian, Logician, and Philosopher." *Proceedings of the C. S. Peirce Bicentennial International Congress.* Graduate Studies No. 23. Lubbock: Texas Tech Press, 1981. Pp. 13–34.

———. "Peirce's Progress from Nominalism Toward Realism." *The Monist,* 51 (1967), 159–78.

———. "The Range of Peirce's Relevance." In *The Relevance of Charles Peirce.* Ed. Eugene Freeman. The Monist Library of Philosophy. La Salle, Ill.: The Hegeler Institute, 1983. Pp. 11–37.

———. "Supplement: A Chronicle of Pragmaticism, 1865–1879." *The Monist*, 48 (1964).

Forster, Paul D. "Peirce and the Threat of Nominalism." *Transactions of the Charles S. Peirce Society*, 28 (1992), 691–724.

Haack, Susan. "'Extreme Scholastic Realism': Its Relevance to Philosophy of Science Today." *Transactions of the Charles S. Peirce Society*, 28 (1992), 19–50.

Harrison, Stanley. "Charles S. Peirce: Reflections on Being a Man-Sign." *Proceedings of the American Catholic Philosophical Association*, 53 (1979), 98–106.

———. "Man's Glassy Essence: An Attempt to Construct a Theory of Person Based on the Writings of Charles Sanders Peirce." Ph.D. diss., Fordham University, 1971.

———. "Peirce on Persons." *Proceedings of the C. S. Peirce Bicentennial International Congress*. Graduate Studies 3. Lubbock: Texas Tech Press, 1981. Pp. 217–21.

Hume, David. *A Treatise of Human Nature*. Garden City, N.Y.: Doubleday Dolphin, 1961.

James, William. *Collected Essays and Reviews*. Ed. R. B. Perry. New York: Longmans, Green, 1920.

———. *Pragmatism: A New Name for Some Old Ways of Thinking*. Cambridge, Mass.: Harvard University Press, 1975.

———. *Varieties of Religious Experience*. New York: Longmans, Green, 1912.

Jauhari, Jamila. "The Physics of Avicenna." Ph.D. diss., Fordham University, 1987.

Locke, John. *An Essay Concerning Human Understanding*. Ed. Alexander Campbell Fraser. Oxford: Clarendon, 1894.

Lonergan, Bernard J. F., S.J. "The Future of Christianity." *A Second Collection: Papers by Bernard J. F. Lonergan, S.J.* Ed. W. Ryan, S.J., and B. Tyrrell, S.J. Philadelphia: Westminster Press, 1974.

———. *Insight: A Study of Human Understanding*. New York: Philosophical Library, 1958.

———. "Insight Revisited." *A Second Collection: Papers by Bernard J. F. Lonergan, S.J.* Ed. W. Ryan, S.J., and B. Tyrrell, S.J. Philadelphia: Westminster Press, 1974.

———. *A Third Collection*. London: Geoffrey Chapman, 1985.

———. "Theology in Its New Context." *A Second Collection: Papers* by Bernard J. F. Lonergan, S.J. Ed. W. Ryan, S.J. and B. Tyrrell, S.J. Philadelphia: Westminster Press, 1974.

Lovejoy, Arthur O. "The Thirteen Pragmatisms." *Journal of Philosophy,* 5 (1908), 1-12, 29-39.

Margolis, Joseph. "The Passing of Peirce's Realism." *Transactions of the Charles S. Peirce Society,* 29 (1993), 293-330.

Murphey, Murray G. *The Development of Peirce's Philosophy.* Cambridge, Mass.: Harvard University Press, 1961.

The New Elements of Mathematics by Charles S. Peirce. Ed. Carolyn Eisele. 4 vols. in 5. The Hague: Mouton Publishers, 1976.

Orange, Donna. *Peirce's Conception of God: A Developmental Study.* Peirce Studies 2. Lubbock, Tex.: Institute for Studies in Pragmaticism. 1984.

Pater, W. de. *Linguistic Analysis and Theology.* Louvain: Acco, 1970.

———. *Taagalanlytische perspektieven op godsdienst en kunst.* Antwerp: Nederlandsche Boekhandle, 1970.

———. *Theologische Sprachlogik.* Munich: Lösel-Verlag, 1971.

Perry, R. B. *The Thought and Character of William James.* II. *Philosophy and Psychology.* Boston: Little, Brown, 1935.

Peterson, John. "Can Peirce Be a Pragmaticist and an Idealist?" *Transactions of the Charles S. Peirce Society,* 27 (1991), 221-35.

Pollock, Robert C. "Emerson and America's Future." In *Doctrine and Experience.* Ed. Vincent G. Potter. New York: Fordham University Press, 1988. Pp. 48-74.

Potter, Vincent G. *Charles S. Peirce: On Norms and Ideals.* Amherst: University of Massachusetts Press, 1967.

———. "The Irrelevance of Philosophy." *Thought,* 49, No. 193 (June 1974), 143-55.

Raposa, Michael L. "Habits and Essences." *Transactions of the Charles S. Peirce Society,* 20 (1984), 147-67.

Riley, Gresham. "Peirce's Theory of Individual." *Transactions of the Charles S. Peirce Society,* 10 (1974), 135-63.

———. "The Self, Self-Knowledge, and Pragmaticism." Ph.D. diss., Yale University, 1965.

Riley, Woodbridge. *American Thought: From Puritanism to Pragmatism and Beyond.* New York: Peter Smith, 1941.

Roberts, Don. *The Existential Graphs of Charles S. Peirce.* The Hague: Mouton, 1973.

Robin, R. S. "Peirce's Doctrine of the Normative Science." *Studies in the Philosophy of Charles Sanders Peirce, Second Series.* Ed. E. C. Moore and R. S. Robin. Amherst: University of Massachusetts Press, 1965.

Russell, Bertrand. *Introduction to Mathematical Philosophy.* New York: Macmillan, 1919.

——. *Principles of Mathematics.* New York: Norton, 1903.

Schneider, H. W. "Fourthness." *Studies in the Philosophy of Charles Sanders Peirce.* Ed. R. P. Wiener and F. H. Young. Cambridge, Mass.: Harvard University Press, 1952.

Semiotic and Significs: The Correspondence Between Charles S. Peirce and Victoria Lady Welby. Ed. Charles S. Hardwick. Bloomington: Indiana University Press, 1977.

Smith, John E. *The Analogy of Experience: An Approach to Understanding Religious Truth.* New York: Harper & Row, 1973.

——. *Experience and God.* New York: Oxford University Press, 1968. Repr. New York: Fordham University Press, 1995.

——. *Experience, Reason, and God: John E. Smith in Dialogue.* Ed. Vincent Colapietro. New York: Fordham University Press, 1996.

——. "The Reconception of Experience in Peirce, James, and Dewey." *The Monist,* 68 (1985), 538–54.

——. *The Spirit of American Philosophy.* New York: Oxford University Press, 1963.

——. "The Tension Between Direct Experience and Argument in Religion." *Religious Studies,* 17 (1981), 487–97.

Strong, E. W. "William Whewell and John Stuart Mill: Their Controversy About Scientific Knowledge." *Journal of the History of Ideas,* 16 (1955), 209–31.

Thompson, Manley, *The Pragmatic Philosophy of C. S. Peirce.* Chicago: The University of Chicago Press, 1953.

Weiner, R. P. Title of selected writings of Peirce. Garden City, N.Y.: Doubleday Anchor, 1958.

Weiss, Paul. "CSP." *Dictionary of American Biography,* 14. 398–403.

About the Author

Vincent G. Potter of the Society of Jesus died suddenly on May 3, 1994. Father Potter was Professor of Philosophy and first holder of the Distinguished Loyola Chair in the Humanities at Fordham University. Academic Vice President from 1988 into 1992, he also served the university as a Trustee and as Chairman of the philosophy department. His talents as a gifted editor were brought to bear as an associate editor of *Thought,* as a member of the governing board of Fordham University Press, and as founding Editor of the press's American Philosophy Series. At Fordham he also served as Editor-in-Chief of the *International Philosophical Quarterly* from 1985 to the day of his death.

Father Potter, a native of New York born on October 18, 1929, was ordained a priest at Louvain in 1960, having received his A.B. and licentiate in philosophy from Bellarmine College and his licentiate in theology from St. Albert de Louvain. His Ph.D. was taken at Yale University. A Jesuit philosopher learned in both the tradition of St. Thomas and in modern philosophy, especially American, Father Potter had uncanny skill at synthesizing such apparently divergent schools of thought. His scholarship included numerous articles and ten books. At the time of his death he was not only preparing for publication this collection of essays, but also had just completed a translation of one of St. Thomas's *Quaestiones Disputatae,* the *De malo,* which is to be published by Oxford University Press.

As a Peirce scholar Father Potter needs little introduction. His publications on the philosophy of Charles S. Peirce, which began in 1966 and were ongoing at his death, have been received with favor both in the United States and in Europe. Active in the Charles S. Peirce Society, Father Potter served as Secretary-Treasurer, Vice President, and, in 1985, as President. He was also a member of the advisory board of the Peirce Edition Project at Indiana University, Indianapolis. On a more personal level was his guidance of students; he mentored at least seven dissertations on Peirce alone. In the end, however, it is Father Potter's work on integrating the epistemological theories of Peirce and Bernard Lonergan that may be his most original contribution to the field of philosophy.

www.ingramcontent.com/pod-product-compliance
Lightning Source LLC
Chambersburg PA
CBHW031241290426
44109CB00012B/393